DATE DUE

May 8			

DEMCO 38-296

Practical Digital Libraries

Books, Bytes, and Bucks

The Morgan Kaufmann Series in Multimedia Information and Systems
Series Editor, Edward Fox

Practical Digital Libraries: Books, Bytes, and Bucks
Michael Lesk

Readings in Information Retrieval
Edited by Karen Sparck Jones and Peter Willett

Introduction to Data Compression
Khalid Sayood

Forthcoming

Digital Compression for Multimedia: Principles and Standards
Jerry D. Gibson, Toby Berger, Tom Lookabaugh, and David Lindbergh

Multimedia Servers: Design, Environments, and Applications
Asit Dan and Dinkar Sitaram

Practical Digital Libraries

Books, Bytes, and Bucks

MICHAEL LESK

M K◄

Morgan Kaufmann Publishers
San Francisco, California

		Copyeditor	Ken DellaPenta
	er Mann	Proofreader	Jeff Van Bueren
	Overton	Design &	Paul C. Anagnostopoulos
	eth Beller	Composition	MaryEllen N. Oliver
	Heirakuji	Illustrator	George Nichols
Cover Photo	Jeffrey M. Spielman/	Indexer	Steve Rath
	THE IMAGE BANK	Printer	Courier Corporation
Cover Graphic	Cherie Plumlee		

Morgan Kaufmann Publishers, Inc.
Editorial and Sales Office
340 Pine Street, Sixth Floor
San Francisco, CA 94104-3205
USA
Telephone 415/392-2665
Facsimile 415/982-2665
Email mkp@mkp.com
WWW www.mkp.com

Order toll free 800/745-7323

01 00 99 98 97   5 4 3 2 1

Library of Congress Cataloging-in-Publication Data

Lesk, Michael.
    Practical digital libraries : books, bytes, and bucks / Michael
Lesk.
        p.   cm.
    Includes bibliographical references and index.
    ISBN 1-55860-459-6 (pbk.)
    1. Libraries—United States—Special collections—Computer files.
2. Digital libraries—United States.   I. Title.
Z692.C65L47   1997
025′.00285—dc21   97-22069
                                                          CIP

In memory of Gerard Salton (1927–1995),
who originated much of the technology of
digital libraries and incidentally introduced
me to the subject

Contents

5   Knowledge Representation Methods   99

6   Distribution   125

7   Usability and Retrieval Evaluation   147

Figures

Preface

Why Digital Libraries, and Why this Book?

In 1938 H. G. Wells dreamed of a world encyclopedia in which all human knowledge would be available everywhere, a "complete planetary memory for all mankind." In 1945 Vannevar Bush had a vision of a scholar consulting any book by tapping its code on a keyboard. Today we can build these systems. This book explains why, how, and what decisions remain. Its purpose is to explain to both librarians and computer scientists the technologies behind digital libraries, the choices to be made in building them, and the way they might function economically in society.

Digital libraries are organized collections of digital information. They combine the structuring and gathering of information, which libraries and archives have always done, with the digital representation that computers have made possible. Digital information can be accessed rapidly around the world, copied for preservation without error, stored compactly, and searched very quickly. No conventional back-of-the-book index compares with the text search engines we now have. A true digital library also provides the principles governing what is included and how the collection is organized. The World Wide Web, the overwhelming example of a shared world-wide collection of information, has been turned into many digital libraries by individuals or groups that select, organize, and catalog large numbers of pages. Unlike earlier generations of online services, the Web is accessible to many without training in information use, which has made digital libraries important to far more people than have ever cared about them in the past. The Duke of

Wellington opposed railways because they would encourage the poor to move about. What would he have thought of everyone having all this information?

Over the centuries the world has changed from one in which few people could even do arithmetic into one in which pocket calculators are given away in advertising promotions. The same change is happening in information. This book cannot tell you what this change will mean, but it will tell you how it is coming about and pose some of the questions that will matter. Most of these issues are mundane: how to convert material to digital form, how to deliver it to users, and what kind of economic support is possible. But some questions will go to the key issues of libraries: what is their value to society, and how can that be preserved in digital form? We need to know not only how to build digital libraries, but why.

Audience

This book is practical. It addresses the problem of a librarian who wishes to digitize material and needs to understand what kinds of conversion technologies are available or who wishes to purchase digital material and needs to know what can be done with it. It also addresses the problems of a computer scientist trying to understand the library applications of some of the relevant algorithms. More important, it addresses the practical problems of costs and economics, which are today more of an obstacle than the technology. Looking forward, it helps both librarians and computer scientists answer questions like "Will we be able digitize video economically?" and "How can we search video on a computer?" And, on the most general level, it points out the issues that will affect libraries and their users as digital technology continues to take over functions traditionally supported by paper and printing press. As I write, there is no other book that combines a broad view of all the problems with the specific detail needed to provide practical assistance to those facing these problems.

Approach

When I started writing this book, some topics seemed particularly important, some less so. It is easy, for example, to find material on computer storage algorithms and databases, so I have avoided that area; Witten, Moffatt, and Bell (1994), for example, have an excellent book on text storage. Image and video storage are more recently developed areas, and although there is some very useful material available (e.g., Peter Robinson's excellent book [1993]), it seemed more important to provide detail in this area. The economics of digital libraries is another area of such rapid change and uncertainty as to require a considerable amount of explanation, as do issues involving intellectual property. Collections and preservation, on the other hand, are fundamentally similar to traditional library activities in this area and can be discussed largely by analogy. It's particularly difficult to provide a survey of what is being done around the world in digital library projects. This changes so rapidly that anything will be out of date by the time it is written, let alone read, so I tried to give examples rather than attempt to be comprehensive as of any particular date.

The overwhelming motive has been a practical one: to give specific details of how things are done or could be done rather than to speak generally about areas. Principles are valuable, and I have included some, but what I have always wanted when searching for information is useful detail about what is going on or how something can be accomplished. A book on carpentry needs to discuss wood, perhaps even some ecology, but if all it does is discuss the threat to the rain forest, it will not help someone who needs to build a bookcase. There are other books that discuss the wonders of the computer age; this book proposes to help you bring them about. And there are other books that discuss the dangers of the computer age; this book proposes to tell you how to avoid them.

Content

This book explains how to build a digital library. The early chapters deal with the problems of conversion and construction. Equipment is needed; Chapter 1 describes the technology involved in libraries and computing and how it has evolved over the years. Technology to index the texts is required, and Chapter 2 describes how text is stored and retrieved in online systems. Some of the material may be images, so techniques for image storage and manipulation are discussed in Chapter 3. Information on sound and multimedia storage is in Chapter 4.

Once the collection is stored, it has to be organized. A landfill of books is not a library. The history of classification and indexing schemes is described in Chapter 5, along with a discussion of what techniques can be used with electronic information. Then, the content has to be delivered to people; Chapter 6 contains information on distribution techniques, including a discussion of how digital libraries will relate to the expanding world of electronic commerce. The last step toward the user is in Chapter 7, on usability of libraries, which also describes how information retrieval systems are evaluated and measured.

Keeping a library collection around is a problem for the digital world as well as for traditional libraries. Digital files are often lost when people do not keep copies, when they are deleted by accident, or if no one realizes the value of keeping them. Chapter 8 discusses collecting and preserving information, both in the traditional and the new worlds.

The biggest problems facing digital libraries today are economic. We know how to build a digital library; that is what the first eight chapters are about. We do not know how to make it economically supportable so that it can be expected to survive. Electronic technology is placing great stresses on the copyright law, the traditional book publishing business, and other aspects of libraries. These stresses are coming at a time when the universities and government agencies that traditionally supported most libraries are themselves under financial pressure. How will we cope with these economic problems? Chapter 9 discusses economics—the ways in which libraries might be funded—as well as the impact of economics and electronics on information availability. Chapter 10 discusses intellectual property rights and their impact on the digital library. Finally, the book concludes with a survey of world activities in Chapter 11 and with a discussion of future issues in Chapter 12.

Acknowledgments

Half the lines in this book have changed since the first draft was written. My thanks to the many people who have helped. This includes, most particularly, my editor at Morgan Kaufmann, Jennifer Mann, whose enthusiasm and comments have been particularly welcome and supportive for months. Elisabeth Beller's work on producing the book has also been essential. The referees, including Dan Atkins, Martin Dillon, Dale Flecker, Edward Fox, Marianne Gaunt, Peter Hart, David Levy, Wendy Lougee, Greg Newby, Scott Stevens, Hal Varian, Donald Waters, and Terry Winograd, have made many useful comments, as have friends of mine such as Michael Bianchi, who read the manuscript. Thanks, in particular, to Sharon Propas of Stanford for her careful checking and comments. I thank them for their help and remind the reader that those mistakes that remain are attributable to my stubbornness. I also thank the many collaborators on my research projects over the years and the community of research scholars of information systems. And, in particular, this book is dedicated to the late Gerard Salton (1927–1995), a great information retrieval researcher whose work has provided us with many of the methods we use today. He had many students who are now leaders of research around the country. In particular, he first introduced me to information retrieval and programming and started me down the path to this book in 1961.

1

Evolution of Libraries

U SERS OF THE World Wide Web are familiar with the ability to find Swiss railway schedules or the list of World Series winners on their screens. To some, digital information is a fantastic resource of new powers; to others, the idea that, in addition to dealing with the 300 pounds of paper used in the United States per person per year, we must now deal with all this online information as well is frightening. Universities worry that undergraduates waste too much time surfing the Web, and everyone is frustrated by the inability to find what they want when they want it.

1.1 *Why Digital Libraries?*

The answer should not be despair but organization. A digital library, a collection of information that is both digitized and organized, gives us powers we never had with traditional libraries. Vannevar Bush, head of the U.S. Office of Scientific Research and Development during World War II, wrote that the great research libraries were only "nibbled at by a few" and that selecting items from them was a "stone adze in the hands of a cabinetmaker" (Bush 1945). What does digital technology offer us instead? Will digital libraries deal with floods of information? Will they help with the information glut, the information war, and the many other buzzwords of the information age?

A digital library can be searched for any phrase, it can be accessed all over the world, and it can be copied without error. This is why digital libraries are coming.

They address traditional problems of finding information, of delivering it to users, and of preserving it for the future. Digital information takes less space than paper information and thus may help libraries reduce costs. But it is more important that they can provide a level of service never before attainable—individual word and sentence search, and delivery of information to the user's desk—information that does not decay with time, whether it is words, sounds, or images.

What does it take to build a digital library? You need to get stuff into it, you need to be able to get stuff out of it, and you need to be able to pay for it. Beyond doing that, what will the digital library mean? What are the social effects likely to be when digital libraries are widely used by scholars and researchers, by students and teachers, and by the general public?

First, the digital library must have content. It can either be new material, prepared digitally, or old material, converted to digital form. It can be bought, donated, or converted locally from previously purchased items. Content then needs to be stored and retrieved. Information is widely found as text stored as characters and images stored from scanning. These images are frequently scans of printed pages, as well as illustrations or photographs. More recently, audio and video, plus interactive material, are accumulating rapidly in digital form, both newly generated and converted from older material.

Next, the content must be found. Retrieval systems are needed to let users find things—relatively straightforward for text but still a subject of research for pictures, sounds, and videos. It must then be delivered to the user; a digital library must contain interface software letting people see and hear its contents. A digital library must also have a "preservation department" of sorts; there must be some process to see that what is available today is still available tomorrow. The user with a knife cutting out pages may not be a problem in a digital library, but computer systems have their own vulnerabilities, including some caused purely by neglect.

Libraries also need a way to pay for digital libraries, and this is a major issue. Certainly, in a transition period the old services cannot be abandoned immediately, and thus new services must be funded in addition to old. Finding a way to fund digital libraries is the most frustrating problem for librarians today, but it may not be the most puzzling problem tomorrow. Digital libraries are going to change the social system by which information is collected and transferred. A digital library is not just a collection of disk drives; it will be part of a culture. We need to decide how the typical citizen will get information, how important information transfer is to democracy, and how we will preserve the accessibility of information that we want and the diversity that we would like. Libraries have a key role to play in these decisions.

So with all the needs for digital libraries, why do we not yet have them? In 1964 Arthur Samuel predicted that by 1984 paper libraries would disappear, except at museums (Samuel 1964). Why hasn't this happened? The biggest reason is that we cannot easily find $3 billion to fund the mechanical conversion of 100 million books to electronic form, plus the additional and probably larger sum to compensate the copyright owners for most of those books. The economics of digital libraries are tangled with those of digital publishing, the entire networking industry, and questions of security and fraud. Other forces delaying the development of digital libraries include the very real preferences of many people who like books the way they are, and who even like catalog cards; the problems of assuring access to those who cannot afford computers or online services; the problems of providing a digital library in an easy-to-use and comfortable form; and the many questions reflecting our sensible reluctance to change a system that works into an unknown one. To some librarians and users, digitizing books is an example of fixing something that is not broken. Nevertheless, costs are declining, current publications are becoming widely available in electronic form, and we are exploring economic methods of supporting digital information. These trends will make electronic terminals the route by which first students and scholars, and then the general public, obtain information.

1.2 *History and Change*

This book is about the practicalities of making a digital library. Sometimes it helps to know where you are coming from and not just where you are going. So this chapter will review both library and technical history, to try to learn what might change and what might survive as we introduce new technology. Santayana wrote, "Those who do not study the mistakes of history are condemned to repeat them," and Marx said that history always repeats itself, the first time as tragedy and the second time as farce.

Today, after all, is not the first time that society has had the opportunity to completely change the way it passes on information. History tells us that there have been many major changes in both the way we distribute and store information and in how it is used in society. The music of Bach has flourished on the harpsichord, piano, vinyl record, and CD; it has been used in church services, concert halls, and shopping mall Muzak. Information distribution has moved from asking your neighbors (still common) to classification systems, reviews, advertisements, and other ways of arranging information and notifying people about it. Indexing and searching systems have been added, first on paper and now in electronic form.

What is perhaps surprising is that technology does not always drive the changes in how information is handled. Technological determinism, the idea that it is hopeless to alter the changes forced on us by new inventions, isn't always right. Sometimes new inventions push us in a particular direction; other times it is changes in society. Books were sold (as manuscript copies) before they were printed. Monks in medieval cathedrals kept libraries and copied books for each other. There was an organized medieval book trade, and when printed books replaced manuscripts as the main item of trade, much of the previous infrastructure remained in place. Moving forward, the 18th century saw massive changes in literacy and in the kind of material that was written and published without a great deal of change in the technology of printing. The 19th century saw much greater technological advance but less change in what people did as a result. Our century has seen a flood of new media, but with a decrease in public participation (more broadcasting, less letter writing). What, then, will happen as a result of the current technology changes?

For more than a decade nearly every word printed and typed has been prepared on a computer. Paradoxically, until very recently most reading has been from paper. Now, digital distribution of email, fax, and of course Web pages has exploded and is breaking this logjam. We would like digital information to be available to everyone, to be preserved for the future, and to enhance our technology, our commerce, and our democracy. Libraries provide us with information in books; they let scholars read the books of centuries ago and deliver current information to businesses. What will they do with electronic information?

If conventional libraries were to just sit and wait, it is not likely that they would become a major provider of digital information. For universities and libraries to retain their status and relevance, they have to participate in the new digital world, as many are doing. There are many social goals that are important for them, beyond the simple ability of libraries to pile up books or disks.

1.3   *Advantages of Digital Libraries*

Digital technology is making it easier to write books, easier to save their content, and, in fact, easier to save everything being written. This will mean that more and more information is available. It will mean that the ability to find information is increasingly important; the possession of it will be less important. Libraries will find it cheaper and easier to store electronic information, as information drifts from paper to computer format. New material is often available digitally today, and it will make up more and more of libraries as time goes on. Digital information can be either easier to generate and fetch or harder. We have a public choice of which goal to pursue. We can find ourselves either with a limited set of sources or a much wider diversity of them. Technology can move us to few resources or to many, depending on how we apply it. We, as a society, need to make this choice so that we improve accessibility and diversity. The same arguments that Benjamin Franklin used to justify the postal service now apply to digital libraries: for a good democracy, the citizens need access to information.

Figure 1.1, for example, shows scanned representations of Cranford, New Jersey: the town on an 1878 map, on a modern U.S. Geological Survey map, in a low-pass aerial photograph, and in a view from a space satellite. The railway line running from left to right, the Central of New Jersey (now the NJ Transit Raritan Line), is the same in all the pictures. Making this kind of data available with a few keystrokes has applications in education, historical research, or land use planning. For example, note the small lake in the bend of the river shown in the 1878 map; it is gone (filled in, presumably) in all the recent maps. Yet someone wishing to dig a deep basement on that spot would probably like to know that it was once underwater.

In building systems, whether of maps or books, we must avoid too much focus just on technology and economics. Libraries are pointless if no one uses them, and Christine Borgman of UCLA has already written why even online catalogs, let alone online documents, are so hard to use (Borgman 1996). Experiments with users have shown that the more someone tells a librarian about what they want, the more likely it is that their quest for information will be successful. Building digital libraries is not just a question of piling up disk drives; it involves creating an entire organization of machines and people, perhaps even a culture, in which people are able to find information and use it. The social implications of a world in which information is distributed almost without institutions are not understood. What does this mean for universities, for education, and for publishers?

Information transport has been a key issue both past and present. How we move information from one person to another, and how we see that it is retained from one generation to the next, are persistent questions. Unfortunately, another persistent issue has been attempts to manipulate this—to try to direct what knowledge will be available to people. Depending on motive and point of view, this may be called "defining a curriculum," propaganda, advertising, or censorship. The Chinese emperor Shih Huang Ti tried to burn all books, hoping that future historians would say that all knowledge started in his reign. As a democracy, the United States has believed that the widest possible distribution of knowledge is best; in 1787, Thomas Jefferson, in a letter to James Madison, wished that "the education of the common people will be attended to, convinced that on their good senses we may rely . . . for the preservation . . . of liberty." But the limits that are imposed (Oliver Wendell Holmes noted that the First Amendment "would not protect a man in falsely shouting fire in a theater") are normally more restrictive on the most widely distributed media. We accept obscenity limits on broadcast TV more than on cable TV; we consider a published libel more serious than a spoken slander. Some countries have tried hard to limit information distribution; the old Soviet Union drove its writers to underground publication (*samizdat*). Today China and Singapore are

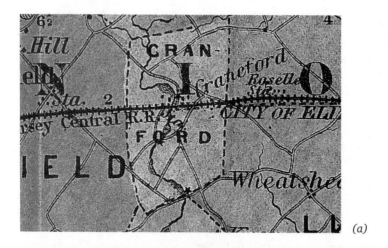

(a)

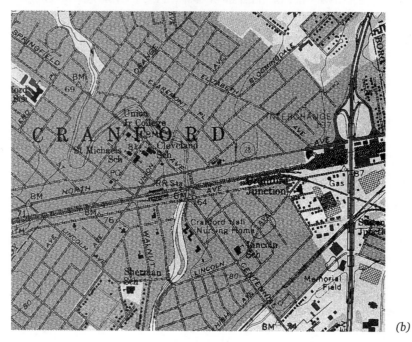

(b)

Figure 1.1   Cranford, New Jersey: *(a)* on an 1878 map, *(b)* on a modern U.S. Geological Survey map, *(c)* in an aerial photo, and *(d)* in a low-resolution satellite photo

(c)

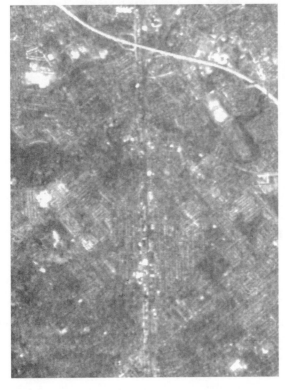

(d)

examples of countries trying to control the spread of electronic information. But electronic media are hard to control, and are often privately rather than government owned.

And in contrast to attempts at restraints, there have been dreams of widely available knowledge, or at least of making knowledge more accessible. The French encyclopedists hoped in the 18th century to produce a single compilation of knowledge, as did H. G. Wells and as have more modern futurists who attempt to make a model of how people will find information. And, for all time, there has been no single source of knowledge. It is not enough to know just Aristotle, and it is not likely to be enough to know just one source on the Internet.

1.4   *Rise of Printing and Libraries*

The works of Homer have been a part of Western culture for over 2000 years. Once, that meant the presence of a bard, who could recite the *Iliad* and *Odyssey* from memory. Later, it meant a manuscript, and still later it meant a printed book. Today, Homer (and all the rest of classical Greek literature) is available on the Perseus CD-ROM. Will that be a change comparable to the invention of printing, as is often suggested?

Printing, of course, made books much more widely available. The early presses, however, were still expensive. Through the centuries, technology, most particularly in paper-making, mechanical presses, and typesetting machinery, steadily lowered the cost of books. A single man at a handpress might print 2500 sheets a day, while modern printing plants turn out hundreds of thousands of sheets per employee. Paper used to cost a day's wages for 24 sheets; now it is so cheap we have to recycle it to minimize the space taken in the garbage. A compositor setting type by hand in the 18th century was expected to set 1000 ens per hour, or 3–4 words per minute. A Linotype operator can set about 10 words per minute, and a modern typist can do 50 words per minute easily. Combining all of these effects, the *London Daily Journal* of March 4, 1728, cost 3 halfpennies for two sides of one sheet, while the *Times* (London) of 1905 cost 1 penny for 24 pages, or a price per page one-tenth as much. Books and newspapers changed from upper-class luxuries into something accessible to everyone.

As books became more common, large libraries started to include hundreds of thousands of books rather than the dozens of books in medieval libraries. Universities have become the owners of the largest nonnational libraries. In the United States, after the Library of Congress, only the New York Public Library and the Boston Public Library have collections to compare with those of the largest university libraries. Table 1.1 shows the holdings of major university and nonuniversity libraries. For international comparison, Table 1.2 shows some of the other major li-

Table 1.1   Number of volumes held

Institution	1910	1995
Library of Congress	1.8M	23.0M
Harvard	.8M	12.9M
Yale	.55M	9.5M
U. Illinois (Urbana)	.1M	8.5M
U. California (Berkeley)	.24M	8.1M
New York Public Library	1.4M	7.0M
U. Michigan	.25M	6.7M
Boston Public Library	1.0M	6.5M

Table 1.2   Number of volumes held

Institution	Earlier	1910	1996	Older Name
British Library	240K (1837)	2M	15M	British Museum Library
Bodleian (Oxford)	2K (1602)	0.8M	4.8M	
Cambridge University	330 (1473)	0.5M	3.5M	
Bibliothèque Nationale de France	250K (1800)	3M	11M	Bibliothèque Nationale
National Diet Library (Japan)		0.5M	4.1M	Imperial Cabinet Library
Library at Alexandria	533K (48 B.C.) (classical; 24 rolls of papyrus approximately equals 1 volume)			

braries of the world (Canfora 1990). The log plot in Figure 1.2 shows the steepness of the growth in university libraries in the United States around 1900 (Rider 1944; Leach 1976).

Although we read in Ecclesiastes that "of making many books there is no end," the concept of the "information glut" and "information overload" is mostly a 20th century idea. Specialization today has destroyed the 18th century ideal of a man who would know everything. William Blake was a poet, artist, and the inventor of copper plate lithography. An exceptional 19th century genius might work in many areas: William Morris made wallpaper, books, furniture, and tapestries, and was best known in his own life as a poet. Today it can take a lifetime to become an expert in a tiny area.

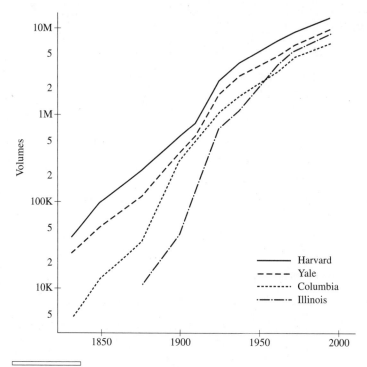

Figure 1.2   Growth of libraries

In 1951 there were 10,000 journals published; today there are 140,000 (Meadows 1993), as shown in Figure 1.3. The concept of being overwhelmed by information was popularized by Derek de la Solla Price (1986). The expansion of the number of journals in recent years and the increase in their subscription costs has been led by the commercial publishers. The effort made by some libraries to collect a very large number of scientific journals encouraged some publishers to charge what would earlier have been thought enormous sums for subscriptions. As a result some journals now cost over $10,000 per year. The increases in prices make continuing problems for libraries. The Andrew W. Mellon Foundation funded a study (Cummings et al. 1992) that documented the loss of purchasing power in libraries over the last 30 years. Each year during the 1970s research libraries bought about 1.4% fewer books, while the number of books published increased more than 2%. Thus, library collections have more and more holes.

What is all this information worth? Public justification for libraries has changed over the years. Once upon a time (in the 19th century) both education and libraries were seen as being important for preserving democracy. Now the idea that encouraging information transfer will help the economy is very popular; state after

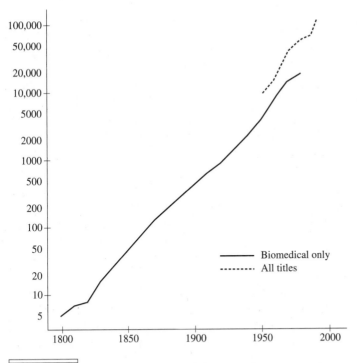

Figure 1.3   Growth rate of scientific journals

state tries to attract business by boasting about the advanced telecommunication services that are available. Nevertheless, it is difficult to prove the value of better access to information. Sometimes people think this is obvious. How could you not want access to information? What is the point of piling up texts and books if they cannot be found again? And yet, all library projects today have great difficulty justifying themselves financially. Why should a university spend 4% of its budget on the library (a typical U.S. number)? Why not 2%? Or 1%? For that matter, why not 10%?

Fritz Machlup and Peter Drucker have written of the importance of information and "knowledge workers" (Machlup 1962; Drucker 1970). But recently there has been considerable controversy about the value of information technology to the economy. This controversy started with Steven Roach (1996), an economist at Morgan Stanley, who suggested that the slowdown in U.S. productivity that started in the mid-1970s, and which most economists attribute to the effects of the oil price increases of 1973, was caused by investment in computers that did not return comparable economic value. Roach argued, for example, that banks that invested heavily in information technology did not show greater profits than banks that did not. He was refuted by MIT professor Eric Brynjolfsson, who found that trucking companies that invested in computers did better than trucking companies that invested in trucks (Brynjolfsson and Hitt 1996). The argument has raged back and forth ever since, with more recent numbers showing better results for computer investment. Thomas Landauer's recent book shows numbers from the communications industries with real productivity gains from capital spending on information technology (Landauer 1995b). And Brynjolfsson claims the return on investment in information technology is 54% for manufacturing and even higher, 68%, for all businesses. Of course, all of these discussions reflect investment in computing for many purposes, not just information handling.

Arguments about the value of information, unfortunately, have little impact on conventional library operations. Many major public libraries have had budget cuts requiring shorter hours or reduced purchases. And many major universities are reducing their library budgets. Why society values information so little is unclear. On the one hand, the greatest success stories of economic growth over the last 20 years are not based on new innovation but on adaptations of research done in other countries. Several countries combine an enviable record in Nobel Prizes per capita with a loss of manufacturing industry as the inventions from these countries are manufactured elsewhere. You would expect information transfer to be essential for business growth. Yet the greatest commercial success is not in the countries that have the greatest libraries in the world. Skeptics ask: if the three largest libraries in the world are in Washington, London, and Moscow, but the largest economic growth is found in Tokyo, Singapore, Bonn, and Seoul, is having a large library all that important for economic success?

Perhaps the greatest boost to the public perception of information value came during World War II. Not only were particular devices, such as the atomic bomb, microwave radar, and the jet airplane invented, but entire academic subjects, such as operations research, were created and applied to wartime problems. The public image of nuclear physicists changed from a group with no public relevance to a status near that of gods. Computers were also invented during the war, although nobody knew it (see Section 1.6.1).

1.5   *Vannevar Bush*

During World War II the most important paper for digital libraries was written: "As We May Think," by Vannevar Bush (1945). Vannevar Bush had been a professor and administrator at MIT and was the head of U.S. science during the war. Bush published his paper in the *Atlantic Monthly* for July 1945. He wrote about the great scientific progress that had been made during the war and said that this represented our ability to use scientists in teams. Until the war, scientists largely worked alone or in small, independent research groups. During the war, large teams of scientists and engineers working together were able to make enormous strides.

Microwave radar, for example, was invented, built, and actually used during the three and a half years that the United States was in World War II. Compare that with the 10 years that it took in the 1970s and 1980s to introduce a new microwave radar transmission system into long-distance telephony. Nuclear physics before the war had the public reputation that Byzantine philosophy might have today: it was an entirely ivory tower subject of no possible practical use. The atomic bomb turned this around (and temporarily resulted in an enormous reputation for physicists). Bush, writing before August 1945, could not mention the bomb, but he had plenty of other examples to write about. He felt the enormous technological progress was a result of learning to organize scientific effort—of changing scientific research from a craft into a factory process and being able to combine the work of many, the mass production of knowledge.

Bush asked to what peacetime purpose we might put this new ability to organize science. He suggested that the best goal would not be another specific engineering goal, such as commercial airplanes, but the general purpose of organizing knowledge. His hope was that scholars could work together themselves. Richard Hamming, inventor of error-correcting codes, once wrote that Newton had seen so far because he stood on the shoulders of giants, but that computer scientists today stand on each other's feet (Hamming 1969). Bush wanted a breakthrough in accessibility of information, using technology to organize and retrieve books, journals, and notes.

In planning his system, which he called the "Memex," Bush relied entirely on bar-coded microfilm. He knew about digital computers, but he had grown up with (and made his reputation on) analog computers, which rely on currents and voltages to model quantities, instead of representing quantities as numbers. Bush was never entirely comfortable with digital machines. He did have several very prescient ideas, however. He suggested that individuals would plant links from one piece of knowledge to another, which he called "trails" of information. These trails are the precursor of today's hypertext and the Web. Bush also emphasized the ease with which you could put your own information into the system. In his article, he described how a handwritten page would be photographed and placed into the microfilm archive. Thus, the Memex could include a regular library (he imagined a 1-million-book research library on film), plus your own notes, plus the notes of your friends. This range of material was not available in one place until recently with the invention of the Web; traditionally your notes were in your office, and the library was a big building across campus. Bush also provided a very straightforward interface, based entirely on pictures of pages. Figure 1.4 shows a diagram of the Memex as envisaged by a *Life* magazine artist in 1945.

Figure 1.4   Memex vision

One thing Bush did not predict was free-text searching. In his vision everything was categorized and indexed by people, often by many different people with varied slants on the items they were describing. He talks about the impact of the Turkish bow on Europe; such an item might be on the "trails" of people studying military history, social history, strength of materials, ethnology, anthropology, and so on. But he did not imagine in his first paper people simply keying in "show me every article with the phrase 'Turkish bow' in it." Bush instead envisaged a community of scholars, all helping each other by indexing and relating all the different items published in a library. We have much better technology than he had; we did not have the community he wanted until the rise of the Web.

The emphasis Bush placed on community and on individual labeling of information was in stark contrast to another leading paper of the late 1940s, Warren Weaver's essay on machine translation (Weaver 1955). In 1947 Warren Weaver, also an MIT professor, suggested that machines could translate languages; he knew of their cryptanalytic abilities and suggested that Turkish could be viewed merely as an encoded form of English and deciphered by machines. Now it is certainly possible that foreign languages can be used as a code. The United States Navy, during the war, used Navajos as "code-talkers" who relayed messages from ship to ship, talking in Navajo (a language not studied in Japan). But translating a foreign language is much harder than deciphering a cipher message. Although Weaver's essay stimulated a great deal of work on machine translation and an entire field of statistical approaches to language analysis, it has not yet produced widely accepted machine translation software.

Weaver did set up a different thread of development of how material stored on computers would be accessed. Bush, remember, thought in terms of human classification and what we today might call "knowledge structures." Weaver thought in terms of statistical processing. For the next 40 years, we continued to have research in both areas. Artificial intelligence (AI) researchers studied ways of representing knowledge in some fundamental way, while the retrieval groups mostly studied ways of manipulating isolated words and treating them statistically. There were numerous discussions about "understanding." AI researchers suggested that until computers could in some sense understand natural language, they would not be able to perform speech recognition or language translation, while the information retrieval (IR) researchers demonstrated that at least information retrieval could be performed to some degree with programs that were fairly straightforward.

The contrast between Bush's emphasis on human classification and the Weaver strategy of pure statistical analysis has lasted for four decades. For most of that time statistical processing seemed to be winning. It did not look as if the creation of large masses of material with manually defined linkages between subjects was ever going to get the resources, whether volunteer or paid, that would make it possible. Text displays with links from one place to another, like cross-references but appearing automatically when clicked with a mouse, are called *hypertext*. Some of the experimental university hypertext systems found that it was hard to create the hypertext resources and that students did not quickly add to them while taking the courses for which the hypertext system was designed. The rise of the Web suddenly reversed this. After decades of increased emphasis on statistics, we suddenly have a revival of interest in manual linkages and a vast number of them actually implemented across the world. This is a social victory for the ideas of Vannevar Bush.

Bush did predict many other technical changes. He foresaw instant photography, photocopying (dry photography), electronic telephone switches, and other hardware advances, nearly all of which have come to pass. He also predicted speech recognition and some other software advances that have run afoul of the fact that although we can manipulate vast quantities of information with computers, we cannot understand it. But the basic conception of storing vast amounts of information and accessing it at will, and the identification of this goal as a target for an entire generation of researchers, is Bush's great contribution to the field.

1.6   *Computer Technology*

Computing technology starts fitfully in the late 19th century, with mechanical machines such as Hermann Hollerith's punched card sorting devices for use with the U.S. Census. Electronic computers and digital storage, of course, are the key inventions that make possible digital libraries.

PUBLIC RECORDS OFFICE

The original Colossus during the Second World War

Figure 1.5   Colossus—first electronic computer

1.6.1   *Processors*

The earliest electronic computer was not a number cruncher but a language processing machine. It was a 1943 machine called Colossus at the British code-breaking organization, Bletchley Park, shown in Figure 1.5. Colossus was destroyed at the end of the war, but it is being rebuilt at the Bletchley Park Museum. The popular misconception that computers started out doing arithmetic arose because the success of the Allied cryptanalysts was kept secret for 30 years after the war. Alan Turing, the founder of theoretical computer science, was one of the mathematicians and designers at Bletchley, and many early researchers knew of the machine and were influenced by it.

Although the existence of Colossus was a secret, the vacuum tube computer ENIAC in Philadelphia was publicized and often considered the beginning of computing. Some of its engineers moved to Remington Rand and there built the first successful commercial electronic computer, the Univac. Univac I filled a room; now much more powerful machines fit on a chip. Figure 1.6 indicates the progress in transistors per chip. For comparison, the ENIAC of 1947 had 18,000 vacuum tubes. There have been advances in computer architecture (notably microprogramming) as well as in device design.

The speed of processors has increased as well, although somewhat less dramatically than their complexity. In 1961 the IBM 7090 executed instructions in

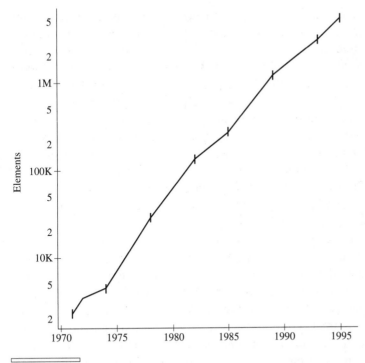

Figure 1.6   Transistors per chip

2 microseconds; a 1-microsecond instruction timing was still fairly common in the late 1970s. With the rise of better processor designs and smaller features on each chip, speeds have now increased to advertised processor speeds of 200 MHz, super-ficially a 200-fold speed increase, although the use of microprogramming means that these numbers are not directly comparable.

1.6.2   *Memory Technology*

The improvements in the technology to store digital information have been among the most impressive in any field. Cheap storage makes digital libraries not only possible, but affordable, and completely changes our view of what we can afford. In the 1960s a researcher could just barely take one long text and store it as ASCII (American Standard Code for Information Interchange—the most common way of representing one letter in one computer byte); today huge volumes of text are stored commercially, and researchers experiment with moderate-sized collections of video.

In general, really fast and accessible memory is more expensive than slower memory. Thus, computers often have hierarchies of memory, with three levels of storage. The best memory involves no large moving objects; it is all electronic, and thus it is *random access memory* (RAM), meaning that all the items in memory can be accessed in the same time. Today the access time is measured in nanoseconds. The next level is typically built of magnetic disks, and since some physical device (a read head) has to move across the disk to access different portions of the disk, it takes substantially longer (milliseconds) to find a particular piece of information. However, once the read head is at a particular point, it can pick up a sequence of bits in times measured in microseconds. Per bit, disks are cheaper than RAM. The lowest level of storage involves demountable devices, such as tape cartridges. It has a still lower cost per bit, but it takes seconds to minutes to retrieve a cartridge and mount the cartridge in some kind of reading device. Memory is measured in *bytes*, with large quantities identified as *gigabytes* or *terabytes*; Table 1.3 offers ways to visualize common storage amounts.

Primary random access memory is now made from semiconductors, while disk drives are now the standard secondary storage technology. IBM built the first magnetic disk in 1956; it held 4.5 megabytes and cost $40,000. Figure 1.7 shows price trends in disk storage and random access memory. Both prices are declining rapidly and at roughly parallel rates. Thus, the justifications for multiple levels of memory, and all the system architecture decisions that go with that, remain the same. This is why similar database software architectures continue to remain valid. Were the relative price changes to break step, database systems would have to be redesigned. Cheap enough RAM would produce in-memory database systems and favor techniques like object-oriented database management systems (OODBMS); sufficiently cheap disks, by contrast, would turn us back to batchlike database system designs.

Disk drive reliability is also increasing, with five-year warranties now commonplace. However, disks are still subject to head crashes, which can destroy the entire disk in an instant, and so all data on Winchester disks should be copied to alternate locations. This also protects against inadvertent commands that erase important data.

Many other kinds of storage have been used or are used by computer systems. What matters for storage is price, size, and durability. Primary offline storage has been magnetic tape, which has increased in density until a modern 8-mm video cartridge used for computer storage capacities holds from 5 to 7 GB per cartridge. Still larger capacity drives are coming. Sony announced in 1996 a new 8-mm drive, fitting in a 3.5-inch form factor and holding 25 GB uncompressed. Yet another cartridge format from Quantum (the DLT 7000) will hold 35 GB in a linear recording format; DLT stands for "digital linear tape." Still larger capacity tapes are used for digital video in studios, holding up to 165 GB per cartridge. The cost of storage on 8-mm video cartridges is about $4/GB, well below even the rapidly dropping disk prices. Magnetic tape, unfortunately, can wear out and should have temperature-controlled storage to maximize its life.

Table 1.3

Unit	Exponent	Amount (bytes)	Example
Byte	1	1	One keystroke on a typewriter
		6	One word
		100	One sentence
Kilobyte (KB)	3	1000	Half a printed page; a tiny sketch
		10,000	One second of recorded speech; a small picture
		30,000	A scanned, compressed book page
		100,000	A medium-size picture, compressed
		500,000	A novel (e.g., *Pride and Prejudice*)
Megabyte (MB)	6	1,000,000	A large novel (e.g., *Moby Dick*)
		1,400,000	A 3.5-inch floppy disk
		2,000,000	A song; a very large picture
		5,000,000	The Bible
		8,000,000	Typical RAM memory size, as of 1996
		10,000,000	A Mozart symphony, compressed
		20,000,000	A digitized scanned book
		50,000,000	A long radio program (2 hours)
		100,000,000	A small magnetic disk
		500,000,000	A CD-ROM; the *Oxford English Dictionary*
Gigabyte (GB)	9	1,000,000,000	A shelf of scanned paper; a section of bookstacks, keyed
		7,000,000,000	An 8-mm tape cartridge
		9,000,000,000	Large magnetic disk drive
		10,000,000,000	A digital movie, compressed
		100,000,000,000	A floor of a library
		200,000,000,000	A large digital videotape cartridge
Terabyte (TB)	12	1,000,000,000,000	A million-volume library
		20,000,000,000,000	Largest disk storage array in 1996
		20,000,000,000,000	Contents (as text) of Library of Congress
Petabyte	15	1,000,000,000,000,000	A scanned national library
		15,000,000,000,000,000	World disk production, 1995
		200,000,000,000,000,000	World blank tape production, 1995

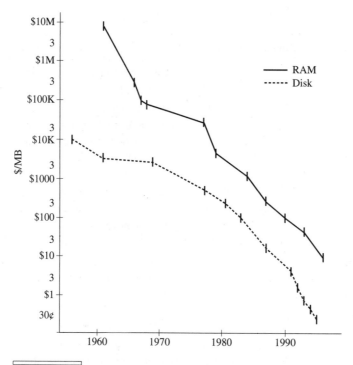

Figure 1.7 Price of memory

The audio CD format looked immediately attractive to computer systems manufacturers, offering a lightweight 650-MB storage device suitable for mass production and extremely durable. CDs, for their first 15 years, could only be written in large factories that had high setup costs but low costs per disk, making them inherently a mass production device. Recently the CD-R, or CD-recordable, has become common. These devices are not physically the same as the traditional CD, since they rely on a different physical mechanism for changing the reflective surface of a disk to encode the bits. However, CD-R disks are read by all standard CD readers. A CD-R device is now under $1000, and the blank disks are about $7, making it possible for many people to write their own CDs.

CDs are admirable storage from the viewpoint of a library. Since they are write-once devices, they cannot be overwritten by any kind of software accident. They are physically durable and do not deteriorate with normal use. Philips originally advertised them as "perfect sound forever," and although this slogan is no longer in use, CDs still do not wear out in any normal sense if properly made. They can, of course, be damaged by sufficiently silly handling (e.g., scratching a label into the disk) or lost by fire or theft, so additional copies are still needed.

Just as CD readers became ubiquitous on PCs, with the vast majority of non-laptop PCs now sold being "multimedia ready" (an advertising term meaning a sound card and a CD reader), the industry began to design the follow-on device, the digital video disk (DVD), also called the digital versatile disk. The stimulation for the DVD came from the movie industry, which could not fit a compressed digital movie at adequate quality into the 650 MB of a CD. Digital video disks will hold 4 to 9 GB on a side, depending on whether they are single- or double-layered, and can also be double-sided, which would mean a total capacity of 17 GB (CDs are single-sided). The primary purpose of these disks will be to sell movies, for about $20 each. If the marketers are successful, DVD readers will be the hot device of the 1997 Christmas season. They offer a promise of extremely large and durable storage, ideal for many kinds of digital library applications.

1.6.3 *Software*

Software technology has also made great strides. Whether software or hardware moves fastest is not clear. Some years ago Donald Hammann investigated the improvements in algorithms to diagonalize matrices, a standard problem in numerical analysis (the solution of mathematical tasks by iterative methods, an important field for many practical problems) (Hammann 1983). His result (shown in Figure 1.8) is that if you have large matrices to diagonalize, and you have a choice between 1947 hardware with modern software and 1947 software running on modern machines, you are better off with the old hardware and new software.

Most important in software has been the rise of the Internet, the electronic network between computers most widely used today. The development of protocols has joined with the use of transmission devices to permit large-scale interconnection between computers. Figure 1.9 is a log plot of the number of Internet hosts (a machine that is accessible from the Internet and contains the necessary software to respond to Internet messages). The growth is now worldwide; the United States may have about half the Internet, but Germany and the United Kingdom run neck and neck for second place, with about 450,000 hosts each at the beginning of 1996. Behind them, despite the relatively small population of each country, are Canada with 375,000 hosts and Australia with over 300,000. The Faeroe Islands have over 500 Internet hosts.

The most important new software technology for digital libraries is the invention of the World Wide Web by Tim Berners-Lee (then at Conseil Européen pour la Researche Nucleaire [CERN]) and Mosaic by Marc Andreesen (then at University of Illinois, now a founder of Netscape). Berners-Lee created the idea of making it easy for people to accumulate pictures and text for access around the world; Andreesen made the interface that got everyone excited. The result was an epidemic phenomenon, as Web pages went from a trickle to a flood over the last two years.

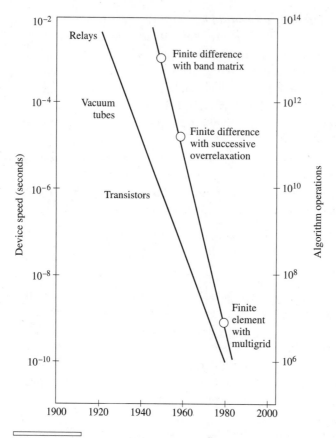

Figure 1.8   Computational progress

There were virtually no Web pages in mid-1993, but by January 1996 there were over 75,000 hosts with names beginning *www*. Many now see the Web as the likely interface for all kinds of information and interaction in the future; we're just not sure about some of the important details, like who will pay. But this is the hope for how to deal with the information glut of today.

In summary, technology has made enormous advances in processors, input and output, storage devices, and connectivity. In 1962 a good university research computer was an IBM 7090, which cost about $3 million, and a student to program it could be hired for $1.50 per hour, so that the machine cost the equivalent of 2 million hours, or 1000 years of work. Not surprisingly, computer time was precious, was shared out among the different users, and was billed by the minute. Today we could buy a better machine for $3000 and pay the undergraduate $6 per hour, so that the machine would cost the equivalent of 500 hours, or less than three months of work. Input is much easier, going directly into an editor instead of via a

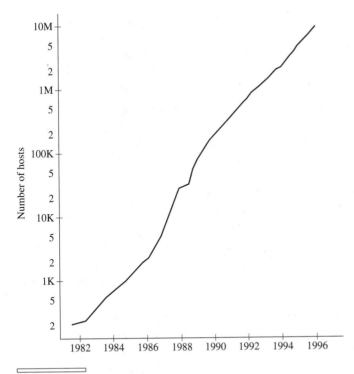

Figure 1.9 Internet hosts

card punch; output is also much higher quality, since the machines of 1962 tended to have only uppercase printers. Not surprisingly, given the cost changes, libraries can now use computers for many functions, so long as the computers save even a little time or provide a little help, and we no longer feel we are technically limited in building systems.

1.7 *Information and Software*

Since Colossus, the first electronic computer, was devoted to crypt-analysis, statistical language processing was the very first application of computing. This kind of processing involves calculations on the frequencies of words and characters; the most elementary kind is simple letter-frequency tables. Next, computers worked on the computation of ballistic tables and other numerical applications. But by the 1950s computers were used to create indexes, including the kind of index/concordance named KWIC (key word in context). KWIC indexes were invented by the late H. P. Luhn, a researcher at IBM. Each significant word was presented in the center of a line of text, with the preceding and subsequent contexts shown.

Luhn envisaged them as an alternative to conventional indexes, but they are too bulky to use effectively in this way. They still have applications in literary analysis; concordances and their uses are described in Section 2.8. Many literary texts have been entered into computers, partly as a way of making them available and partly for other kinds of literary studies. For example, Michael Hart created Project Gutenberg, in which volunteers have entered hundreds of texts. Hart's goal, which he has been working toward since 1971, is to have 10,000 public domain texts digitized by the year 2000, in plain ASCII format; so far he has about 600.

Although machine translation work in the early 1950s proved to have only limited utility, work started on syntactic analysis to improve these programs. The syntactic work led to systems that tried to do question answering, retrieving specific data from tables of numbers in response to an English question. Early promising work by researchers like Daniel Bobrow (then at MIT) and William Woods (then at Bolt Beranek and Newman [BBN]) has been slow to lead to practical applications in digital libraries. Experiments done by IBM indicated some sobering problems. In the process of learning how to use a traditional query language on some database, the user learns some important information about the database, such as what the questions are that the database can answer. Users left without any such guidance tend to ask questions that the database system cannot answer, even including such questions as "What should I do next?" Once it is recognized that users of a natural language query system still have to take a course in the database content, it seems to be less important that they also have to learn a new format to ask questions. Database interfaces also improved, with systems like QBE (query by example) becoming simple to use.

Instead of question answering, information retrieval of whole texts became common with the boom of the Web (see Section 1.6.3). Thousands of people and institutions have posted valuable information on Web pages; the Web now holds about 2 TB of text (something like 2,000,000 volumes if printed out as books). Material on the Web can be found with the search engines run via Webcrawlers (Ross and Hutheesing 1995). These programs seek out every page they can find on the Web, bring back all the text on it, and compile an index. Among the programs that do this as of late 1996 are Lycos (CMU), Alta Vista (Digital), Open Text, and Excite (Architext). For many purposes, these are now the quickest and easiest way to find information. As of August 1996, for example, Alta Vista was indexing 30 million pages from 275,000 Web servers, and it was used 16 million times a day.

Webcrawlers, or *spiders*, are programs that spend evenings retrieving every Web page that they can reach, looking at it for any references to any other Web page, and picking that page up as well. In this way they try to collect every single page and in fact compete by boasting of how many pages they found. They make full-text indexes to all of this text and provide search services free. Alta Vista operates very rapidly, searching its file in a few seconds, because it keeps the entire inverted file in RAM (see Section 2.4 for a discussion of how such text searching is done).

Access to the Web is slow enough that real-time interaction is hard to achieve, giving a strong motivation to the idea of *agents* or *knowbots*, programs that would run around the Web and execute where appropriate. In particular, a Web page could supply a program to run on the user's computer and thus achieve much faster response time and also offload the computing load from the server machine to the machine of the person who actually wanted to see the result. People hesitated to do this at first for practical reasons (how to get a program that could run on the many types of machines users might have) and for security reasons (how to be sure that this program would not do anything unwanted). James Gosling of Sun Microsystems designed Java, a language that can be interpreted, getting around the problem of which machine it had been compiled for, and that is sufficiently limited in its capabilities (no file reading or writing) to be safe to execute. Java *applets* (the name for a piece of code run as an application inside a Web browser) are now interpreted by software like Netscape and can be used to provide interactive services. The Web is clearly the model for the widespread digital library that Bush (and others) envisaged.

1.8 *Summary*

There seems little sign of any slowdown in the development of storage technologies. Disk prices drop as sizes increase. The largest storage system mentioned in a recent boasting contest was 23 terabytes (TB) at Lawrence Livermore National Laboratory, along with a press release from Wal-Mart about a record-breaking 11 TB data warehouse. Perpendicular magnetic recording or other new technologies may produce another factor of 10 in disk capacities. Processors are also getting faster and so are networks. Recently the U.S. government has announced plans to spend $500 million on a new high-speed backbone for the Internet, connecting top universities and research labs. Display devices are also steadily improving, albeit more slowly. The 640×480 screen of a decade ago is now more likely to be 1280×1024, with 1800×1440 readily available and 3000×2000 displays existing as prototypes. Larger flat screen displays are likely to start replacing conventional monitors, with savings in weight and desk space.

We do not know, however, what people want to do with even the technology we have today. Many questions remain unanswered about how information will be or should be used, including questions about access methods for finding information and about content and what is or should be available.

How users will choose to find information is a problem that has not been studied enough. Some people search for what they want, knowing fairly accurately what it is; others browse around, looking for something interesting. Some use automatic searching tools, while others want to trace manual links (the Bush–Weaver dichotomy is still around). Some would even like formal models or classifications of what is online. How do we continue to cater to all these methods of access? For example, how do we provide searching of images? Or efficient browsing of video and audio?

The content that libraries should provide is also unclear. Some material is available as searchable, formattable text. Other information is only available as pictures of printed pages (or of real scenes). Users want both, but different retrieval techniques are required, making it hard to provide unified systems. Some of the contents of a digital library will be new material, delivered electronically to the library; other information will be converted from older forms. The libraries need to merge both kinds of collections.

For some materials, digital versions are going to be all the user needs. In fact, for some objects they may be the only form that is created. For other materials, digital versions may only be finding aids, with the user eventually getting the original form for deeper study. Even in paper libraries, art historians use books or slides to identify works whose originals they would then travel to see. For which users and which materials will digital representations be inadequate?

Most important for a library is to have the right content for its users. The Web today contains some 2 TB of information, the equivalent of a 2,000,000-volume library. But is it the most valuable content, and if not, how can we get the right content? Can we even agree on what the right content is? Some wish to exclude some kinds of material (whether it is terrorist information, pornography, or unapproved political sentiments). As well as exclusion, inclusion can also be a problem. Much material on the Web is low quality; can we make it possible for people to use the Web effectively to get high-quality answers?

Access to users, as well as to documents, also matters. Not everyone is a computer expert. How do we see that everyone—including those without computer skills and those with less money—still has access to information? We have justified digital libraries and networks with the same arguments for public education and informed voters that we used in the past. In the future, if these arguments matter, digital libraries must be accessible and the systems must be designed to provide information universally, not to isolate people from the information they need.

To begin discussing these questions of how a digital library is used, the next two chapters will deal with the technology of content retrieval for text and images, explaining how to build a digital library that can find pages and pictures for users. Later chapters will deal with the more institutional aspects of libraries—collections, preservation, and economics. The chapters on usability and on the future of digital libraries will return to some of the social questions and discuss how we might organize the system for better support of society as a whole.

2

Text Access Methods

TWO BASIC METHODOLOGIES support digital libraries today. One is the ability of computers to manipulate text; the other is their ability to manipulate images. A page of text can either be represented as the sequence of characters on the page or as the picture of the page containing the characters. This chapter discusses the technology that handles characters; the next chapter will deal with the technology of images. (For a really excellent and detailed survey of methods for searching large text files, see Witten et al. 1994.)

The ability of computers to manipulate text includes searching, formatting, and other operations. Where once the creation of a concordance, an index of the occurrences of every word in a work or set of works, might have been a life's work, it is now entirely mechanical. Similarly, searching for exact character strings is now trivial. In the mid-1970s the Bell Telephone Laboratories company newspaper started running word puzzles for amusement (e.g., "list three words that contain the letters *btl*") and was surprised when a group of people with a machine-readable dictionary proved able to answer these puzzles as fast as they could be typed in. Today everyone with a personal computer and CD-ROM dictionary could do this.

The most notable success of computing has been in document preparation, with the word processing industry now dominated by programs such as Word or WordPerfect. Almost nothing in a commercial setting is typed on traditional typewriters any more, let alone written by hand. As a by-product of this machine conquest, almost everything now written is available in machine-readable form, and its reuse in other ways is easy and widespread.

2.1   *Computer Typesetting and Online Databases*

The new word processing technology has produced vast online databases. These came originally as by-products of computer typesetting. For some years in the past, it had been possible to control typesetting equipment from paper tape. Monotype machines, for example, typically worked by having the operator punch a paper tape of instructions, which was then used to drive the actual casting machine. The use of computers for typesetting started in the late 1960s, adapted from this process. Standard reference books, which were reprinted and were extremely expensive to reset, were the first places for applying computer typesetting. *Books in Print*, as an example, was one of the earliest U.S. machine-composed books. Newspapers also led in their use of computer setting; they could take stories from news wires and put them into printed form without editors or compositors.

Technology for computer typesetting has changed over the years. In the early years of computer composition, filmstrips with images of specific letters were manipulated by the computer. As each letter was read into the machine (typically from paper tape) the filmstrip would be moved so that a light could shine through the letter, exposing some photographic paper and thus making up the page. Either the paper or the optics had to be moved after each letter to arrange to get the next one in a different place, so such typesetters were relatively slow. Then cathode ray tube (CRT) screens came into use. Letters were placed on the screen, and then the whole page was exposed in one place. This saved the time to move the paper, but there was still a photographic process; what came out of the machine went into some kind of developer, finally producing a sheet of photographic paper, which could be used in offset printing.

Most recently, we have seen the advent of laser printers. These printers, derived from xerographic copy machines and invented at Xerox PARC in the 1970s, dispense entirely with the idea of creating a physical plate. Instead, an optical image of the material to be reproduced is projected onto a drum coated with a material that becomes electrically charged when exposed to light (various forms of selenium are used), so that the image of the page in light and dark creates an image of charged and uncharged drum regions. Electrically charged ink particles are then picked up only by part of the drum and thus transferred to the page to be printed. The image is generated in the first place with a laser turned on and off by electrical circuitry, rather than from a CRT or from a page (thus the name *laser printer*). Laser printers started as one-at-a-time output machines, replacing complex chain printers for computer output, but now large machines built on this principle, such as the Xerox Docutech or Kodak Lionheart, can print high-quality (600 dots per inch) multicolor images so rapidly (135 pages per minute) that entire books can be printed on demand. They are still not quite competitive either for the very highest quality printing jobs (1500 dots per inch is easily achieved by the offset industry) or for very long press runs, but they are taking over all office applications. The newest developments are in the direction of color printers, for which color laser printers are still competing with inkjet printers (color laser printers offering somewhat better saturation and speed at higher cost) and also with dye sublimation printers, which provide extremely high-quality color.

Simultaneously with the development of printing technology, the software to format the documents has developed. Starting in the mid-1960s at MIT, programs that let people print formatted documents onto electric typewriters were developed. The MIT software led to research progress through various new programs, such as the nroff/troff programs at Bell Labs, scribe at Carnegie Mellon University (CMU), and TEX at Stanford. These programs, originally devoted to justifying right margins and numbering lines (both tasks extremely annoying to manual typists), were letting users choose type fonts and letter sizes and many other characteristics of print appearance by the mid-1970s.

Two models of printing software followed. Some word processing software is keyed to the exact appearance of the text: their commands reflect choices such as "italic" or "point size 12" and their output is hard to adjust in format. Nor do they indicate whether something is in italics because it is an author name, or a title, or a heading, or a foreign word, or what. They tend to be simple to edit, following the model of "what you see is what you get" (WYSIWYG) originally developed for the Bravo text processor at Xerox PARC in the early 1970s and followed by most commercial word processing systems. The other model, pioneered at Bell Labs, describes the document in terms of content: text is labeled as "heading" or "footnote" or whatever, and a separate set of formatting instructions decides that a heading might be 12 point Helvetica bold or some such description. Such text is harder to type but easier to use for purposes other than the original (e.g., reformatting into multiple columns). The present development of the first model is PostScript (discussed in Section 3.4), and of the second model, SGML (discussed in Section 2.2).

Of course, once the text is keyed for printing, it can be saved for many other uses. Large text databases were accumulated fairly rapidly from such sources as online newspapers; the electronic file of the *Toronto Globe and Mail* dates to 1964. The text retrieval industry developed based on dialing up large central database systems and phrasing interactive queries. Such systems started with government research in the 1950s and 1960s; for example, Dialog, the biggest such commercial system, derives from a NASA project named RECON.

Figure 2.1 shows that the number of online databases has been growing steadily for the last 15 years. The slight falloff in the last few years may represent competition from CD-ROMs and the Internet (Williams 1996).

Figure 2.1   Online databases

The variety of material available today is immense. The complete text of many newspapers, most abstracting and indexing journals, and a great many current magazines are available in digital form. All of this is a by-product of the commercial printing industry. In general, although things change rapidly, we can say the following:

1. For-pay online systems have good coverage of magazines; some scientific journals, particularly in medicine; all abstracting and indexing services since about 1970; and most major newspapers since 1990.

2. For-pay CD-ROMs include many major reference works such as encyclopedias and dictionaries; the many journals in CD-ROM are usually images, although a few are text.

3. Free resources on the Internet include a great many technical reports, current papers, and a variety of material ranging from student papers to major works of pre-1920 literature.

Most books and journals are still not on the Internet in full text form; this will change, but it is an economic problem, not a technical one.

2.2 *Text Formats*

As mentioned before, text can be stored in a variety of formats. Even the basic alphabet is not firm. For languages that only use the 26 letters of the Latin alphabet (most notably English), the ASCII standard has won out over alternatives (5-bit teletype code, 6-bit binary coded decimal [BCD], and 8-bit extended binary coded decimal interchange code [EBCDIC]). ASCII is a 7-bit code, leaving 1 bit of each 8-bit byte unused. However, there are a great many languages that need additional symbols, whether just a few accent marks (most of Western Europe's languages) or thousands of new symbols for ideographs (Chinese and Japanese). Standards groups are working on all these questions, and a new Unicode standard is likely to become the official representation, covering the characters for all major languages with a 16-bits-per-character representation.

Much more important than the character set is what to do to signal how the letters are to be handled. In the WYSIWYG style the letters are marked with direct typesetting information: font, size, position, and so on. This is normally done by putting very specific typesetting codes (in older systems often labeled with codes like "upper rail" from the description of hot-lead machines) around the letters. As mentioned, though, in such environments it is not possible to revise the formats. Publishers have "style manuals," which describe the formats of their books and magazines; to convert from one to another is impossible if only the output format, and not the meaning of the input, is described in machine-readable form.

More and more, therefore, large publishing groups are using higher-level descriptive systems. In these, each input character is in some way marked as to the intent of the character. Three main standards are worth discussing: MARC (Machine-Readable Cataloging), SGML (Standard Generalized Markup Language), and HTML (Hypertext Markup Language). In each case, it is possible to look at the environment of a character and decide what that character means.

This point bears not just on publishing convenience but on the entire philosophy of text retrieval and display: who should be in control? Often the author writes a string of words, the publisher chooses what they will look like on the page, and the reader just reads. Not always, however. Some authors, particularly poets, have cared a great deal about the exact appearance of their words on the page. If the reader gets the document in a format like SGML, however, it can be rearranged into a format of the reader's choice. Sometimes this seems clearly good; for example, someone with poor vision can choose to reformat with larger size print, making the document easier to read. Or, someone reading from a screen can adapt the presentation to the size of the screen (or the window in use). However, this limits the control of the author and publisher over the appearance of the material, which can cause problems: a page design carefully laid out for optimum readability (e.g., with references to pictures placed relative to text, or detailed tables) may be destroyed by a reformatting user, leading to a difficult-to-absorb text. So publishers and authors may object and wish to retain control of the appearance of the document. We do not yet know what the socially acceptable solution is going to be. Will readers be given complete freedom to rearrange material (even, perhaps, to the extent of choosing to hear the document read aloud), or will publishers and authors demand some control over the appearance of documents and avoid systems that risk losing it? Each choice might be appropriate in a different context.

Finally, properly tagged text is essential for some kinds of retrieval. If people searching the file are to be able to search for particular words in the title, or for author names as opposed to names mentioned somewhere in a document, it is necessary to have the fields labeled properly in the database.

Of the standards mentioned above, the oldest is MARC, designed at the Library of Congress in 1969. MARC is used primarily for bibliographic records, but it is typical of a number of record-oriented formats. In MARC, each line contains a code saying what it is, followed by the text. For example, code 100 is a personal author, and code 245 is a title. Part of a sample book record might look something like

```
100a Lockley, Ronald Mathias.
245a The private life of the rabbit :
245b an account of the life history and social behaviour of the wild
rabbit
260a London :
260b Corgi,
260c 1973.
300a 174, [8] p. :
300b ill. ;
300c 20 cm.
500a Originally published, London: Deutsch, 1964.
```

The key fields shown are the author (100), title (245, divided at a colon), place of publication (260a), publisher (260b), and date (260c). In addition, the number of pages, size, and original publisher are shown. The full record would also have the Dewey and/or Library of Congress class, and other data. MARC, as can be seen, is a very record-oriented language, with very rigorous formats. It is tailored to bibliographic entries for library catalogs and thus does not support many of the features needed in full documents (equations, tables, footnotes, and so on).

By contrast, SGML is a much more flexible standard. In fact, SGML is only a syntax and a philosophy. It says that information is to be tagged meaningfully and that tags are to be contained within angle brackets. Thus, an SGML sequence might look something like

```
<title>Huckleberry Finn</title><author>Mark Twain</author>
```

in which each field to be tagged is surrounded by two tags in angle brackets, one indicating the start of each field and the other the end. The end tag is the same as the start tag except that it is preceded by a slash. The tags must be nested correctly—the following line is illegal:

```
<title>Huckleberry Finn<author></title>Mark Twain</author>
```

Tags can contain other information. For example, you could have `<author type=pseudonym>` or `<figure graphicfile="F11830.gif">`. On the other hand, a tag can be freestanding, without any data (e.g., `<thinspace>`).

In addition to information in tags, SGML also deals with the definition of special characters. These are preceded by an ampersand and ended by a semicolon, as in the example `&pound;` for the sterling currency symbol £.

The content of tags is flexible, but there are several popular standards for them. These include the American Association of Publishers (AAP) Electronic Manuscript Standard, the Department of Defense Continuous Acquisition and Life-Cycle Support (CALS) rules, and the Text Encoding Initiative (TEI) standard. Many publishers have defined their own document type definition (DTD) to reflect their particular needs and requirements. Here is a sample of the TEI labeling:

```
<stage>Enter Barnardo and Francisco, two
    Sentinels, at several doors</stage>
<sp><speaker>Barn<l part=Y>Who's there?
<sp><speaker>Fran<l>Nay, answer me. Stand
    and unfold yourself.
<sp><speaker>Barn<l part=i>Long live the King!
<sp><speaker>Fran<l part=m>Barnardo?
<sp><speaker>Barn<l part=f>He.
<sp><speaker>Fran<l>You come most carefully
    upon your hour.
```

Some complexities of printing are still settling down in SGML. Mathematical equations in SGML are very complex, and I think that a language similar to UNIX eqn is likely to succeed. Very roughly, eqn is a format in which equations are typed as they would be read aloud. The Web doesn't handle equations yet, so the syntax is still to be decided. For tables, a format with a great many internal labels such as `<row><cell>xx</cell><cell>xx . . .` is winning over the UNIX tbl-style of separating the format from the table data. Similarly for bibliographic citations the idea, from UNIX refer, that the user should have a separate bibliographic file with just data, and specify the format elsewhere, is losing to the SGML scheme in which the user tags each item but specifies the order. It will be harder to convert from one citation style to another than in refer, but it will be easier to control the exact appearance as you are typing. At least there are content labels on the fields. For graphs and images, importing PostScript seems to be the winning strategy.

The formatting language used on the Web is HTML (Hypertext Markup Language). HTML is syntactically a very similar language to SGML, with the same kinds of formats. The major relevant difference is that HTML supports hypertext links. These are specified in a format such as

```
<A HREF="http://www.cis.ohio-state.edu:80/text/faq.html">
```

just as with ordinary formatting tags. Their meaning, however, is that they point to another document or another place in the same document. See Section 5.4 for a more detailed discussion of hypertext.

Since most word processors follow the WYSIWYG model, it is more difficult to find one that makes it easy to enter SGML labels. Some publishers claim that it can be twice as expensive to enter material formatted correctly in SGML than it is to use an ordinary word processor. Although some aspects of the formats can be converted automatically, there is no way to supply automatically the information about the labels that is needed for proper SGML.

2.3 *Linear Text Searching*

No one has the time to read an entire library. Everyone must use some method of deciding which items to read. Although there is much dislike for the searching process, and many users insist they find what they need via browsing or serendipity, searching is really essential for proper use of any library, especially a digital library being accessed remotely, with no one at the next table to ask for help. Given a large collection of online texts, how can the reader find what is wanted? This divides into several basic questions:

1. What kind of vocabulary is used to describe the content? This may just be the text, as it appears, or there may be synonyms, indexing, or other kinds of content labeling.

2. What kind of connectives, if any, are used to handle searches that involve more than a single word or term? The most common form is Boolean logic (i.e., "ands" and "ors"), but some systems use less logic; they have perhaps more natural forms of multiple-item search.

3. How do you actually find a particular item in the text? There are many algorithms, and one important ingredient in digital libraries is knowing how to do the searches. The next few sections will deal with the different search algorithms.

To understand searching, remember a little bit about computer speeds. It normally takes a computer a few microseconds at most to pick up a single character, examine it, and decide what to do next. By contrast, suppose you need something from a disk. Retrieving a disk block at random requires waiting for a *rotational latency*, the time required for the disk to spin around to the place where your data is recorded, perhaps 20 milliseconds. Thus, most of the time involved in a retrieval system is spent waiting for the disk to revolve, and minimizing the number of disk accesses is the way to keep the process running fast.

There are several basic search techniques: linear search, inverted files, and hash tables. Linear search routines start at the beginning, go character by character through the text, looking for whatever it is that is wanted, and stop at the end. The entire file is processed. Inverted file search routines make an index and only retrieve the blocks that contain the right matches. Hash table searching algorithms compute a good guess at the location of the items you want. Finally, signature files require a linear scan again, but they condense the material being searched so that the scan is faster.

The first search algorithm is linear scanning, simply going through the file from beginning to end looking for a string. On UNIX systems, this is done by a command grep, which has become a pseudonym for the process.

Linear scanning is slow, but it can be used to search for more than just a single string. String searching is often extended to a more flexible kind of request called *regular expressions*. They can be retrieved without backing up, and a large amount of computer theory has been developed around how to do this. Regular expressions are a limited extension to strings. The simplest form of regular expressions are "wild card" characters. For example, the period can be used to match any character. Thus a search for a.c matches any three characters beginning with *a* and ending with *c*. Another common operator is a repeat operator (e.g., a+ matches one or more adjacent instances of the letter *a*). A more complete regular expression list might be operators such as

.	matches any character
a*	matches any number of *a*'s (including none)
a+	matches one or more *a*'s
a?	matches zero or one instances of *a*
[a-d]	matches any of the characters *a, b, c,* or *d*
(a)	matches the expression inside parentheses
a|b	matches either expression *a* or *b*

Regular expressions include strings as the simplest case, so the expression cat matches the corresponding word. The expression [a-zA-Z]+ matches any string of letters, and the expression (dog|cat)? matches either the word dog or the word cat, or nothing. By convention, whenever there is a choice, the longest possible expression is matched.

Searching for regular expressions involves moving through the entire file, character by character, and keeping track of the matches. If there are choices, the computer must know what possibilities the current string might match. For example, a search for [a-z]+s (all words ending in *s*) against the string mess will produce a choice at each *s*; is this the final *s* or just another letter in the [a-z] substring? The first one is in the substring, the last is the final letter, but this can't be known in advance. If the computer keeps track of both alternatives, the search is called *nondeterministic*. Usually the search is converted to a more complex deterministic algorithm in which the set of choices is represented by a "state" in a finite automaton, speeding up the algorithm. Further details on regular expressions can be found in Aho, Sethi, and Ullman (1986).

If you know you are looking for a specific string of letters with no operators, you can do better. The Boyer-Moore algorithm was the first technique that did a linear scan but did not look at every character. Suppose you are looking for a long word like *aardvark*. The algorithms above would start looking at each character coming along to see if it was an *a*; if it is not, they continue with the next character. But suppose the computer looks to the eighth letter ahead. If the word *aardvark* begins here, the eighth letter must be a *k*. Suppose it is a *t*. Then the word *aardvark* doesn't start at this point. In fact, it can't start anywhere in the next eight letters, since there is no place in the word for a *t*. The search can skip eight letters ahead, without even looking at the intervening seven characters.

In practice this may not be very valuable; it may be that reading the characters takes most of the time, and whether they are looked at or not is unimportant. In other circumstances, especially if the processor has something else to do, the Boyer-Moore algorithm or one of its refinements may be a useful speedup.

Over the years there have been attempts to build special-purpose hardware searching devices, usually implementing some kind of string or regular expression matching. They have ranged from the IBM HARVEST system of the late 1960s to more recent systems by GE and TRW. These devices provide a hardware implementation of a finite state machine and a way to load an expression into it. They then stream large quantities of data past the device, which picks off the ones it wants. This may help in unloading a central CPU, for example, and it is possible to put such a device into a disk controller, providing a kind of searching right off the disk stream. Most of the attraction of these devices is the same as any other kind of linear search: no internal storage of the file in order to search it, and very flexible searching parameters.

The most ambitious linear search attempt to date is the use of the Connection Machine, a parallel computer with thousands of simple processors, to do text scanning (Stanfill and Kahle 1986; Stanfill, Thau, and Waltz 1989). In these experiments, thousands of processors each get some part of a file, and they can search their part very rapidly (Stanfill and Thau 1991; Stein 1991). So long as the entire file is simultaneously accessible, the Connection Machine could search it rapidly. The main advantage of a system like this is not in single-query search, however; it is in an application where a great many queries are being searched at once, so many that effectively the whole database has to be read anyway (because the set of matches will cover most of the disk blocks used to store the data).

All linear search algorithms have some properties in common. They require no space beyond that used by the original file (except for space proportional to the query size, not the file size). They can use the file the instant it is written; no kind of preparatory work is needed. They can search for complex expressions, not just strings. But they all get slower as the file to be searched gets longer. Even the hardware or parallel systems, fast though they are, will be slow on large enough databases.

2.4   *Inverted Files*

All of the algorithms mentioned in the last section take time proportional to the length of the string being searched. If the file to be scanned doubles in size, they take twice as long. This is acceptable if you are looking through a short file, but it is not a good way to search billions of characters in a big text database. Instead, the standard technology uses *inverted files*. Inverted files are like the index at the back of a book: the elements to be searched for are extracted, alphabetized, and are then more readily accessed for multiple searches.

Thus, given a text such as "now is the time for all good men to come to the aid of the party," an inverted file program needs a preparatory phase in which it makes a list of each word and where it appears. Start by numbering the bytes in the text (blanks are indicated by an underscore for clarity):

```
Position: 0 1 2 3 4 5        10        15        20        25        30
String:   n o w _ i s _ t h e _ t i m e _ f o r _ a l l _ g o o d _ m e n _

Position: 33  35        40        45        50        55        60
String:   t o _ c o m e _ t o _ t h e _ a i d _ o f _ t h e _ p a r t y
```

The words are then labeled with their byte position, as in the following list:

Word	Byte Position	Word	Byte Position	Word	Byte Position
now	0	*good*	24	*the*	44
is	4	*men*	29	*aid*	48
the	7	*to*	33	*of*	52
time	11	*come*	36	*the*	55
for	16	*to*	41	*party*	59
all	20				

And this list is then sorted into alphabetical order, yielding

Word	Byte Position	Word	Byte Position	Word	Byte Position
aid	48	men	29	the	44
all	20	now	0	the	55
come	36	of	52	time	11
for	16	party	59	to	33
good	24	the	7	to	41
is	4				

This permits a fast alphabetical lookup of each word, followed by a direct retrieval of the relevant part of the string. On average, to find an item in a list of N items takes $\log_2 N$ steps; this is much faster than reading an entire long file. Even for N of 1 billion (10^9) items, for example, $\log_2 N$ is only 30. To achieve this search time, use *binary search*; start at the middle of the list, and see whether the item sought is in the first or second half of the list. Then find the middle item of that half, and repeat until the item is found.

Another possibility with an inverted file is simply to do a two-stage linear scan: suppose the inverted file contains 10,000 items. Write a new file containing every 100th word and its position in the inverted file. Scan that shorter list linearly to locate the approximate position of the sought term, and then scan the 1/100th of the large list. For 10,000 items, binary search should take about 14 probes, and two-stage search will take 50 in each list, or 100 total. However, since there are fewer random probes (requiring a disk seek) and more continuous reads, the performance difference is likely to be small. It is not uncommon to find the cost of reading the next item off a disk to be, say, 1/30th the cost of reading a random item, so that 2 seeks and 100 reads require only as much time as 5 seeks, much less than 14.

Inverted files are the basis of the large systems used today. Nothing else can manage files of gigabytes or terabytes with adequate response time.

On the other hand, inverted files have disadvantages. They cannot search for arbitrary expressions. Typically, systems based on inverted files can only do searches based on the beginning of words. Thus, one will find options for searching for keys like `plate?`, meaning all words that begin with those five letters (*plated, plates,* and so on). To do the reverse—to find all words that *end* with a particular string—will normally require another complete inverted file with the words sorted on their ends, not their beginnings. Inverted files also must be computed before the searches can be done; this can be a long, slow process (basically, it is a sort and will take $N \log N$ time units for N words in the file). Most importantly, it means that updates cannot be accessed immediately; as the file is changed, it must be reindexed to create a new set of inverted files. Often supplementary files are used to allow updates to be accessed immediately, at the cost of requiring two searches.

Inverted files may take a lot of space. The overhead for inverted file systems ranges from 25 to 200%. Space needs can be lowered by using *stopwords,* typically the 50 or 100 syntactic function words that comprise about half the word occurrences in English. Assuming that users will rarely wish to search for words like *the* or *and*, a great deal of space in the inverted file can be saved by not bothering to keep track of them. On the other hand, more space is required if information must be stored about the context or position of each word. For example, some systems can search for a word that appears in a book title or for author names (which must be done with field labels since items like *bond* can plausibly be either a name or a word). This is called *fielded searching* and normally is done by indicating with each word occurrence what part of the text it came from. Here, as mentioned previously, is a reason why it is important to have text tagged so that the computer identifies which part of the input file serves which functions.

Today, inverted files dominate all the large retrieval systems and all the CD-ROM systems. They mesh fairly well with what people expect. The low cost of modern random access memory has permitted the Web search engine Alta Vista to keep the entire inverted file in RAM, part of the reason for its fast retrieval.

2.5   *Hash Coding*

Another form of searching that does not involve scanning an entire file is *hash coding*. The idea behind hash coding is that it would be convenient, given a word, just to compute where it appears in the file. If each letter appeared the same number of times in English, one could just say that words starting with *m* would be halfway through the inverted file. However, this is not true. One solution would be to keep careful files on the fraction of words starting with each set of letters, but because of the interletter frequencies this is difficult. For example, *th* is more common than you would expect by looking at the letter frequencies separately, whereas initial *ts* is less common than you would expect. Simpler is to take each word and compute a *hash function* from it. A hash function is similar to a random number generator; it tries to produce a flat output, in which each possible value for the function has about the same probability. However, it is reproducible—given the same input, it reproduces the same output. Thus, a hash storage system works by taking each input word, computing its hash function, and storing the word and whatever auxiliary information is needed in the location pointed to by the hash function.

Consider a simple (but not very good) hash function like "add up all the values of the letters in each word." Then, for the same string we had before ("now is the time for all good men to come to the aid of the party"), and assigning $a = 1$, $b = 2$, and so on, we would get hash values as follows:

Word	Value	Word	Value	Word	Value
now	52	good	41	the	33
is	28	men	32	aid	14
the	33	to	35	of	21
time	47	come	36	the	33
for	39	to	35	party	80
all	25				

One problem is immediately apparent. Even for such short words, we find the bucket locations (i.e., number of values) ranging up to 80. That seems silly to store only 16 words. To make such a list a standard length, the easiest thing to do is divide by some number and take the remainder. It is good if that number is a prime, since it will spread out the remainders more evenly. Let's arbitrarily pick 19 buckets in the hash table. Then the hash function is "add up the letters, and take the remainder modulo 19." The result is

Word	Value	Word	Value	Word	Value
now	14	good	3	the	14
is	9	men	13	aid	14
the	14	to	16	of	2
time	9	come	17	the	14
for	1	to	16	party	4
all	6				

So the contents of the buckets are

Bucket	Word(s)	Bucket	Word(s)
1	for	9	time, is
2	of	13	men
3	good	14	the, aid, now
4	party	16	to
6	all	17	come

Now we already have all the standard problems of hash storage. The words *the,* *aid,* and *now* all wound up at 14—it is said they have *collided.* Meanwhile buckets 7 and 8 have nothing in them. Since the aim is to spread out the values evenly across the 19 buckets, this shows that our hash function wasn't very good. Let's try something slightly better: multiply each letter value by its position in the word. This yields

Bucket	Word(s)	Bucket	Word(s)
2	*time*	12	*to, aid*
3	*good*	13	*the*
4	*all*	14	*for*
8	*men, of*	16	*come*
9	*is*	18	*now*
11	*party*		

There are still two collisions; this is normal for hash storage systems. To search this list, repeat the hash computation on the word sought, and look in the resulting bucket. In general, results very close to the desired one-probe-per-item can be obtained. The bucket is normally organized into a *collision chain* of cells, putting the items in other cells that are empty. Either a linear search or a secondary hash function searches through the collision chain for additional items. Hash systems can provide faster retrieval than binary search. They are very common in exact match computer applications (e.g., looking up words in computer languages like FORTRAN). Surprisingly, we do not know who invented hashing. It was certainly known in the 1960s (Morris 1968), but, although it is not an exact derivative of any noncomputer storage mechanism, nobody has claimed the invention. The hash algorithm described here is not really very good (e.g., just adding the letter values collapses anagrams), and an implementor should consult papers such as one by Savoy (1990) that compare better algorithms.

The disadvantages of hash storage for digital libraries relate to the sensitivity of the storage algorithm to the exact spelling of the word. Since the goal of the hashing algorithm is to spread the words as randomly as possible, variants like *plated* and *plating* will be very far apart (in this last hash table, at 1 and 16, respectively). Hash tables are thus a bad way to search for a set of words sharing a common root. Since many retrieval systems wish to do searches for words with common beginnings, hash tables for words are rarely used in large systems despite their efficiency advantages. Hashing shares with inverted files the need to spend time processing a file before it can be used and the need for storage overhead.

Updating in hash tables shows some asymmetries. Adding an item is straightforward, but deleting an item that was involved in a collision requires either (1) the reorganization of the collision chain to be sure that everything can still be found, a difficult operation (since the list of items that hashed into this chain is probably hard to find), or (2) the abandonment of that memory cell, filling it with a dummy entry that just says "keep looking." The upshot is that hash table systems are not good for a database that involves a lot of changes if any large fraction of the changes involve deletions.

There is a variant of hashing called *perfect hashing*, in which collisions are avoided, for a particular list of words, by selecting a hash function with no collisions on that list (and which maps the list into a list of exactly the right length). Instead of handling collisions at search time, an auxiliary table is made to adjust the hash function so that they do not come up (Cormack, Horspool, and Kaiserswerth 1985). Unfortunately, perfect hashing requires a stable list of words. Since practical digital libraries get updates, perfect hashing is not usually relevant. Even with perfect hashing, the words still must be stored in the hash table and checked to be sure that the right one is found; perfect hashing still allows the possibility that an incorrectly typed search term hashed to the same location as a different word.

2.6   *Other Text Search Issues*

Textbooks on data structures include other forms of file organizations, including tries and signature files.

Tries, developed by Edward Sussenguth (at Harvard) and others in the mid-1960s, are instantly generated inverted files. Moving letter by letter through a list of words, each letter points to a list of items. First you choose the correct first letter, which points to a list of items by second letter, and so on. Tries have the advantage that updating is easy, both additions and deletions; retrieval is relatively fast; and prefix searches (all words beginning with a given string) are easy. However, both storage overhead and the time to process the data into the trie are disadvantages. Tries are not popular in digital libraries.

Signature files are another data structuring technique that can sometimes be applied to digital libraries. This model is the closest analog of edge-notched cards. Each record is replaced with a short string containing codes reflective of the content of the record, which are then linearly searched. The codes are generated with hash routines so that they make very efficient use of the possible space. Nevertheless, searching any kind of linear file is eventually going to be slower than searching an inverted file.

Since digital libraries are usually searching files of text, the kind of numerical or exact-match technologies used in databases are not sufficient. A search for *library* should probably retrieve documents using the word *libraries,* and similarly for other morphological changes. Roughly speaking, there are something like three variants of the typical English word (albeit perhaps with widely different frequencies). In declined languages such as Russian there may be many more variants.

Suffixing even of English is more complicated than just matching prefixes. Consider, for example, the following:

Root	Derived Word
cope	coping
	copes
copy	copying
	copies
cop	copping (a plea)
	cops

Nonregular English derivations include such changes as *absorption* from *absorb* or *slept* from *sleep.*

It is possible to do some of the simpler transformations merely from the complex word (e.g., removing final *s* or *ing*), but it is much more accurate to do this in the context of a dictionary of stems. Otherwise it is hard not to start turning *nation* into *nate* or to work out that *determination* should come from *determine* while *termination* comes from *terminate* (see Lovins 1968 or Paice 1990 for suffix analysis rules). A common simplification is right truncation: searching for every string beginning with a certain set of letters. This introduces inaccuracies, but it is adequate for many systems and easily understood by the users.

Prefixes could be removed also, although they are less important in English. Again, a dictionary of word stems is valuable in deciding why *in-* might be removed from *inadequate* or *inaccurate* but not from *infer.* Prefixes are more likely than suffixes to change the meaning of a word; removing *in-* often reverses the meaning of a word (but do not forget that there are exceptions like *inflammable*). Truncation from the left, a possible alternative to prefixing, is more expensive than right truncation in the typical retrieval system; it will require the entire word-indexing software to be redone with the strings handled in reverse order.

Sometimes users might wish to have variable characters in the middle of words to allow, for example, looking for *aeroplane* and *airplane* by typing something like a?plane at the search system. This can be quite expensive to implement and comes up less frequently, so it is often omitted from system design; again, cheaper RAM memory has allowed some of the Web search engines to support this kind of operation.

Other possible ramifications of text search include the ability to search for phonetically similar strings. Although dating from 1916, the best known system for this is Soundex, a translation algorithm that attempts to reduce similarly sounding words to the same string. Words are replaced by four-character strings, each of which has an initial letter and then three digits. The letter is the initial letter of the original string; the digits represent successive consonants in the word, grouped into classes:

1	BFPV
2	CGJKQSXZ
3	DT
4	L
5	MN
6	R
0	—

The zero is used to fill out strings when there are not enough consonants. Note that all doubled letters (including doublings of class members) are treated as single codes. Thus *Jack* becomes J200, as would *Jock* or *Jak*. But *Jacques* would be J220 (because vowels are interposed between the *cq* and the *s*).

Free-text search systems of the sort described in the last few sections are a rapidly growing business. Some of the leading text retrieval software companies and their recent revenues are shown in Table 2.1 (Text Retrieval 1996). The growth of the entire text retrieval industry is shown in Figure 2.2.

String-matching software also has other applications. Searching databases of genetic sequences using string-matching techniques is now of major importance in computational molecular biology. The greater tolerance for insertions and deletions in this context has caused alternate algorithms, such as dynamic programming, to be more heavily used than in text searching.

Table 2.1

Company	1995 Revenues
Dataware	$41 million
Fulcrum	$31 million
Information Dimensions	$29 million
Verity	$21 million
Excalibur	$19 million

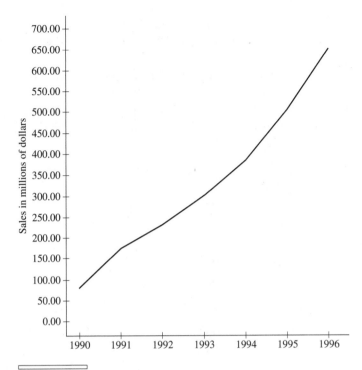

Figure 2.2   Text retrieval sales

2.7   *Thesauri*

As will be discussed later under retrieval evaluation (see Section 7.6), there are two kinds of mistakes that a retrieval system can make: errors of omission (a relevant document is not found) and errors of inclusion (a nonrelevant document is retrieved). The first kind of error is called a *recall* failure, and the second is a *precision* failure. Conventionally in simple keyword searching, a recall failure can occur when the same concept is expressed in two different words. The user might ask for information on *words* and the document might talk about *terms* or some other equivalent. Precision failures can arise by the presence of ambiguous words: the user might have asked for *rock,* meaning music, and be given documents about geology. The use of a thesaurus is a possible answer to these problems.

With a thesaurus, a single label is applied to each concept. The most familiar form is the *Roget's Thesaurus,* a list of 1000 concepts with a list of words for each. A variant of this format is used in information retrieval. Thesauri give a single label for each separate idea, and then a list of equivalent terms. Most commonly, the label is not a number as in *Roget's,* but a phrase. Thus, for example, in *Medical*

Subject Headings (MeSH) the word *neoplasms* is used for *cancer* and its equivalents. Thus, the same label can be searched for no matter what word was used in the text, improving recall.

As an example of a thesaurus, consider the ERIC (Educational Resources Information Clearinghouse) thesaurus; an excerpt is shown below. The user starts with the bold words in the left column (the *entry vocabulary*) and the system recommends or offers the terms in the central column as legal descriptors. The entry vocabulary is alphabetically arranged.

```
DEBATE
        CIJE: 246      RIE: 240    GC: 400
BT      Language Arts
RT      Persuasive Discourse
        Public Speaking
        Social Problems
        Verbal Communication
```

Debate Judges
```
USE     JUDGES
```

Deceleration
```
USE     ACCELERATION (PHYSICS)
```

In this excerpt, BT means "broader term," RT means "related term," and USE means "use instead."

Each category label is unique in the thesaurus. Each label has one and only one meaning, so that a search can be unambiguous within the limits of that label definition. However, there are ambiguities in the best-written texts, and there are certainly opportunities to choose different topics as being worth recording about a document. There are going to be different decisions about what the proper focus of emphasis should be or about the extent of some label definition. Thus, even the use of a proper thesaurus, combined with professional assignment of index categories, will still leave some retrieval problems.

It is also expensive to use thesauri in information retrieval systems since there is today no automatic way of assigning the categories. Manual indexers, as used in the retrieval systems Medline or Westlaw, involve considerable cost and some delay. Only elaborate and well-funded retrieval operations can afford this. Many smaller digital library operations cannot use manual indexing and thus find little use for thesauri. Early experiments by Cleverdon (Cleverdon, Mills, and Keen 1966), Salton (1968), and others showed sufficiently little benefit from manual indexing to cause most online systems to decide that thesauri were not worth the trouble.

Could syntactic processing improve retrieval? Surface structure parsers, which identify the correct structure of each sentence, would seem to help with labeling content of documents. This promise has been held out for decades, but with relatively little progress. What is wrong?

1. Surface structure parses are ambiguous. Sentences such as "time flies like an arrow" with its five possible analyses (consider the parse of the sentence "fruit flies like a banana") are still relatively simple compared with many longer sentences. Given the isolated sentence "I saw the man in the park with the telescope," there is no way even for a human reader to decide whether the telescope belongs to the narrator, the man, or the park.

2. Surface structure parses don't tell you what you need to know. For example, "the pig is in the pen" and "the ink is in the pen" have the same surface structure parse, but if that is all you can say about the two sentences you are not helping with the actual problem of deciding between the different meanings of *pen*.

3. Surface structure does not take account of context. "John went home; you should, too" may ask you to go home, but not necessarily to the same place that John went. A more common example is the failure of surface structure parsing to deal with pronoun reference. A system may not realize that *car* is the object of *drive* in the sentence "if a car breaks down, you can't drive it any further" if it cannot decide the referent of *it*.

4. Surface structure may be too restrictive. Given a query for "optical character recognition," a parser might deduce that the sentence "special character sets have been designed for easier recognition by optical or magnetic check-reading machines" does not contain that phrase, but it is probably relevant to the query.

Karen Sparck-Jones and Martin Kay discussed the paradox that linguistics seemed to be of so little use to libraries and retrieval (Sparck-Jones and Kay 1973). Their discussion is unfortunately still valid. Part of the problem is that much of linguistics has been devoted to syntax, while many of the problems of information retrieval derive from semantics. Retrieval can work reasonably well with strategies that do not use word order at all, sorting the words in a document into alphabetical lists. By contrast, knowing the syntactic structure of the sentences, without knowing the words, would be useless for finding anything.

An exception is the work of Salton on phrase detection. He was able to make considerable progress on identifying phrases for the purpose of improving the precision of retrieval systems (Salton and Buckley 1991). Salton's later work used weighted term matching for global selection and then local context of the terms to improve precision. Salton used distinguishing words based on the trailing context; thus, "Kennedy, elected President in . . . " can be distinguished from "Kennedy, appointed Justice in . . . " to separate articles referring to John F. Kennedy from those referring to Anthony M. Kennedy. This yielded impressive performance numbers using entire articles from the *Funk and Wagnalls' Encyclopedia* as queries; working with shorter queries is more difficult.

Part of the difficulty with trying to disambiguate language is that much ambiguity is deliberate, left in the text either because the speaker would rather have the ambiguity or because it is not worth the trouble of being precise. For example, spoken sentences with acoustic ambiguities, in which a given sound can be correctly transcribed into either of two words, are called puns ("Why did Cinderella buy a Polaroid camera? She was tired of waiting for her prints to come."). There are syntactic ambiguities ("Police help dog bite victims."). And there are semantic ambiguities, when a given word might be read two different ways ("How do you identify a dogwood tree? By its bark."). More often, of course, ambiguity is unintentional but unimportant; do you care that you cannot tell at the beginning of this sentence whether "more often" modifies only "unintentional" or also "unimportant"?

2.8 *Document Conversion*

How do documents get into retrieval systems in the first place? Overwhelmingly, they arrive from computer word processing systems, as virtually everything written today is prepared on a computer. However, sometimes old documents need to be converted into machine-readable form. There are two general strategies for doing this: keying them or scanning them. Scanning is followed by optical character recognition (OCR) to obtain a character-by-character text, although accuracy is sometimes too low without postediting.

It would seem that scanning would generally be much cheaper than keying. Rekeying costs perhaps $1 per KB for a single keying and 50% or so more for careful checking or rekeying. The cheapest prices are not likely to be from U.S.-based keying operations. Given that a good typist can do 50 words per minute, at 6 bytes per word the actual input rate is perhaps 300 bytes per minute or 20,000 bytes per hour. However, there is nearly always markup, labeling, and other costs. (The extra cost of markup and tracking is why double keying does not cost twice as much as single keying.)

In keying historic materials, often it is desired to retain the original spelling and any mistakes, rather than correcting them to current standard. To do this, it may actually be effective to have the keying done by people who do not know English (or whatever the language of the document is). They are less likely to replace older spellings by modern forms.

Scanning is, in principle, cheaper, even for pages that are sufficiently fragile that each one has to be handled individually. Scanning, OCR, and correction for one page (perhaps 2000–3000 bytes) recently cost about 40 cents per page, or 20 cents per KB, provided that not too much postediting is required. Manually fixing

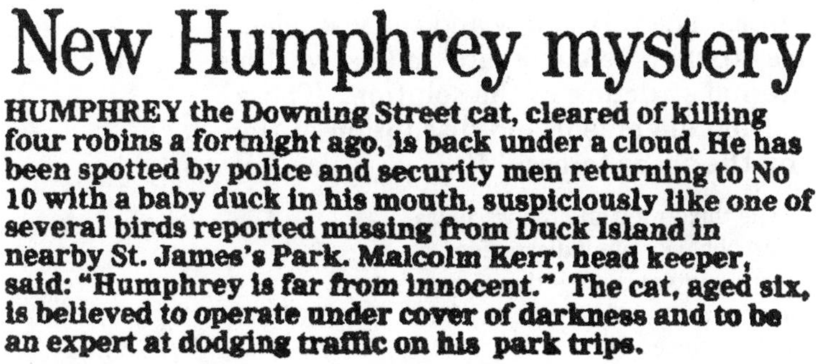

New Humphrey mystery

HUMPHREY the Downing Street cat, cleared of killing four robins a fortnight ago, is back under a cloud. He has been spotted by police and security men returning to No 10 with a baby duck in his mouth, suspiciously like one of several birds reported missing from Duck Island in nearby St. James's Park. Malcolm Kerr, head keeper, said: "Humphrey is far from innocent." The cat, aged six, is believed to operate under cover of darkness and to be an expert at dodging traffic on his park trips.

New Humphrey mystery
HUMPHREY the DownLng Street cat, cleared of klllI'ig
fotir robins a fortnight ago, Ia back under a cloud. He has
been spotted by police and security men retilrning to No
10 with a baby duck in Ms mouth, suspiciously like one of
several birds reported missing from Duck Island In
nearby St. James's PariL Malcolm Kerr, head keeper,
said: "Humphrey Ia far from Innocent." The cat, aged six,
Ia believed to operate wider coe'er of darkness and to be
an expert at dodge tram# on 'lie park trips.

New Humphrey mystery
 HREY the Downing Street cat, c
four robim a fortnight ago, is back under a cloud. He has
been spotted by PoUce and security men returning to No
10 with a baby d-uck in his mouth, suspiciously Uke one of
several b@ reported   ftom Duck Is@d in
nearby St. James's Park. Maloolm Kerr, head keeper,
said, "Humphrey is far fmm bmocent.' The cat, aged s@
is believed to operate under   of darkness and to be
an expert at dodging trame on his park trips.

Figure 2.3   OCR on newspaper text

mistakes at a rate of one or two per line can cost as much as rekeying. As an example of how badly OCR may function on some text that does not look all that bad to the eye, Figure 2.3 shows an image at top (from the *London Daily Mail*) and two different commercial OCR program results below. OCR programs do much better on higher-quality printing on better paper; Figure 2.4, for example, is a sample of a passage from an American Chemical Society journal. The only mistake is in the footnote.

OCR results have been improving steadily. The University of Nevada–Las Vegas has run regular comparisons between OCR systems. This year their test involved 5 million bytes of text, from corporate annual reports, newspapers, legal documents, business letters, and magazines. Resolutions for scanning ranged from the typical

increase in shear rate. The thixotropy and the viscoelasticity and non-Newtonian behavior are indicative for changes in the internal structure of the solution. Those changes originate from alignment and disruption of the rodlike micelles by the shear forces.[41,42]

increase in shear rate. The thixotropy and the viscoelasticity and non-Newtonian behavior are indicative for changes in the internal structure of the solution. Those changes originate from alignment and disruption of the rodlike micelles by the shear forces.41~2

Figure 2.4   OCR on printed journal page

fax machine (about 200 dots per inch) to 400 dots per inch (dpi). They found character accuracies of 97–99% for the different quality documents over several OCR programs. Each year, accuracy is improving, albeit slowly. The best 1996 program did 98.83% correct on English business letters; the best 1995 program did 98.61%. In some cases, speed is decreasing (although faster processors mean that users still see quicker results). The recognition speeds ranged from 25 to 200 characters per second (Rice, Jenkins, and Nartker 1996). With word accuracies of about 95%, there is still a lot of correction to do.

Fortunately, some information retrieval algorithms are very resistant to OCR errors. This makes sense since a word that is of great importance to the content of a document is likely to be repeated, and the OCR program may well get at least one of the instances correctly. Tom Landauer (University of Colorado) performed studies on Latent Semantic Indexing (see Section 5.5) that showed good retrieval performance with up to 50% of the words degraded. The experiments took place on a collection of medical abstracts, and LSI showed a 20% advantage over plain keyword search, even with half the words misspelled. Similar studies were done by Craig Stanfill (Stanfill and Thau 1991) at Thinking Machines and more recently by Bruce Croft (Croft et al. 1994) and Claudia Pearce (Pearce and Nicholas 1996). Croft found significant degradation in his results, which are word-based; Pearce and Nicholas, working with an N-gram-based indexing system, were able to achieve remarkably good retrieval even with 30% character errors (an appalling result, meaning that the average word is garbled). Whatever the ability of OCR to cope, scanning old paper has high handling costs. Considerably cheaper scanning can be achieved either with modern paper that can be sheet fed or with microfilm. Sheet feeding or microfilm scanning will cost perhaps 10 cents per page, depending on how much indexing information has to be keyed along with it.

Any estimate of conversion cost is likely to be grossly low if considerable editorial work is required. The easiest conversion is material that is self-describing (so that no large number of identification labels must be keyed along with the basic text), not full of typographic variations that must be tracked and not requiring careful reproduction of nonstandard spelling. Tables, equations, and other nontext materials also raise scanning costs.

Much literary material has already been converted and made available by commercial vendors. Chadwyck-Healey, for example, sells a set of five CD-ROMs containing all published English poetry up to 1900, the full text of the Patrologia Latina, and other literary information. Other material comes from government-organized projects, such as the full texts of French classic literary works prepared at the University of Nancy as the TLF (*Trésor de la Langue Française*). Still more material comes from a mix of smaller government-funded projects or university efforts and is deposited in such places as the Oxford Text Archive or specific archives such as the Rossetti file at the University of Virginia. Universities have other efforts, such as the CLIO system at Columbia, which attempts to put the material needed for the basic courses online. Finally, totally volunteer efforts such as Project Gutenberg have put additional items into machine-readable form.

Keeping track of all this material was a bit chaotic over the years. Early in the days of computer-readable texts, *Paradise Lost* was keyed three times by people who did not know it was being done elsewhere. More recently, however, the Center for Electronic Text in the Humanities (CETH, Rutgers and Princeton) has maintained an online catalog of materials for humanists. Since this catalog is on the Research Libraries Information Network (RLIN), many people without access to RLIN rely on the search systems for the Internet, which will find many of the works sought after. A serious issue, however, is the quality of editing of each of the files. For many humanities researchers, it is important to have accurate, well-edited texts online; versions adequate for popular reading are not enough. Not enough evaluation has been done of the editorial quality of some online texts, particularly those contributed by volunteers. And in some cases the desire to avoid copyright problems has resulted in the use of 19th century texts instead of modern and more accurate texts that are still in copyright.

Among the earliest uses of computers in the humanities was the compilation of concordances. Concordances, alphabetical lists of each word in a document, had been made by hand over the years for a few books such as the Bible and Shakespeare. With computers, it suddenly became possible to do concordances rapidly and easily, and they blossomed for many kinds of texts (e.g., the concordance to the works of the Roman historian Livy done in 1966 by David Packard). Students, using either concordances or searching tools with full text, can write papers on subjects like "the concept of fire in the works of Galileo" much more effectively than is possible without a machine-readable copy. It is possible to find each use of the word and then consider the word, the context, and the underlying concept. Computers also make possible looking at the use of new words in an author's work or looking at the development of an author's vocabulary over time (if many works are available).

Among other applications for online works, one of the most popularized is stylistic analysis to determine authorship. The original study in this area was by the famous statistician Frederick Mosteller to identify the authors of the Federalist papers (originally published with a pseudonym) based on the use of words by Hamilton, Madison, and Jefferson (Mosteller and Wallace 1984). Similar studies have been done on parts of the Bible, proposed new works by Shakespeare, and others (including most recently an investigation of the authorship of the best-selling novel *Primary Colors*). A related application of computerized text analysis identifies psychologically important terms (e.g., body parts) in texts and counts them, thus producing a kind of characterization of text that is not easy to do by traditional methods. Computers are also excellent at comparing different editions of the same work. Previously, when the literary scholar Charlton Hinman wished to compare different copies of Shakespeare's First Folio, he had to build a special machine that flickered between images of the same page in two different copies.

Other applications include educational use of online text for learning languages. Computer-aided instruction is good at vocabulary drill, for example, and can be extended with the use of full texts to teach syntactic structures in foreign languages. The computation of reading levels and thus the preparation of texts aimed at particular grade levels are also easier with mechanical assistance.

It is possible that scholarship will be moved in the direction of extremely detailed textual studies by computer text processing. It is now relatively easy to count the number of lines of Keats that do not contain the letter *j*, while it is not all that much easier than a century ago to discuss the importance of religion in Shakespeare's plays. We must rely on human judgment to decide whether the first kind of study is worth doing and in what balance compared to the second.

2.9 *Summary*

Text processing on machines is now a mature industry. We can get large volumes of current text in ASCII form, and the Web search engines are examples of what can be done with it. Many traditional paper-abstracting and indexing services, for example, now see most of their usage online, and there are online versions of many current publications. This chapter has reviewed how such systems are built and what some of the uses of machine-readable text have been. Not only are such systems practical, but they are cheap, and they can be substantially cheaper and easier to use than paper storage.

The technology of inverted files currently dominates the industry. We can do as detailed a text search as we wish; modern systems can search up to terabytes

(10^{12} bytes) with adequate response time. Even if the Web were to get much larger (and remember that the current content of the Web in ASCII is already within a factor of 100 of the largest libraries), we could still manage to do the necessary searching for full text. For smaller files, some of the alternative search mechanisms have advantages and are useful in writing programs to manage user files.

Every word can be found with a search engine. This can be good or bad. My name is rare; a search for Lesk will find either me or one of a small number of my relatives. Those searching for someone named Bond have a much harder time with search engines; there are many people with that name, much use of the word in chemistry or glue manufacture, and many Web discussions of the James Bond movies. Similarly, some concepts are easy to search for; others are shadowed under more popular meanings of the same words or may not have a single obvious descriptive term. Word searching may not be enough when the relationships between words are important. Venetian blinds, for example, are quite different from blind Venetians. And the inability to specify that a name is an author's name may result in the retrieval of many documents written by others who mention the searched name as a reference.

Progress will have to take the form of more concept-oriented searching, as some search engines are already beginning to advertise. Such systems will have to rely on some combination of detecting word relationships, using thesauri, and otherwise trying to access conceptual ideas rather than just word strings. Some of these problems will be discussed in Chapter 5; others are open research problems. More immediately, however, libraries must face up to material in which we do not even have full ASCII text, namely, scanned pages of books or journals.

3

Images of Pages

BESIDES ASCII, THE other way digital books arrive in libraries is as scanned pages. Some material is either not available as ASCII code or not appropriate to store that way. Most is stored as images, portraying a picture of the original. This chapter discusses how image files are created and how they can be accessed and used. For material that is not in ASCII, this is the way most digital libraries today store information. Often, for content such as photography, which is basically pictorial rather than textual, this will be the format used for many years to come.

Even for material that is fundamentally made of words, software systems today often provide access to images of text, not to ASCII code. The reader sees a scanned version of the printed page—the same familiar image, down to the headings and typestyles. The software is simpler to build since it does not vary with subject matter. Thus, the advantages of the image format are familiarity and ease of creation. The disadvantages are that searching must depend on other cues than the text itself (often a separate index or OCR file) and that the image is usually much bulkier than the text would be. A typical printed page from a book would contain some 2 KB in ASCII, while the same page as an image will be 30 KB or so, even compressed. For example, Figure 3.1 shows a comparison: the word *cat* uses three bytes; the line drawing is about a kilobyte; and the scanned photograph is 13 KB compressed with the JPEG algorithm (for a discussion of JPEG, see Section 4.2).

Images are much less adaptable than text: a reader with poor eyesight or viewing a bad screen or under bad light conditions cannot choose a larger character size, for example. Cut-and-paste downloading to capture the material for later use is also more difficult (although both Xerox PARC and the Bibliothèque Nationale de France have experimented with bitmap editing systems).

Figure 3.1   Size of representation

Images are often the choice for older material; post-1980 material will be available in machine-readable form, since hot-lead machines have completely given way to computer typesetting. A library wishing to convert old material to machine-readable form, however, is likely to have no economic alternative to scanning, since keystroking costs 10 times as much as scanning. Scanning is so cheap, in fact, that its cost is comparable with the cost of building shelf space to hold books.

3.1   *Scanning and Fax Machines*

Scanning technology has improved dramatically through the 1990s in accessibility and usage. Handheld scanners are now available for PCs, and there are over a million scanned images on the Web. Much of the improvement has been a consequence of the development of photocopiers and facsimile machines, resulting in widely available hardware to move pieces of paper through electronic gadgets and produce digital representations of them.

There are several kinds of scanning machines available. The most familiar are flatbed scanners, which place the image on a glass window and move a scanning head past the image. Typically the window will scan 8 × 14 or A4 paper, although they will accept small images as well, and these machines do exist in large sizes (up to 24 × 36 inches). They will normally scan color, grey-scale, or bitonal (one bit per pixel) and will do so at resolutions up to 400 or 600 dpi. Flatbed scanners now cost under $1000 with good quality and interface software. Such scanners do a simple bitonal scan at a dozen seconds per page or so. They can be equipped with sheet feeders to handle paper of acceptable strength.

Scanning machines are based on charge-coupled device (CCD) sensors: a linear array of CCD sensors, perhaps with color filters in front of them. The scanning array has many devices, since to achieve 300 dots per inch across an 8-inch page, the scanner needs a 2400-element row of sensors, but it is physically small and optics are used to reduce the image to the size of the array. Although flatbeds move the scanner past the image, there are also scanners that push the paper past the imaging device. Flatbeds are preferable for scanning from books or fragile paper, which cannot be moved easily by machine.

As an example of the use of such a scanner, I fed a 900-page book (out of copyright!) through an HP Scanjet 4C, at 15 seconds per page; since I needed to change the stack of paper every 10 or 15 minutes and often missed the change, it took most of a day, rather than the expected two hours. Quality was high enough for an OCR program to work quite reliably (it took overnight to do all 900 pages). An automatic deskewing program was used to align the pages. To use the stack feeder, however, the binding had to be cut off the book to turn it into a pile of loose pages. Some items, of course, should not be treated this way, but then each page would have to be placed by hand (efforts have been made to build page-turning robots, but so far they are impractical).

Other kinds of scanners pass the pages across the scanning head rather than moving the scanning head. Many of these scanners are faster, but they require that the paper be somewhat stronger and in better condition. They may also be double-sided, flipping the paper over and sending it past the scan heads again. Often they are only 300 dpi bitonal (i.e., they are made to scan printed or typed documents and not color drawings or photographs). These scanners might well operate at 1–2 seconds per page, at a cost of $5000 to $10,000. Another kind of paper-moving scanner is a desktop device that feeds a single page through a small scanner, again intending print only for OCR. These are now cheap enough to be bundled with keyboards.

There are also extremely cheap scanners, less than $100, which operate as handheld devices, swiped over pages to be scanned. In this case alignment is very unlikely to be accurate, but the applications are usually not very demanding for output quality. At the other extreme, scanners with costs of $70,000 and up also exist; these scan in pages per second instead of pages per minute, and are normally used in commercial applications to handle large volumes of standard-format documents (credit card slips, bank checks, and the like).

Quality of scanning is normally expressed in resolution, measured in dots per inch. For comparison, fax machines scan 200 dots per inch (horizontally only), while laser printers print at 300 dots per inch. Scanning is inherently more demanding of resolution than printing, since a printer can align the letters it is printing with the basic grid of pixels it can print. It is worth a factor of two in resolution to be able to align the letters with the ink spots printed by the machine. Thus, you would expect to need 600 dpi scanning to preserve the quality of a laser printer page at 300 dpi. Quality that good may not be necessary if the only goal is readability. Figure 3.2 shows progressively poorer resolution in scanning. The readability also depends on the type size; this document was about 6 point type, about as small print as will normally be encountered. With this type, the 100 dpi

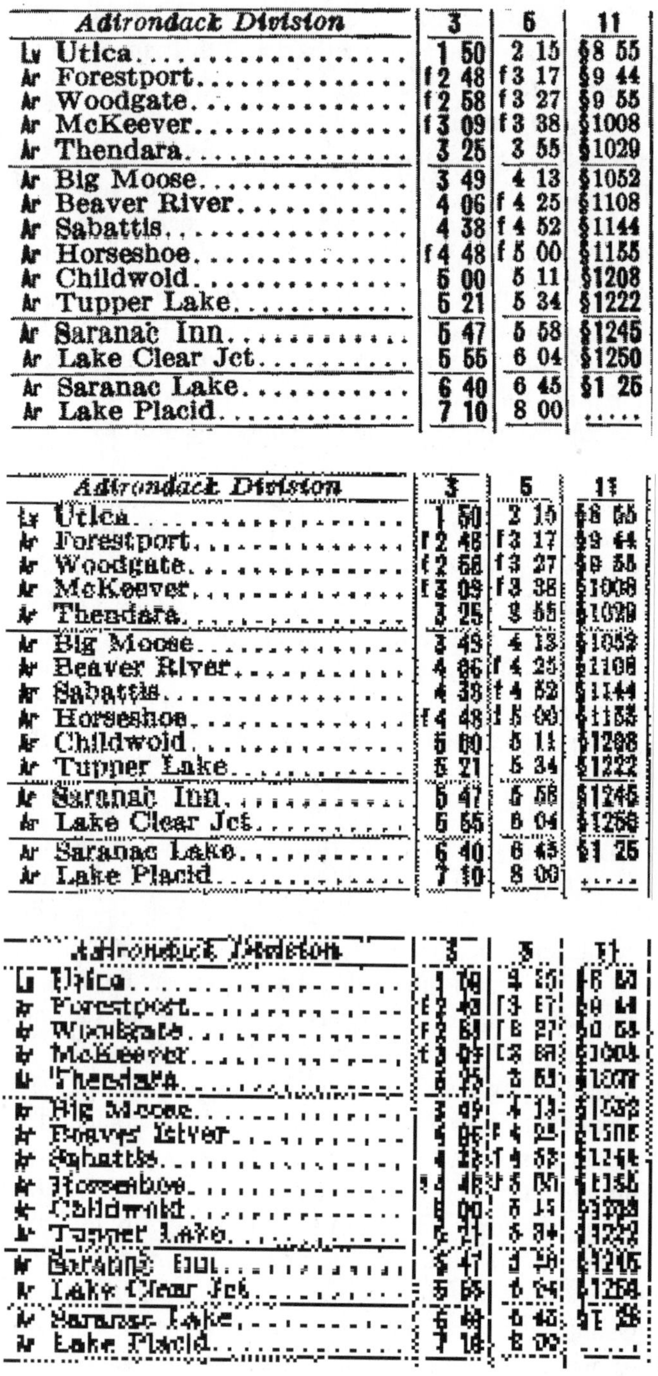

Adirondack Division	3	5	11
Lv Utica	1 50	2 15	$8 55
Ar Forestport	f2 48	f3 17	$9 44
Ar Woodgate	f2 58	f3 27	$9 55
Ar McKeever	f3 09	f3 38	$1008
Ar Thendara	3 25	3 55	$1029
Ar Big Moose	3 49	4 13	$1052
Ar Beaver River	4 06	f4 25	$1108
Ar Sabattis	4 38	f4 52	$1144
Ar Horseshoe	f4 48	f5 00	$1155
Ar Childwold	5 00	5 11	$1208
Ar Tupper Lake	5 21	5 34	$1222
Ar Saranac Inn	5 47	5 58	$1245
Ar Lake Clear Jct	5 55	6 04	$1250
Ar Saranac Lake	6 40	6 45	$1 25
Ar Lake Placid	7 10	8 00	.....

(a) 300 dpi

(b) 150 dpi

(c) 100 dpi

Figure 3.2   Resolution of scanning

image is almost unreadable. Librarians and others normally consider 300 dpi to be a minimum-quality resolution for scanning, and many argue for 600 dpi or even higher.

To understand the appearance of the scans in Figure 3.2, consider that a minimum letter representation as a bitmap for display is about 5 × 7. This means that 10 bits across the letter are needed for scanning. An average letter that is printed in 8 point type is about 4 points wide, or 18 letters per inch. Thus, resolution of 180 dots per inch, or about 200 dpi, should be enough to provide readable quality, and 300 should be good enough to provide some margin. So, for example, the Archives Division of the State of Oregon states the following in its administrative rules: "(1) Office documents containing fonts no smaller than six-point shall be scanned at a minimum density of 200 dpi. Documents containing fonts smaller than six-point, architectural and engineering drawings, maps, and line art shall be scanned at a minimum density of 300 dpi."

Microfilm scanners for libraries comprise an important subclass of scanners. Microfilm is physically strong and standard format (either 16-mm or 35-mm). As a result it can be scanned faster than paper, with microfilm scanners running in times measured in seconds per page. Companies such as Minolta, Mekel, and Sunrise build microfilm scanners, with costs in tens of thousands of dollars. Libraries have traditionally used 35-mm microfilm; most other users have moved to 16-mm film. Normally, microfilm is black and white, high contrast, and thus only bitonal scanning makes sense. The grey-scale or color information was usually destroyed when the film was made. Microfilming can be done in color, but the higher cost of the film, its lower resolution, the scarcity of color illustrations in old books, and the greater care that would be needed in the filming all mean that color film is rarely used.

3.2   *Image Formats for Scanned Printed Pages*

Plain text images can be stored in a variety of formats. Various computer operating systems or display control software systems (such as window managers), for example, have their own standard image representations, designed to be rapidly loaded onto a screen. In most library applications, however, compression is most important. Compression can be either perfectly reversible (lossless), or it can change the image slightly to obtain a higher degree of compression (lossy). Often librarians prefer lossless compression to avoid any information loss merely to save on storage, which is becoming increasingly cheap.

Scanning books or journals, and then wishing to compress bitonal images of printed pages, is exactly the same problem faced by the groups standardizing

facsimile transmission. Facsimile standards, issued by the international telecommunications groups, have moved through several stages. The most recent version is
known as Group IV, issued by a group once known as CCITT (a French acronym
for Consultative Committee on International Telecommunications Technology) and
now called ITU (International Telecommunications Union). Often the compressed
bits are surrounded by a TIFF (Tagged Independent File Format) heading section,
which serves to inform programs using the file what the file structure is. TIFF can
be used to describe many different kinds of image files; it is not limited to Group IV
fax compression.

All image compression algorithms take advantage of some redundancy in the
image. The basis of fax compression is that pages are made of letters, which
are made up of printed strokes of conventional width. Thus, the normal background is white, with intervals of black of fairly predictable length. Furthermore,
consecutive scan lines often have similar black-white patterns. For example, in encoding the letters *I*, *L*, or *T*, all of which have vertical strokes, the same number
of black bits will appear in the same place on several successive horizontal scan
lines. Thus, CCITT Group IV fax combines horizontal and vertical compression
algorithms. The horizontal compression is based on run-length encoding, using
Huffman coding (see Section 7.3.1) separately on the black and white bits of the
line. A set of precomputed tables of Huffman codes tuned for the typical widths of
letter strokes is written into the standard. Vertical compression is based on adjacent
line coding. The standard contains codes for "this section of this line is like the
last line, or like the last line shifted one bit right or left." Group IV fax is generally
the most effective compression technique for printed pages. Table 3.1 shows the
number of bytes in a scanned page image (of a large page covered very densely
with relatively small print) compressed in different ways. With more normal pages
a TIFF image around 25–30 KB per page is common. Given the tape storage cost of
$4 per GB quoted in Section 1.6.2, this means that tape storage of three copies of
a typical library book (30 KB per page and 300 pages, or about 10 MB per book)
would be about 10 cents. At these rates, the dominant cost is going to be the human and machine time involved in writing the tapes, not the physical costs of the
medium.

Table 3.1

Bytes	Format
1,065,016	Uncompressed
293,076	GIF (equivalent to run-length encoding)
264,694	LZW (equivalent of UNIX compress)
144,026	TIFF Group IV

3.3 *Display Requirements*

To read images on a screen can be difficult. As explained above, the typical resolution for scanning is 300 dpi, but the typical computer workstation screen resolution is 72 dpi. This means that either the optical quality is lowered by a factor of four to get the page to have the same size or that only part of the page will be visible. In terms of resolution, an 8.5 × 11" page scanned at 300 dpi requires 2560 × 3300 bits, and the screen might be 1024 × 768 or 1152 × 900, again far too small. There are several strategies that can be taken to deal with this:

1. Often the page is smaller than the computer screen (books are often printed on paper measuring 6 by 9 inches, and a workstation might have a screen 14 inches across and 10 inches high). This permits some expansion. Typically the page has a blank margin that can be trimmed off as well, allowing still more expansion.

2. Various interface techniques let the user navigate around the page, including scroll bars, zoom controls, or a small version of the page with an enlarging lens (see Section 7.4).

3. Users can be asked to buy bigger screens. Screen sizes of up to 1800 × 1440 are available today. However, there are still going to be people with laptops (or old computers) who will wish to access the digital library.

4. Antialiasing can be used to improve the quality of the display.

Antialiasing is a computer graphics technique that uses grey scale to give apparently better resolution for bitonal images. When a black-and-white image is placed on a computer screen, the original image design rarely aligns perfectly with the boundaries of the pixels that make up the screen. Clearly those pixels that correspond to entirely white parts of the image should be white, and those that are covered by black parts of the image should be black. For those pixels that are partly covered by the black part of the image, however, it improves the appearance of the image if they are grey rather than forced to be either black or white. To understand this, consider the two representations of a diagonal line shown in Figure 3.3.

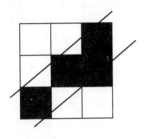 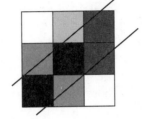

Figure 3.3 Antialiasing

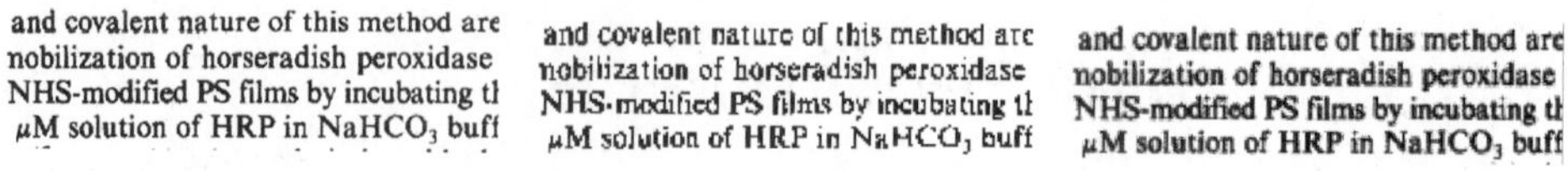

and covalent nature of this method are nobilization of horseradish peroxidase NHS-modified PS films by incubating tl µM solution of HRP in NaHCO₃ buff	and covalent nature of this method are nobilization of horseradish peroxidase NHS-modified PS films by incubating tl µM solution of HRP in NaHCO₃ buff	and covalent nature of this method are nobilization of horseradish peroxidase NHS-modified PS films by incubating tl µM solution of HRP in NaHCO₃ buff
(a)	*(b)*	*(c)*

Figure 3.4   Antialiased text: *(a)* 300 dpi, *(b)* 100 dpi bitonal, *(c)* 100 dpi antialiased

Assume that the area between the two diagonal strokes is supposed to be black. Note that in the left-hand figure all pixels are either black or white, with a result that the line is really approximated in a rather jagged manner. In the right-hand figure the use of grey for the partially included pixels gives a somewhat better rendition.

This is shown for text in Figure 3.4, in which the same image is shown as scanned at 300 dpi, as reduced to 100 dpi bitonal, and as shown with 100 dpi resolution antialiased. As can be seen, the antialiasing adds significantly to the readability and appearance of the text.

None of these alternatives is really a substitute for larger and higher-quality screens. In addition to the dot resolution, screens also differ in refresh rate (the higher the better, with most computer terminals now above 60 Hz) and in color quality, which will be described later (see Section 4.2).

3.4   *PostScript, Acrobat, and Reprinting*

Many people, of course, still prefer to read on paper. It is more portable than even a laptop, except for very large books. It is less dependent on electric power and less of a risk in places where either electric shock or theft may be a problem. More importantly, it is comfortable to move around and adjust in position, and it is higher resolution, as explained above.

Printing selected library contents onto paper would seem straightforward, and for plain text documents it is. For more complex documents it can be difficult, and for years fast printing of routine text conflicted with the ability to print high-quality graphics. In the 1980s Adobe Systems introduced PostScript, a general graphics language adapted to drawing letters from fonts. PostScript is now a standard language for interfacing to many kinds of printers, and it is perhaps the closest thing we have to a completely accepted standard for materials in machine-readable form. However, it is a graphics language, not a text language. It describes the appearance of a page, with the letter positions and the particular size and style of each letter all specified. Thus, it is more difficult to reuse PostScript-encoded material for other purposes than it is to reuse SGML or other text-coded materials.

PostScript, in principle, is a very powerful and complex language. It defines fonts and logos by software that can generate any kind of graphical appearance.

PostScript includes a complete set of control commands in which any program can be written; I once wrote a text justification program in raw PostScript. It also contains procedures for printing characters in fonts, which are also defined in the same language. These two parts of PostScript are usually kept fairly separate: fonts are defined and then characters are printed from the fonts. PostScript includes color definition and color printing commands.

PostScript also allows the representation of arbitrary bitmaps, as from scanned images. The typical printer, however, is much slower at dealing with such bitmaps than it is with text, and some printers may run out of memory if they are asked to print too many bitmaps, or too detailed a bitmap, on a page. Under some circumstances it may be faster to convert images directly to more printer-adapted languages such as HP's PCL (Printer Control Language). However, such languages are not likely to be portable across different manufacturers and should be avoided for general-purpose use. Alternatively, companies such as Adobe and Xionics manufacture hardware and software to assist printers in handling PostScript and printing faster.

PostScript is the basis of an Adobe software package called Acrobat, which serves as a page-viewing interface. Acrobat, distributed free, displays a format named PDF (Portable Document Format). PDF, like PostScript, preserves a particular page appearance. Unlike languages like SGML or HTML, PostScript and PDF do not let the user decide what the page will look like; control of appearance stays with the author. For some purposes, this makes document entry and display simpler, albeit less flexible.

PDF is not exactly PostScript. PDF lacks the general-purpose programming language, and PDF includes provision for interactive viewing events (e.g., the user choosing which page to display next). However, Adobe provides software to print PDF or generate it (Acrobat Exchange and Acrobat Capture). The philosophy of both PostScript and PDF is similar: the creator of a document specifies what it should look like and the reader gets that appearance. Thus, neither is suitable for an application in which, for example, people with limited vision wish to reprint everything in triple-size normal type.

3.5 *Indexing Images of Pages*

How do you find anything in images of pages? Unlike ASCII text, none of the kinds of database construction described previously are possible with images. The traditional library instance is to write text descriptions of each picture and then index the text. In the context of page images, this means finding an alternate source of index information for the pages, which may, in the worst case, involve library cataloging of the material. If the images are pages in books, this may not be too bad, since a relatively small amount of cataloging will cover a large number of pages, at

300 pages per book. However, because of the difficulty of flipping through a set of computer images compared with flipping pages in a book, users will prefer if items can be located fairly accurately. This means indexing to the table-of-contents level.

Another alternative is to find an index made for other reasons. For example, the Adonis CD-ROMs (which include page images of 650 biomedical journals) include journals that are covered by the Medline indexing system. The Adonis images need only be labeled by journal, volume, and page. Users can search Medline, retrieve a page location, and then use Adonis to find the image of that page. Similarly the IEEE journals on CD-ROM are covered by a published index to them prepared by Inspec (IEE). The older the material involved, unfortunately, the less likely it is that such an index will exist.

With normal pictures of people or scenery, users might browse through *thumbnails* (small-size versions) of the images. But thumbnails of text pages are unreadable. If OCR worked extremely well (or was corrected manually to a high level), recognized page images could be treated as in the previous chapter. Although OCR reaches an adequate level of performance on very clean modern printing or typing, it is not accurate enough on old print or deteriorated paper to be a replacement for the imagery. What OCR can do, however, is provide a text to be used for indexing and searching. There are search algorithms that are fairly resistant to occasional errors in the text, and these will permit text-searching techniques to be used with image databases.

This approach has been suggested for at least two decades. It was first tried seriously at the National Agricultural Library in the mid-1970s and is at the base of the RightPages system of AT&T Bell Laboratories and UCSF (University of California–San Francisco) plus the TULIP effort of Elsevier. However, it has several practical disadvantages:

1. In order to highlight matching terms (often considered a very desirable feature of a digital library system), the OCR program must indicate the exact location of the characters recognized. Few provide this information; AT&T achieved it by writing its own OCR software.

2. The OCR errors make it impossible to guarantee performance to the users, and faced with a system making apparently incomprehensible errors, users are likely to retreat from it in fear.

OCR was discussed in more detail in Section 2.8. Results are improving, although you still cannot dispense with proofreading. There is even work now on OCR for old printing, being done by Gary Kopec of Xerox PARC.

There are still other possibilities for navigating images. For some documents it may be possible to find alternative ways of displaying guidance on reading images. For example, Figure 3.5 shows an example of an 18th-century newspaper page. The full page is not suitable for display because there is not enough resolution on a

Figure 3.5 Newspaper page from the 18th century

typical screen to show the entire page and be able to read any of it. In order to read a story, it has to be enlarged to a level at which only a small part of the page will fit on a screen, and thus the user will lose all context about what has appeared where. Some other means of letting the user navigate around the page is necessary.

The answer is to take advantage of the newspaper format. Although the print on this page is too poor for OCR, the horizontal and vertical rules used by newspapers can be found and then used to cut the page image into stories. The easiest way to locate such lines in low-quality images is not to look for continuous strings of bits, but to calculate average horizontal and vertical bit densities per scan line. In this case, for example, the first step is to find the vertical lines, which are continuous down the page. For each vertical column of pixels, count the dark ones and divide by the length; this will show the vertical rules despite breaks in them. Then, having divided the page into columns, repeat the calculation for each horizontal scan line within a column. That quickly divides the columns into stories. Images of the first few lines of each story can then be used to indicate what it is, a sort of menu of the paper (shown in Figure 3.6).

Clicking on one of these first headings brings up the image of the full story (by showing the page centered on that story). Imagine the user clicks on "TUBEROSE ROOTS"; the result is Figure 3.7.

Using this technique, people can browse the image files without any OCR text. The full newspaper page does not need to be read. Other cues that can be

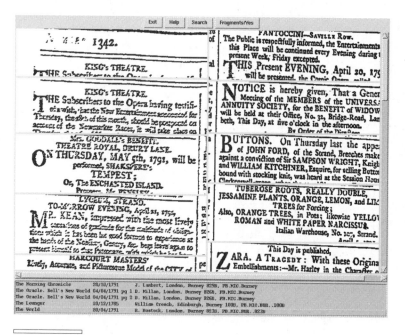

Figure 3.6   Heads of newspaper stories

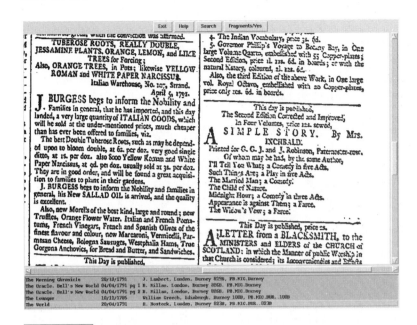

Figure 3.7   Detailed story

used to help locate stories include the position of material on the page. In these newspaper pages, for example, major international news is typically at the top right, while the top left is theatre reviews and announcements. Systems based on features like this will permit users to scan sets of newspaper pages without any indexing.

3.6   *Shared Text/Image Systems*

Some systems involve both ASCII and image pages. Publishing systems, for example, sometimes involve text preparation by keyboarding but manual pasteup of the final pages, taking photographs and line drawings and adding them to the page with glue or tape. Another motivation for mixed ASCII and image systems is the complexity of displaying pages that contain pictures; it may be easier to divide the task and rely on image display to convey the pictures.

The Chemical Online Retrieval Experiment (CORE) project involved extracting the illustrations from the scanned pages. This project had access to the information (derived from the typesetting system) that makes up the database of the American Chemical Society (ACS) and that provided the complete text of the articles. But this information did not provide the graphic elements of each page. Although half the pages have no graphics, there was an average of about one illustration per page, and about a quarter of the area of the average page is not text. The illustrations are essential to the understanding of the article; online full-text systems that leave out the illustrations are often used merely as finding aids, rather than as replacements for the paper. The CORE project had to get these illustrations by finding them in the page images. Since the total project needed to find 399,000 figures and chemical structural diagrams in 80,000 articles with 428,000 page images, it had to be an automatic process.

Pages could have four things beside text: tables, equations, figures, and schemes (chemical structural drawings). The equations and the tables are in the database derived from keyboarding, so the need is to find figures and schemes. Both figures and schemes are visually similar: they are both line drawings. Figures may include chemical structures, spectrograms, diagrams of equipment, and so on; schemes are usually just chemical structures. They must be sorted out, however, since the schemes and figures can be moved past each other in the course of typesetting; that is, Scheme 1 may be referred to in the article before Figure 1 but may appear after it on the page. Figures are always at either the top or bottom of the page, while schemes can appear in the middle of a text column (but often appear at the edge of a page as well). Despite an attempt to avoid OCR in general, the only really reliable way of sorting figures from schemes is to find the caption by looking for the word "Figure" as a bitmap.

Page segmentation is a well-studied problem (Fletcher and Kasturi 1987; Wang and Srihari 1989; Srihari et al. 1994), but often the previous work involved halftones or other material that is locally different from text printing. Nearly all the chemical illustrations are line drawings, and there is a continuum between some tables or chemical equations and some figures or schemes. The CORE project, therefore, wrote its own programs to deal with graphics extraction, based on the regularity of lines in normal text. Figure 3.8 shows a part of a journal column, and Figure 3.9 plots the number of black bits per scanline moving down the page. Each scanline is one horizontal trace across the page; Figure 3.9 shows the number of black dots in each trace. The column begins with a normal figure (a line drawing), which runs from scanline 200 to 800, with irregular low values of bits per scanline (the bump at 150 is the heading line on the page). A five-line caption follows, the five regular bumps from scanline 800 to 1000. There follows an unusual dark figure (1100 to 1700), with a two-line caption (1700 to 1800). The remainder of the column (1800 on) is lines of text, and regular bumps appear in the plot. The regularity of this density plot of ordinary typeset text separates it from the irregular density characteristic of figures. For speed, the CORE project used only overall measures of bit density, not exact character matching (except for the word "Figure" as mentioned earlier).

The first step in graphics extraction was to align the page accurately on the axes. Skew can be produced in scanning, either because the pages have not been cut accurately from the journal or the pages were fed through the scanner on a slight angle. Any correction algorithm must recognize the possibility that the page

7162   *The Journal of Physical Chemistry, Vol. 92, No. 26, 1988*

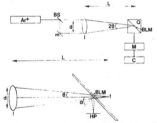

Figure 1. Schematics of the system used for observing holographic interferometry in BLMs. Ar⁺ = argon ion laser; BS = beam splitter; m = mirror; Q = quartz cuvette; BLM = bilayer lipid membrane; M = microscope; C = camera; HP = holographic plate; f = focus; l = lens; and *d* = interbeam distance.

Figure 2. Complex interferometric fringe pattern observed in a thick GMO film prior to thinning to a BLM.

Second, advantage has been taken of fluorescence to produce distinct interference patterns of molecules that are incorporated onto the surface of a BLM. The power of holographic interferometry is demonstrated in the present report by showing differences between thick lipid films and true BLMs, as well as by determining the shapes and sizes of cadmium sulfide (CdS) particles in situ generated on glyceryl monooleate (GMO) BLMs. Evidence is also provided here, by holographic interferometry, for the presence of Merocyanine 540 on the surface of GMO BLMs.

Experimental Section

Merocyanine 540 (Sigma), glyceryl monooleate (GMO, Nucheck Co.), cadmium chloride (Aldrich), and hydrogen sulfide (Matheson) were used as received. Water was purified by means of a Millipore Milli-Q system.

BLMs were formed across a 1.00-mm-diameter hole in a thin (0.10–0.15 mm thick) Teflon film, placed diagonally in a rec-

Figure 3.8   Column of text

begins or ends with a figure containing lots of white space. In the CORE project the left edge of each scanline was found, and then a vertical line was run down the left edge of the page and pushed as closely up against the text as possible, to find the skew angle. The page must be within one degree of correct orientation for figure extraction to work. Another method for deskewing was discussed by Baird (1987). Baird takes a set of parallel lines across the page and measures the dispersion of the measurement of the number of dark bits. Where this dispersion is maximum (that is, some of the lines are running through only white space and some through as dark a set of bits as they can find), the lines are aligned with the text baseline. This

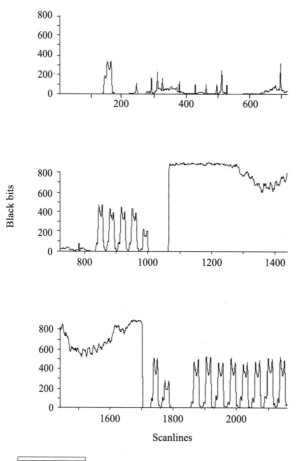

Figure 3.9   Density function

is a more robust method (it will work with ragged left and right margins) but takes longer.

After deskewing, the page was broken into double-column and full-width regions. Normally the ACS pages are double-column; each could contain one full-width region, either for a title-author block or for a wide table or figure. Looking at the *vertical* density plot (how many black bits in each vertical stripe down the page, taken in thirds) identifies the column boundaries and locates the transitions between double-column and full-width areas. Eventually, the page was cut into at most five regions (two columns at the top, two columns at the bottom, and one full-width section).

Each region was then scanned for figure captions, using exact bitmap matching for the word "Figure" (since the journals use different typefaces, different masks are

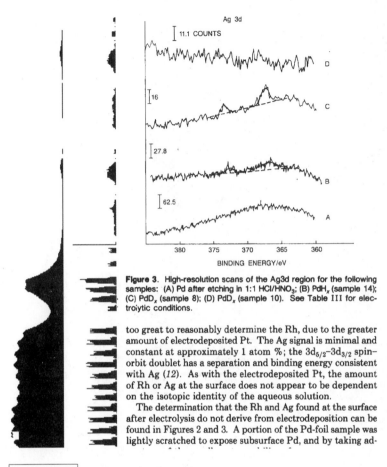

Figure 3. High-resolution scans of the Ag3d region for the following samples: (A) Pd after etching in 1:1 HCl/HNO₃; (B) PdHₓ (sample 14); (C) PdDₓ (sample 8); (D) PdDₓ (sample 10). See Table III for electrolytic conditions.

too great to reasonably determine the Rh, due to the greater amount of electrodeposited Pt. The Ag signal is minimal and constant at approximately 1 atom %; the $3d_{5/2}$–$3d_{3/2}$ spin–orbit doublet has a separation and binding energy consistent with Ag (*12*). As with the electrodeposited Pt, the amount of Rh or Ag at the surface does not appear to be dependent on the isotopic identity of the aqueous solution.

The determination that the Rh and Ag found at the surface after electrolysis do not derive from electrodeposition can be found in Figures 2 and 3. A portion of the Pd-foil sample was lightly scratched to expose subsurface Pd, and by taking ad-

Figure 3.10   Correlation function

used for different journals). Each region also has its horizontal densities computed, and the program computed a function that detects a regular pattern. This function is known as the *autocorrelation function* because it relates the density pattern to a shifted version of the same density pattern. In the same way as you can walk comfortably along a set of ridges (such as a corrugated road) if your stride matches the interval between the bumps, this function has a maximum value when the shifted pattern differs from the original by one line spacing. Thus, it can be used both to detect the existence of the regular pattern and to detect the distance between lines. Given the line spacing, and the autocorrelation function, a threshold is applied to select which parts of the page are graphics. Figure 3.10 shows a sample column with the density function plotted just to the left of the text and the autocorrelation function at the far left.

7270 *J. Org. Chem., Vol. 56, No. 26, 1991* Dahan and Biali

of the OH groups (δ = 8.19 ppm) as compared with 1 (δ = 10.2 ppm) can be ascribed to the weakening of the hydrogen bond between the OH groups as a result of the presence of the boat conformation in 2.[7] It is interesting to note that whereas there is a large chemical shift difference for the diastereotopic methylene protons of calix[4]arene ($\Delta\delta$ = 0.71 ppm),[8] the $\Delta\delta$ value for 2 is relatively small and therefore under slow exchange conditions these protons appear as a somewhat unresolved AB quartet at 200 MHz.

(b) **IR Spectrum.** The IR spectrum of calix[4]arenes is characterized by a low stretching OH frequency (3150 cm^{-1}) due to the presence of a circular hydrogen bond.[2] A marked deviation of the calixarene from the cone conformation into a boat form should result in weakening of the hydrogen bond and a shift of the stretching frequency into larger wave numbers. Indeed, Böhmer and co-workers[9] have shown that the OH stretching frequency of calix[4]arenes bridged at two para positions at nonvicinal rings 3 shifts to higher frequencies with the decrease in length of the bridge and the progressive distortion of the cone conformation. For example, for systems 3 (n = 5–9) the OH stretching frequencies are ν_{OH}(KBr) = 3410, 3340, 3250, 3260, and 3210 cm^{-1}, respectively. For calixarene 2 ν_{OH} (KBr) is 3290 cm^{-1} and is analogous to the frequencies found for system 3 when n = 6 or 7.

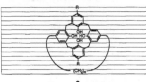

3

(c) **Molecular Mechanics Calculations.** Molecular mechanics calculations of calixarene 2 were performed using the MM2(85) program.[10] According to the calculations, the boat and 1,3-alternate conformations are of similar steric energies and are the lowest energy conformations. The 1,2-alternate and symmetric cone conformations have much higher steric energies and lie 5.3 and 31.2 kcal mol^{-1} above the boat conformation. It should be noted, however, that the calculations do not take into account properly the hydrogen bonds. Since these hydrogen bonds are likely to contribute mostly to the relative stabilization of the boat and cone conformations, the underestimation of the strength of the hydrogen bonds should result in an overestimation of the steric energies of both conformations. Once this factor is taken into account, it is possible to reconcile the results of the calculations with the experimental result (i.e., exclusive population of the boat conformation).

The calculated structure for the boat conformation of 2 is remarkably similar to the crystallographic conforma-

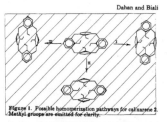

Figure 1. Possible homomerization pathways for calixarene 2. Methyl groups are omitted for clarity.

tion determined for 2-DMF (Table S1 in the supplementary material). The main difference between the experimental and calculated structures is in the O···O nonbonded distances which are overestimated by the calculations by 0.3–0.4 Å possibly due to the partial neglect of the hydrogen bonds.

Dynamic Stereochemistry of 2. Due to the lower ideal symmetry of the boat conformation of 2 (C_2, symmetry) as compared with 1 (C_{4v} symmetry), several homomerization pathways of the macrocyclic skeleton are possible for 2 whereas for 1 only the inversion process need to be considered. The stereodynamics of the all-cis stereoisomer of resorcinol-based calixarenes 4 which according to the X-ray analysis also exist in a boat conformation[11] have been analyzed by Högberg.[2,12]

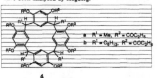

a R^1 = Me, R^2 = COC$_2$H$_5$
b R^1 = C$_5$H$_{11}$, R^2 = COC$_2$H$_5$

4

Three processes can be considered for the dynamic process operating for 2. In the first process (I in Figure 1) there is an exchange between the "perpendicular" and "coplanar" rings without including the passage of the OH groups through the macrocyclic cavity. This process does not exchange the "axial" and "equatorial" methylene protons. In the idealized transition state a cone conformation of C_{4v} symmetry is obtained. Since the result of this dynamic process is that the molecule looks as if it was rotated by 90°, this process is called pseudorotation.[13,14] The second process (ii) involves the passage of the rings through the molecular cavity (a ring-inversion process)[13] and keeps the identity of the rings ("perpendicular" or "coplanar") unchanged. The third process (iii) can be formally considered a combination of processes i and ii and

(7) Wolff, A.; Böhmer, V.; Vogt, W.; Ugozzoli, F.; Andreetti, G. D. *J. Org. Chem.* 1990, 55, 5665.
(8) Araki, K.; Shinkai, S.; Matsuda, T. *Chem. Lett.* 1989, 581.
(9) (a) Goldmann, H.; Vogt, W.; Paulus, E.; Böhmer, V. *J. Am. Chem. Soc.* 1988, 110, 6811. (b) Paulus, E.; Böhmer, V.; Goldmann, H.; Vogt, W. *J. Chem. Soc., Perkin Trans. 2* 1987, 1609. (c) Böhmer, V.; Goldmann, H.; Vogt, W.; Paulus, E. F.; Tobiason, F. L.; Thielman, M. *J. J. Chem. Soc., Perkin Trans. 2* 1990, 1769.
(10) Allinger, N. L. *QCPE MM2(85).* See also: Sprague, J. T.; Tai, J. C.; Yuh, Y. H.; Allinger, N. L. *J. Comput. Chem.* 1987, 8, 581.

(11) Erdtman, H.; Högberg, S.; Abrahamsson, S.; Nilsson, B. *Tetrahedron Lett.* 1968, 1679. Nilsson, B. *Acta Chem. Scand.* 1968, 22, 732. Tunstad, L. M.; Tucker, J. A.; Dalcanale, E.; Weiser, J.; Bryant, J. A.; Sherman, J. C.; Helgeson, R. C.; Knobler, C. B.; Cram, D. J. *J. Org. Chem.* 1989, 54, 1305.
(12) Högberg, A. G. S. *J. Am. Chem. Soc.* 1980, 102, 6046.
(13) Anet, F. A. L. *Top. Curr. Chem.* 1974, 45, 169.
(14) It should be noted that in the initial report on the ring inversion barrier of a calix[4]arene (Happel, G.; Mathiasch, B.; Kämmerer, H. *Makromol. Chem.* 1975, 176, 3317) the ring inversion process was (incorrectly) dubbed "pseudorotation".

Figure 3.11   Classified page

Finally, Figure 3.11 is the result: the figures and schemes were spotted correctly by the program and marked out (using different boxing to represent the figures and schemes separately).

3.7   Image Storage vs. Book Storage

The steady decrease in imaging costs compared with the steady increase in building construction costs raises the question of when they will cross— when will it be cheaper to scan books than to build shelves for them? The quick answer is that today scanning is comparable in cost to central campus libraries, more expensive than off-site deposit libraries, but may be cheaper than physical storage for consortia of libraries (and for individual libraries in a few years). In doing this comparison, one should fairly contrast only the cost of the bookstacks; libraries also contain offices and reading rooms, whose cost may not be related to the book capacity.

Three different possibilities for library storage are scanning, on-campus storage, and an off-site depository. What do these cost?

1. The first good measurement of the cost of scanning books was the CLASS project at Cornell, which found the pure scanning cost to be about $30 per book, or about 10 cents per page (Kenney and Personius 1992). The CLASS work scanned 19th-century mathematics textbooks, and did so by cutting the book away from the binding and placing each page by hand on a flatbed scanner.

2. Two recent on-campus bookstacks are the extension to Olin Library at Cornell, costing about $20 per book, and the extension to Doe Library at Berkeley, costing about $30 per book. In both cases they are almost entirely stacks, but both are underground (and, in the case of Berkeley, built to withstand an earthquake of 8.0 on the Richter scale).

3. The Harvard Depository costs about $2 per book, for an off-site storage building with good book storage facilities but no architectural decoration. The Depository is about 35 miles from the main campus, and book retrieval costs $4 per volume retrieved.

What these numbers say is that for a book that is never or rarely used, off-campus storage is cheapest. Of course, the users may not consider the service good if books require 24 hours to retrieve, but the British Library has managed for a generation with one-day retrieval for most of its books, partly by an adroit shelving policy that keeps the most used books more rapidly available.

Figure 3.12 at top shows the Harvard Depository ($2 per book), and below the new Tolbiac building of the Bibliothèque Nationale de France ($90 per book). Using a large library as an architectural monument may make sense for reasons as varied as a university emblem or political prestige, but money spent on monumentality should not be confused with money spent on library service.

If the choice is between scanning and on-campus storage, the costs are comparable for a single library today. This statement is oversimplified, and several points should be made:

1. The CLASS scanning project cost was low, inasmuch as it was done by the library itself; contracted-out scanning such as JSTOR, discussed below, has been more expensive. Digital images require some kind of digital storage and delivery technology, although with disk space at 25 cents per megabyte and 10 MB per book, the storage is only about $2.50 per book. The cost estimates for underground stacks are higher than for above-ground buildings.

(a)

(b)

Figure 3.12   *(a)* Harvard Depository; *(b)* Bibliothèque Nationale de France

2. The CLASS scanning project cost was high, inasmuch as it used books that were old enough that their pages would not go through a sheet feeder. The cost estimates for pure stacks are low since they do not provide any reading rooms or offices, and certainly to find central campus space for a new library adjacent to an old library will usually require substantial architectural costs (such as underground building). Most importantly, multiple libraries can share digital copies (albeit for out-of-copyright works) without any loss of service quality to any of them, which is not possible with physical copies (unless the libraries are located near each other).

For comparison, the CORE project, which scanned modern printing on good paper, could use a sheet feeder. The illustrations in the journals we scanned were overwhelmingly line drawings, so we scanned bitonal at 300 dpi. We could achieve about 15 pages per minute through our scanner, which cost about $15,000 back in 1990, and paid somebody about $12.50/hour to stand in front of it. Unfortunately for the economics, we only had about 300,000 pages to scan as the American Chemical Society did about 130,000 pages for us. As a result, the scanner was idle most of the time, and the cost to us was perhaps $20,000 total, or 7 cents per page, most of which was amortized hardware cost. A scanner with similar performance would be about $6000 today.

And a more conventional new library is one at the University of Kentucky, which holds 1.2 million books and 4000 reader seats for $58 million, with construction costs of about $165 per square foot. A survey done by Michael Cooper gives construction costs ranging from $21 to $41 per book (Cooper 1989). Cooper reports that the amortized cost of keeping a book on a shelf for a year is $3. If the book has to be retrieved by library staff, this introduces additional costs. The New York Public Library finds retrieving and reshelving costs of about $2 per book. Harvard needs to add another $2 per book for its Depository, to cover the shipment back and forth for 35 miles.

Don Waters has summarized the costs in the appendix to Garrett and Waters (1996). Waters found the costs for electronic storage and retrieval to be higher (over $2 per volume for storage and $6 per volume for retrieval), but judged that the costs for the paper library would rise about 4% per year, while the computer costs declined 50% every five years. Under these assumptions, the costs of the digital and traditional library operations cross over in about five years. In ten years electronic storage has a major cost advantage, with access costs of $2.70 per book rather than $5.60 (as estimated by Garrett and Waters 1996). He finds that for single libraries, a depository solution is cheaper today and will be cheaper for five years to come. In ten years it may be cheaper to scan books, even for a single library. Table 3.2 compares depository and digital archive costs.

Electronic libraries have some less easily quantified advantages over paper libraries. Books are never off-shelf or inaccessible because someone else is using them

Table 3.2

	Year 1	*Year 4*	*Year 7*	*Year 10*
Depository Library				
Storage costs per volume	$0.24	$0.27	$0.30	$0.34
Access costs per volume	$3.97	$4.46	$5.02	$5.64
Digital Archive				
Storage costs per volume	$2.77	$1.83	$1.21	$0.80
Access costs per volume	$6.65	$4.76	$3.51	$2.70

(unless publishers adopt per-user license agreements). More importantly, books do not become inaccessible because they are stolen, and they are not torn or damaged while used. Many users may not be on the premises (reducing the building costs). Access to electronic books can be faster than to paper, although since users do not pay for access today, it is not easy to recover cash from them in exchange for this faster access. Most importantly, access can involve searching and thus much more effective use of the material.

Sometimes electronics has even more advantages. Extremely fragile items that must be provided in surrogate form can be distributed widely once digitized. Many more people will be able to look at the *Beowulf* manuscript as electronic images than would have been able to travel to London and to justify to the British Library their need to handle the unique and extremely fragile manuscript. Furthermore, the scanning of this manuscript has been done using advanced photographic techniques including UV scanning and backlit scanning, so that parts of the electronic images are legible even where the corresponding portions of the original manuscript are not legible (the *Beowulf* original was damaged by a fire in the 18th century and further damaged in repair attempts after the fire). See Section 11.3.

Of course, the most attractive situation is where many libraries can share the costs of digitizing material. The Andrew W. Mellon Foundation is funding project JSTOR to implement this strategy. JSTOR began by scanning 10 journals in economics and history back to their first issue and has now expanded its scanning to 100 journals. The journals were selected because they are widely held in American libraries. Both page images and cleaned-up text are to be available. The intent of JSTOR is to see if libraries can, in fact, relieve shelf space crowding by substituting use of the electronic images for the paper (Bowen 1995). JSTOR has contracted its scanning to a company in Barbados, and is paying 39 cents per page for scanning, OCR, and correction. In addition, there are costs in cleanup and quality control in the United States, which are harder to quantify.

Another possibility is that material can simply be purchased from the supplier in electronic form. Publishers issue many journals on CD-ROM, particularly in areas such as biomedicine, where the Adonis system covers several hundred journals. Some industrial libraries already spend more than 50% of their acquisitions budget on electronics; for some pharmaceutical libraries this is approaching 80%. Elsevier has suggested that for virtually any journal they publish they will be prepared to provide CD-ROM versions, and if the library also subscribes on paper, the extra price for the electronics might be as low as 10%.

A dissertation by William Lemberg (1995) goes into digitization costs for all U.S. library holdings in some detail and suggests that over the next 100 years there is a savings of $44 billion to be achieved by digitizing approximately 22 million documents (and discarding more than 400 million duplicate paper copies of them). The long time period considered makes this result very sensitive to his assumed 8.25% discount rate. Also, he assumes that libraries would make no payments for copyright for electronic documents, just as they do not now pay extra to loan a paper document. Only about $2 per book on average is available to pay out without destroying the economic benefit of digitization.

Electronic libraries also have some disadvantages. Users accustomed to paper may dislike or fear on-screen books or find the screens difficult to read. If readers must provide their own equipment, this is expensive (although many colleges already ask every student to buy a computer), and if they have low-quality screens, reading may be still more difficult. If, on the other hand, the library is providing the reading equipment, there may be times when it is overloaded, and users must wait to get at it. It may also be broken or under maintenance, so that although a single book is never off-shelf, it may well be that a great many books are sometimes unavailable because of a machine failure. The Bellcore Library has an electronic catalog; at first it was unavailable on Sundays as a result of maintenance schedules. The idea that the catalog was unavailable even though the room was open would not make any sense to a traditional librarian.

3.8 *Summary*

The previous chapter discussed our ability to build libraries of books stored as characters, derived from printing operations or other keying. This has been practical for some time, and large companies sell this service. This chapter concludes that digital libraries of images are also practical today. Collections of hundreds of thousands of printed pages and tens of thousands of photographs have been created and are being used successfully. The costs are not trivial, but they are becoming comparable to the costs of conventional storage.

Part of the question about replacing items with digital media is whether a digital version of some document is entirely suitable as a replacement for the original, or whether it is merely a finding aid. Art historians, for example, usually feel that they must see originals to do their research, and any substitutes (including printed reproductions in books) are just finding aids. Many readers of journals feel the same way; they print out anything longer than a page or so.

For straightforward reading of text, and with adequate screens and interfaces, computer versions can be a suitable alternative. Experiments (to be described in Section 7.2) show that reading from screens is as effective as reading from paper. Given the convenience of fingertip access, libraries can look forward to user preference for online rather than paper materials.

Image systems, however, have more difficulty than text systems in achieving an interface users will like. They need to transmit more data than text systems, and they require greater screen resolution. Many systems today are thus perceived by the users as too slow and too hard to read. Users may be disappointed in a digital library system even if the problem is in their own hardware (e.g., a computer with a screen that is too small).

Whether image representations of printed books are merely a waystation on the road to text systems is not yet clear. Perhaps, as OCR improves, and as the spread of the Web causes the attachment to paper formats to wane, we can expect these page image systems to become less important. However, as an intermediate step in the conversion of already printed material, they are likely to retain their importance until perhaps a few million old books have been converted worldwide.

4

Multimedia Storage and Access

L IBRARIES DO NOT JUST consist of text pages, whether ASCII or image. The current rage for multimedia encourages us to plan for collections that include sound, video, software, and everything else imaginable. Unlike the optimistic conclusions in the last two chapters, for which there were suitable methods and successful examples of digital libraries with millions of pages of ASCII and hundreds of thousands of images, building systems for multimedia is harder. In particular, video remains a problem for libraries. The ubiquitous VHS cartridge is fragile and poor quality. Color photographic film is expensive. And digitizing video today produces such volumes of material that it cannot yet be stored really cheaply, nor do we have good ways of searching it once stored. This chapter will discuss where we stand on handling nontextual material; it may not be straightforward today, but there is active progress. This is probably the area of greatest current research interest and progress.

4.1 *Sound Formats: Vinyl, Tape, and CD*

The simplest form of nontext material to deal with is audio. Audio has been collected by libraries for years; the Library of Congress even has thousands of player piano rolls. The once-standard vinyl record gave way to cassette tape and then to CD. In one of the faster complete replacements of one technology by another, CD made vinyl obsolete in about 10 years. Cassette tape still survives since its players are cheaper and more common in automobiles.

There are two common levels of formatting for audio, a high-quality standard for music and a low-quality one for voice. The format for storing music is driven by the entertainment industry, which now uses digital encoding for both studio and consumer formats. Ideally we would like recorded sound to approximate a live performance in its impression on the listener's ear; a typical person can hear up to 15–20 KHz and a dynamic range of 30–60 dB in loudness. KHz (kilohertz, or thousands of cycles per second) is a measure of frequency. Middle C on a piano keyboard is 0.256 KHz, the A above it is 0.440 KHz, and most people cannot hear above 20 KHz, although dogs can. When digitizing sound, the frequency range in KHz determines the sampling rate, and the dynamic range (see below) determines the number of bits per sample. Since it requires a minimum of two samples per cycle to give the ear a clue to the existence of a frequency, the sampling rate must be double the highest frequency that is to be captured. Thus, to represent the range up to 15 KHz requires 30,000 samples per second or higher. In other words, a value of the sound wave intensity must be recorded about every 30 microseconds (30 millionths of a second). The decibel scale raises the sound intensity by a factor of 10 every 10 decibels, so that a 65-dB sound is 10 times as large as a 55-dB sound. Roughly, 30 dB is a quiet room, 40 dB is conversation, 60 dB is loud music, 80 dB is a noisy car, and 100 dB is painful (e.g., an express subway train rushing through a station). To represent the difference between the 30 dB quiet parts and the 60 dB loud parts of a musical performance requires a range of 1000 in amplitude, or at least 10 bits of dynamic range. Music is typically handled by computers in CD format: 44,000 samples per second at 16 bits per sample on each of two audio tracks, comfortably above what is needed to represent what the average ear can perceive. This means that audio CD players must handle 176 KB per second (the standard 1X CD-ROM reader). This format is sufficiently high quality in terms of both acoustic range and accuracy that most people accept it as the best representation, except for a few audiophiles who insist that analog sound has a different and preferable texture.

Voice, by contrast, is normally acceptable at much lower sound quality. The standard for voice is the telephone line, which clips the sound signal to the range 300 to 3300 Hz and which has a relatively low amplitude range as well. In fact, digital telephony is normally done at 8000 samples per second with 8 bits of amplitude data per sample, or 8 KB per second. There is also no stereo needed to represent one voice. The frequency range of digital voice in this format is only up to 4000 Hz, which means that many high frequencies (particularly in women's voices) that are quite audible are suppressed. This makes telephony harder to understand than, say, FM radio, which can transmit the entire hearing range. The FM carrier bands are 150 KHz wide, divided into three signals, with the basic mono signal able to carry up to 40 KHz (the other bands are the stereo sideband, which carries the difference of the left and right channels, and a sideband set aside for a separate Muzaklike service that some stations offer). In order to expand the intensity or loudness range, the 8 bits of the amplitude data do not store a plain numerical amplitude (which would mean a range of only 24 dB) but a companded amplitude. *Companding* means that the 8-bit numbers used to code the intensity of the signal are translated to a range of amplitudes that is arranged so that small amplitudes are represented more accurately than large amplitudes. Effectively, the number stored is the logarithm of the actual amplitude. The standard representation is called "mu-law" and is adequate for understanding speech.

Recording and playback of sound are easy since most current workstations include sound digitization and generation cards. The digitization of the telephone equipment business has meant that chips to do mu-law translation are readily available, and thus the sound cards are widespread. Nearly every computer is now sold as "multimedia ready," which means, among other things, that it includes a sound card. Typically it is necessary to provide volume levels to the sound equipment or other controls. Although there is no standard for the controls comparable to that of the basic sound format, the SoundBlaster card format is the most common.

It is possible to compress voice below 8 KB per second while retaining most of the intelligibility. The most common standard is GSM, the compression used in a particular kind of digital cellular telephone system. GSM compression is about a factor of five beyond mu-law (160 bytes are turned into 33 bytes). This corresponds to a speech coding rate of 1.6 KB per second. Considerably better compression can be done (research projects for years have reduced speech to 300 bytes per second), but it becomes more difficult to do the compression and decompression in real time, and the compressed sound quality deteriorates, especially as any sounds other than human speech are being transmitted. Thus, they are not acceptable for recording radio programs, for example, which may have incidental music or animal noises. GSM is reasonably tolerant of such nonvoice sounds.

The usual sound formats do not contain any labeling information (audio CDs have a place for it, but rarely contain any). Thus, libraries attempting to catalog and store sound cannot do so within the sound format itself but must do so outside. It is unfortunate for libraries, for example, that audio CDs do not come with a small ASCII burst at the start describing the music and the performers on the disk. Audio is also less likely to be self-identifying than printed pages (that is, it is less likely that a cataloger can work entirely from the item itself, rather than requiring information about it from other sources).

In practice, libraries are rarely manipulating collections of commercially recorded music. Music publishers do not usually grant permission for such use, and as a result, although libraries store and lend audio CDs as physical objects, they do not often have the right to network them or otherwise transmit them. Thus, "audio libraries" often mean speech libraries, which are more likely to have been recorded on cassette recorders, as by-products of some oral history or anthropological research project. These materials can often be stored at voice quality. At 8000 bytes per second, an hour of sound is about 30 MB. Since a typical conversational speed is about 100–125 words per minute, an hour of talking includes 6000–7000 words representing about 35 KB of text. Thus, recording sound rather than storing the text spoken requires 1000 times as much disk space. Much more serious, however, is that there is no easy way to search sound recordings. Nor can people browse sounds with anything like the facility that they can scan pictures. Thus, large sound archives typically require detailed cataloging, which is far more costly than the recording and storage of the sound.

Voice on the Internet is now booming with the realization that you can make phone calls across the Internet. People wishing to avoid long-distance phone calls are experimenting with using the speakers and microphones on their machines to make phone calls using packeted voice across the Internet. At present the quality is poor, since the Internet does not have real-time service guarantees. The Internet also features CD stores offering samples of many of the CDs, for example (with licenses), and the RealAudio format is used for various kinds of audio libraries. Some libraries provide voice samples on the Internet. For example, the Vincent Voice Library at Michigan State University provides, among other works, speeches by presidents, from Grover Cleveland to Bill Clinton. Sound is easy to store and index; it is hard to search, however, and the copyright problems with music are even worse than print. Yet it is attractive to think of large libraries of both speech and sound, accessible across the Internet.

Users of a sound library would also like to be able to search sounds in many ways. Queries can be imagined to search music by composer, style, instruments that are playing, or even by the musical theme being played. Or you might search for emotional content: romantic music, martial music, or funeral marches. To date relatively little work has been done in these areas.

There are some steps for sound processing that can be taken automatically once a digital representation is available. Perhaps the most common form of sound manipulation is changing the speed of the speech. Normal conversation is about 125 words per minute, but people can understand much faster rates (reading speeds of 400 words per minute are not unusual). Thus, it is often desired to accelerate a spoken passage. Simple time compression will also shift the pitch of the sound, making it less intelligible. However, it is relatively easy to accelerate speech while retaining the same pitch. Ordinary listeners can adapt to understand double normal speed. Blind students, who must spend large amounts of time listening to speeded-up speech, learn to understand four times normal speed.

Another easy strategy is segmentation. Particularly with professional speakers (as on the radio), you can expect longer pauses between sentences than between words, and between paragraphs than between sentences. As a result a computer measuring the amount of silence in a recorded segment (just looking for low-intensity values) can detect interparagraph breaks. By then reading the first sentence in each paragraph, it is possible to give an abbreviation of a journalistic text. It would seem possible to analyze the pitch and intensity of a spoken text and decide what the speaker thought was important, and thus abbreviate it more effectively in those cases where the style of writing is not such as to put a summary sentence at the beginning of each paragraph. Algorithms to do this, however, are not yet available.

4.2   *Pictures: GIF and JPEG*

The storage of pictures other than images of printed pages introduces other complications. These pictures are likely to contain color, and their use is less predictable. There are over a hundred different standards for image representation. The most common are GIF, JPEG, and ImagePac.

GIF (Graphics Interchange File) is a common format, although it may become less so as a result of a claim by Unisys that they have a patent on the Lempel-Ziv compression algorithm used in GIF. GIF uses a 256-element color space, which adapts well to typical computer screens but falls far short of the color range in naturalistic scenes. The compression in GIF comes from two sources: one is the use of Lempel-Ziv compression on the image data, and the other is the reduction of the color space to 256 possible values. Since Lempel-Ziv is a lossless compression scheme, GIF is lossless on bitonal or grey-level images (so long as there are only 256 grey levels); it is lossy on color images for which it reduces the number of colors. GIF is particularly well adapted to computer-generated drawings, since these are likely to use only a few colors. It is not as well adapted to photographs of people or real scenes, since these have a great many colors. To improve GIF compression performance, it is necessary to reduce the number of colors in the scene (below 256). For many scenes, there is little perceived quality loss in reducing to 64 colors (especially on computer displays without good color capabilities).

JPEG, named for the Joint Photographic Experts Group, solves many of these problems. It is also a publicly defined and usable standard, with fast decoding software. The JPEG algorithm is fairly complex and depends on breaking an image into 8×8 pixel blocks, calculating spatial Fourier coefficients to represent the information in each block, and throwing away some of the high-frequency information to compress the image. Spatial Fourier coefficients are a way of describing how rapidly the information in the picture is changing as one moves across the picture. The lowest spatial Fourier coefficients describe features that are flat across the block or across half of it; the highest coefficients describe aspects of the block that are changing back and forth at each pixel. Keeping only the lowest coefficients is equivalent to viewing the picture from a greater distance or squinting at it. JPEG is a lossy compression algorithm and also adjusts the color map; JPEG compression of a picture with only five colors will produce a compressed image with many more colors. JPEG is a generally stronger algorithm than GIF and is adapted to a wider variety of pictures, including, in particular, naturalistic scenes. JPEG is perhaps less well adapted to very sharp computer-generated images, since its Fourier transform methods limit high-frequency detail.

Another image compression technique is ImagePac, the method used in Kodak's PhotoCD (Seybold 1996). ImagePac is less frequently used today, since it was originally (and is still perceived as) a Kodak proprietary product that could not be implemented by others. Librarians and many other customers are skeptical of any format that is tied to one company; they fear possible restrictions on future use. ImagePac, like JPEG, is tuned for natural scenes. It stores luminance data more accurately than chrominance, thus preserving detail better than color. The Kodak PhotoCD format deals with the problem of fast decompression by storing five different resolutions of each picture. Thus, the user can quickly access a low-resolution version for scanning and only later access the high-resolution version. The five resolutions are 128×192, 256×384, 512×768 (considered the base resolution), 1024×1536, and 2048×3072. There is also a higher-resolution version, Kodak Professional PhotoCD, in which the top resolution is 4096×6144. Even this, however, does not represent all the detail available in a high-quality 35-mm slide, let alone a larger format negative.

Wavelet compression is the next step forward. Like JPEG, the wavelet algorithms are based on spatial Fourier transforms taken over the picture, but unlike JPEG they are taken over the entire picture rather than blocks within the picture. The weighting assigned to different Fourier coefficients decreases faster with frequency, leading to a more efficient use of the code space. Wavelets represent fine detail better than JPEG and achieve high compression. Again, they are lossy.

Figure 4.1 (Color Plate) shows the effect of reducing the number of colors in a picture. This photograph was selected to show the effects of color quantization; in a scene with fewer colors (or without natural colors and their variations), color quantization would be less noticeable. Note the effect on GIF compression. Table 4.1 shows the size of the GIF images for different numbers of colors.

One possibility (not used in these examples) for improving image quality is *dithering*. Dithering is a process of representing a color or grey level by using dots of different values that average to the color wanted. For example, newspaper halftoning is an example of dithering: a grey level is suggested by using black dots of different sizes with larger black dots for a darker grey and smaller dots for a lighter grey. Figure 4.2 is a comparison of bitonal images dithered and thresholded; as you can see, dithering helps considerably (at the cost of raising the size of the GIF file from 16,613 to 38,349 bytes). The left picture uses dithering; in the right picture all pixels lighter than a given grey level are made white, and the rest are made black, which is called thresholding.

As mentioned, GIF is best for computer-generated images, such as the kind of transparencies often used in talks that contain only a few words and a very small number of colors. JPEG is better for normal scenes that contain a wide range of

Table 4.1

Number of Colors	Size
2	16,613
4	33,038
7	47,544
10	59,301
20	87,317
50	123,770
256	197,839
all	88,156 (JPEG)

(a)   *(b)*

Figure 4.2   *(a)* Dithering vs. *(b)* thresholding

colors, and where color fidelity matters. ImagePac (PhotoCD) offers somewhat less compression than these methods but high fidelity, and it is a complete commercial product requiring less system design. A suitable retrieval system can be built with any of them, and it is possible to write software that asks what format an image is and then adapts to it, so that the user does not need to know which format was used. The binary computer file containing a GIF image, for example, will begin with the characters *GIF*, and a binary computer file containing a JPEG image will begin with the octal (base 8) value 377 followed by octal 330.

As with sounds, pictures are compared with what we are used to seeing. Computer displays, and all other forms of representation of images including photographs, are limited in dynamic range (intensity) and in color gamut by comparison with the abilities of the human eye. For example, the difference in intensity of the light from a scene in bright sunlight and a scene in a dimly lit room is 10,000:1, yet the eye can adapt and recognize colors and shapes in each situation. Photographic paper, on the other hand, can only capture a range of about 100:1. Slide (transparency) film is much better, and in this case computer displays are better also, usually able to display a range of 256:1.

The range of colors people can see is also large compared to many reproduction technologies. It is not possible today to make devices that reproduce the entire color space, and although it is possible to make systems that are sensitive to infrared or ultraviolet colors beyond what the eye can see, that is not useful for reproducing normal objects. But as Edwin Land (the founder of Polaroid) demonstrated, the eye is extremely good at visualizing colors from a small amount of color information, so it is possible to make computer displays and conventional printing equipment that display only some of the colors the eye can see, but yet are usable. Sometimes limited displays may appear washed out because of an inability to display sufficiently saturated colors. Figure 4.3 (Color Plate) illustrates the so-called color gamut, standardized in the 1931 CIE (Centre Internationale d'Eclairage) Standard Colorimetric System.

The arc-shaped space represents the colors that can be seen. White is in the center; along the edge of the arc are the saturated pure spectrum values from red to blue, and moving toward the center shows the progressively less saturated colors. The eye can see as much of this figure as can be printed. Any system using three dyes or three phosphors will always show a triangular part of the space at best. The marked out areas in the figure show different kinds of color production systems and what they can show. A good color film (e.g., Kodacolor or Ektacolor) will distinguish quite a lot of it. Computer displays usually show somewhat less than the best color film, and offset printing even less still. Newspaper presses can show only a small part of the color space. If you are only doing a few brightly colored items (e.g., cartoons), the lower-quality displays may be adequate; for serious color work considerably better effort is needed. For color output the various technologies differ in the characteristics again; some printers may lack saturation, while others lack the ability to produce subtle tone differences. The best digital color printers are dye sublimation printers, but they are both slow and expensive (although getting less so). Color laser printers, working from the technology of color laser copiers, are becoming dominant.

Brightness and contrast of images also cause problems. Often a scanned image, when put on the screen, looks either lighter or darker than the user expected. The problem is that most computer displays are not linear in their intensity; doubling the signal going to the electron gun more than doubles the apparent brightness of the picture. The coefficient of the curve that relates signal strength to brightness is called *gamma*. For some materials, exaggerating the contrast may be good; bitonal images, for example, don't depend on shades of grey. But for realistic depictions of normal scenes, it is desirable to have the right relationship between the brightness levels indicated in the image and those seen on the screen. This is particularly true

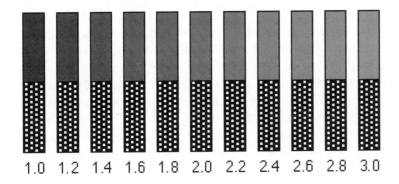

Figure 4.4   Gamma

if the user needs to compare brightness levels made by dithering with those done with grey level.

Suppose that an area of a scene has 50% intensity (midway between white and black). It can either be printed as a grey level of 0.50 or as a dithered area in which half of the bits are black. Ideally, these would have the same appearance. In practice, on a typical screen, they will not. Many screen manufacturers correct or partially correct for gamma problems of this sort, trying to make the apparent brightness reflect the intent of the original picture. Figure 4.4, for example, taken from the web page

```
http://www-cgi.cs.cmu.edu/afs/cs.cmu.edu/user/rwb/www/gamma.html
```

shows the extent to which gamma is represented correctly on the page you are reading. Move far enough away from the page that you see the bottom dot representation as grey. The bars on the left are darker on top; the bars on the right are lighter. The bottom half of each bar is a 50% dither. If the gamma correction that went all the way through the printing was right, the middle bar will look as if the top and bottom are equally dark. To understand whether your workstation corrects gamma properly, fetch the online URL above and look at it on your screen.

How can libraries store pictures and sounds? Traditionally these are cataloged by writing textual descriptions of them and then processing the text. There are thesauri, such as the Getty's *Art and Architecture Thesaurus*, that attempt to cover some kinds of images. However, there is no generally accepted classification to help with subject searching. Instead, much searching of artworks, for example, is based on the painter's name, the title, or the physical size of the work.

Obviously, art collections are often searched for landscapes showing a particular area or for portraits of a particular person. But in addition they may be searched for seasons of the year depicted (a Christmas card publisher will want winter landscapes), or for style of painting, or for religious subjects, or even for moral messages. How would someone in an art library who was looking for a painting related to electioneering, and who could not remember the specifics of William Hogarth's *Four Prints of an Election*, find them? How could we imagine doing this without any manual processing or textual descriptions? This seemed impossible for many years, until the IBM QBIC project demonstrated that it was possible to organize pictures based purely on their bit patterns.

QBIC gathers a variety of features about each picture and uses them for search and retrieval. Effective picture browsing is possible with low-grade attributes of pictures such as color and texture. The QBIC system (Flickner et al. 1995) used the following features:

1. *Color.* QBIC computes a histogram of the colors. It computes 64 color values and, for each color in the original, counts the closest of the color values.

2. *Texture.* QBIC uses the following texture features: *coarseness* (how large the features in the picture are, measured by shifting windows of different sizes over the picture), *contrast* (the variance of the grey-level histogram), and *directionality* (the degree of peaking in the distribution of gradient directions).

3. *Shape.* QBIC uses the size of items, circularity, eccentricity, and major axis orientation. It relies partly on manual tracing of features in the picture and partly on color areas to decide which areas represent features. QBIC lets people draw sketches and use them to retrieve pictures.

Continuing from QBIC, other work has involved finding images based on blobs of different sizes and colors and creating rules for finding a particular kind of image. This work has been done, for example, at Columbia (Chang and Smith 1995) and Berkeley (Ogle and Stonebraker 1995). Figure 4.5 (Color Plate) is from Berkeley and shows the various images retrieved by a model of "horses" (note, for example, that one picture is a woodchuck viewed sideways).

4.3 *Automatic Speech Recognition*

Automatic speech recognition has been a goal from the beginning of computational linguistics and received a great deal of attention in the 1970s when the Advanced Research Projects Agency (ARPA) sponsored considerable work on speech understanding. At that time the situation was very frustrating. There are four parameters that strongly affect the difficulty of speech recognition:

1. Whether the speech is normal continuous speech, or the user is required to speak in discrete words, pausing between each

2. Whether all speakers are supposed to be recognized, or the system has been trained on the voice of one person who will be the only user

3. Whether the dialog can be about anything, or the vocabulary and subject matter (and possibly even the syntax) are restricted to a small number of words, usually dozens

4. Whether the speech is over a telephone (which limits the speech to a bandwidth of 300–3300 Hz), or the speech is recorded from a quality microphone in a quiet room

The rule of thumb in the 1970s was that unless three of the four parameters were in your favor (the second choice in each item above), then your speech recognition task was probably hopeless.

In more recent years there have been great strides. Much of the recognition work is based on dynamic time warping plus hidden Markov models (see Peacocke and Graf 1990 for details). Carnegie Mellon University (CMU) reports a system that does speech recognition at 70% to 90% word accuracy with continuous, arbitrary speakers (Huang et al. 1992). Alex Waibel (1996) discusses speech recognition systems that accept a large vocabulary of continuous speech from any speaker and have word error rates of 10%. Some of the improvement is faster computers and processing, some is improvement in algorithms, and some is a recognition that there are particularly easy tasks to which a system may be tailored. In particular, the job of speaking computer commands, which typically are spoken in a discrete way and are picked from a set of fewer than 100 words, can be done more accurately than typing from dictation. Dictation systems are still usually slower to use than typing (because correcting even 10% of the words may take longer than just retyping a line), but they are gaining much acceptance and are now a standard way of trying to ameliorate the effects of carpal tunnel syndrome.

Rudnicky, Hauptmann, and Lee (1994) present improvements in the word error rate (lower numbers are better) for speech recognition systems in Table 4.2. Note that these error rates are still fairly high. A word error rate of 5% is a rate of about one word per sentence. And these machines can be rather expensive: the winner in a recent ARPA contest got 93% right out of 20,000 words (all test utterances entirely from the dictionary), but the machine had 100 MB of RAM.

However, we have become adept at finding applications in which the domain of discourse is so restricted that speech recognition can work effectively. A computer program can be designed to use only a few dozen commands, for example, and the names can be chosen to be fairly distinct when pronounced (Church and Rau 1995). Audio-based retrieval is even less explored (but see Wilcox, Kimber, and Chen 1994), and CMU is working on transcribing speech for traditional text search.

Recognizing *who* is talking is a slightly different problem from recognizing what is being said. It has been studied for years, often with the idea of identifying

Table 4.2

Task	Speaker Independent?	Continuous Speech?	Date		
			Late 1970s	Mid-1980s	Early 1990s
Alphabet	Yes	No	30%	10%	4%
Digits	Yes	Yes	10%	6%	0.4%
Constrained query	No	Yes	2%	0.1%	
Complex query	Yes	Yes		60%	3%
Dictation, with 5000-word vocabulary	No	No		10%	2%
Dictation, with 5000-word vocabulary	Yes	Yes			5%
Dictation, with 20,000-word vocabulary	Yes	Yes			13%

people for authorization purposes such as unlocking doors. In speaker verification of this sort, the speaker can be asked to speak some particular phrase (or one of a number of phrases) that has been recited before. ITT, for example, sells a product called SpeakerKey and points out that users much prefer voice identification to passwords, particularly those passwords recommended by cryptographers that are hard to guess and thus hard to remember. At present, however, speaker verification is slower and more sensitive to environmental noise or other problems.

On the other side of the law, Aleksandr Solzhenitsyn, in the early pages of his novel *The First Circle*, describes a group of researchers asked by the KGB to identify a potential traitor from voice recordings. This is a harder problem: the person speaking cannot be asked to say something that has been recorded before. Instead, voice properties must be used to decide who it is. Despite various testimony in the courts about "voiceprints," this is still a difficult problem. Michael Hawley's 1993 thesis, for example, describes algorithms for separating the voices of two radio announcers (Hawley 1993).

The ability to identify voices would be useful beyond questions of security. National Public Radio correspondents, for example, each have a particular specialty. Someone looking for information about the Supreme Court, for example, would want stories read by the voice of Nina Totenberg. The computer and communications industries are covered by Dan Charles and John MacChesney, respectively. So voice identification would provide a degree of subject indexing of the sound if transcripts were not available.

4.4 *Moving Images: MPEG and Motion JPEG*

The storage of television and the cinema is perhaps the most important question for the entertainment industry. Given the acceptance that the CD format has achieved, abandoning it for the next standard (DVD) needed the strongest technical justification. And that justification was the simple inability to do high-quality moving-image storage adequate to hold a full movie on a CD.

The film industry has been seeking to digitize its work for many years. Part of the justification is actually in the creation of movies. To make a movie by pointing cameras at actors costs around $2500 per second (a typical two-hour movie, 7200 seconds long, would indeed cost about $20 million). To make a movie by hiring animators to paint cels (single drawings) costs about as much. At 24 frames per second and half a dozen cels per frame, each second requires 100 or so cels, and getting high-quality artwork painted, even in the Philippines, is likely to require $250 per painting. What about a totally synthesized movie? Suppose each frame is a 3000×3000 image (quite high quality). Each frame is then 10 million pixels, or 2.4×10^8 pixels per second. Suppose 1000 arithmetic calculations were needed to compute each pixel. These must be floating point operations, the kind of arithmetic that is not done on simple integers, but on the kinds of numbers that have many digits of precision. What does a floating point operation cost? It is easy to buy a machine that can do 1 million floating point operations per second (a *flop*) for $10,000; amortize it over 12 months, and for $10,000 you can get 3×10^{13} flops (33 million seconds in a year) or $$3 \times 10^{-10}$ per operation. So if each second needs 2.4×10^{11} flops, and a flop costs $$3 \times 10^{-10}$, then computing one second of film would cost $70, or much less than the alternatives.

As of 1996, few movies are completely synthesized, although progress is certainly being made. Looking at the films shown at different SIGGRAPH (ACM Special Interest Group on Graphics) meetings, a viewer of the 1980 conference would have complained about failures in the ray tracing algorithms, while a viewer today would complain about plot and characterization. Movie viewers today are well aware that large parts of movies such as *Jurassic Park* are synthesized, and the entire movie *Toy Story* was computer generated.

Even movies that are not created digitally can still be stored and distributed in a digital format. How much space will that take? The pixel numbers above were for a very high-quality format that would be suitable for theatre projection. Home television sets are much lower quality; in the United States they have 525 horizontal lines and resolve perhaps 350 dots across each line. VHS videotape is of this quality. If we assumed a 500×500 image and 8 bits per pixel, at 30 frames per second (broadcast television), that would be a raw rate of 60 million bits

Table 4.3   Disk space for one minute

Mode	Storage
Script	0.001 MB (1 KB)
Sound recording, mu-law	0.48 MB
Video, H.261 codec	0.84 MB
Video, MPEG-1	11 MB
Video, MPEG-2	40 MB

per second. There is also much discussion of high-quality television, now defined as 1440×960 resolution at 60 Hz frame rates, and a $16:9$ screen aspect ratio (this is a compromise between current TV and old movie aspect ratios of $4:3$ and "wide screen" movies at $2:1$). Superficially this means 12 times as many bits per second.

Video storage demands look particularly large compared with text. In a minute, an actor might speak 125 words, so that even with a sentence or two of stage direction, the script for a minute would be under 1000 bytes. Table 4.3 shows how this can expand. The H.261 algorithm, one of the methods for encoding video (the word *codec* means *coder-decoder*), used at 112 KB per second, is not able to do high-quality coding of images with lots of motions; it is best for a videoconferencing application where people are sitting relatively still.

Compression of television is essential; this can rely either on compression within each frame or, in addition, rely on the similarity of consecutive frames. Simply sending one JPEG picture per frame, and using 10 KB per picture, would be 2.4 Mbits per second; this is known as motion JPEG. Such a technology would make no use of frame-to-frame compression. To take advantage of frame-to-frame redundancy, video compression should use the MPEG algorithms, named for the Motion Picture Experts Group. MPEG-1 is the best known. MPEG-1 is commonly used at a data rate of 1.5 Mbits per second and includes compression both within each frame and from one frame to another. At 1.5 Mbits per second, image quality may not be quite good enough for entertainment video; motion is a little jumpy as the program catches up at major scene changes. However, MPEG-1 is adequate for many instructional videos or other "talking heads" applications such as videoconferencing. MPEG-1 starts with 30 frames per second of 352 wide by 240 high pixels (chosen so that U.S. NTSC at $240 \times 352 \times 60$ fields per second and European PAL at $288 \times 352 \times 50$ fields per second have the same bit rate) and separates the frames into luminance (grey level) and chrominance (color), reducing the color resolution to 176×120, much as is done by Kodak ImagePac. Individual still-frame coding is very similar to JPEG. However, there are three kinds of frames: I-frames, which are encoded entirely as a still image, with no reference to previous frames; P-frames, which are predicted from previous frames (by using difference coefficients to give the JPEG parameters); and B-frames, which are predicted from both present and future frames (typically interpolating between them). An I-frame must be sent every 12 frames so that the system can start from scratch at least every half-second. In order to use the B-frames, the system must transmit the frames out of order, so that when each B-frame is received, the bounding frames on each side are known.

MPEG-2 is higher quality and often uses bit rates of 4–9 Mbits per second. It codes motion at larger block sizes, increases the precision of the JPEG coefficients, and was designed to deal with 720 × 480 pixel sizes. The practicality of either of these algorithms depends on the amount of material that must be stored. At MPEG-1 rates, a 650-MB CD-ROM can hold about 3000 seconds of video. Unfortunately, that is only about 40 minutes, and a typical modern movie is two hours. MPEG-2 requires even more storage; a two-hour movie would take perhaps 3 GB. Thus, the need for a new kind of storage device, targeted at a few GB; this has produced the DVD.

Improvements on MPEG-2 are likely to require considerable storage and processing capabilities in the decoding device. One way of improving the compression rate of movies would be to start transmitting pieces of the background and asking the display device to save them. Thus, as the camera panned back and forth across a room, it would not be necessary to retransmit the areas of the background that remained static. Today, however, it is not clear what kinds of display devices would have this kind of storage capacity (or the ability to do the real-time computation needed to create 24 or 30 images per second).

4.5 *Indexing Images: Motion Segmentation*

If indexing static images is bad, indexing or browsing real-time images would seem to be even worse. Things are not as bad as they seem, however, since the storage system has access to a few pieces of trickery: segmentation, image classification, closed captioning, and voice processing.

Although people can scan video at faster-than-normal speeds, much faster than they can listen to speech, it is still useful to divide a video into sections and let people understand the structure of the film or video. This is surprisingly easy. Segmentation can be done by looking at frame-to-frame differences. In one sample experiment (Lesk 1991), I took a one-hour video, reduced it to 1 bit per pixel, and counted the number of pixels that changed from frame to frame. The number was either about 1% for frames that continued the same scene, or about 30% for a cut (it is not 50% because the frames, on average, are somewhat lighter rather than somewhat darker). A threshold at 10% is quite accurate at dividing a video at the places where the director or editor made "cuts" in composing the program. More careful segmentation work has been reported from Singapore (Zhang, Kankanhalli, and Smoliar 1993).

Given a division of a video into a series of scenes, a system can then present one sample image from each scene and use that as a browsable overview of the program. The user can then click on any image and see the full video starting at that point. Figure 4.6 shows an example of this kind of interface, applied to a video of a technical talk in which the cuts are primarily between the speaker and the projection screen. The screen is divided into a top and bottom half. The top half shows two images. On the left is the current image, which changes in real time as fast as the machine and transmission link can manage, giving the impression of ordinary video. On the right is the most recent viewgraph shown. In the bottom half, four scenes are shown: the present scene, one previous scene, and two coming scenes. That is, the next-to-left bottom picture will always resemble the top-left image, since both are the current scene (although the top-left window is video while the bottom windows change only when the scene changes).

In this case, still further progress is possible by image classification. There are two basic kinds of scenes in this video: the person (David Clark of MIT) speaking in the room and the viewgraphs that he was projecting. It is relatively easy to tell these apart. Figure 4.7 shows the grey-level distribution of the pixels from frames from these two kinds of scenes. Each curve plots the number of times each grey level from 0 to 255 appeared in the frame. The top curve shows the viewgraph distribution, with strong peaks (since the viewgraph contains mostly either white or black), while the bottom curve shows the distribution of grey values for a picture of Professor Clark, whose image has the usual range of densities found in a photograph. As one would expect, pictures of the speaker show a natural distribution of grey values, with a reasonably flat distribution through the middle grey levels. The viewgraph screen is either dark or light and shows a bimodal distribution. Measuring the standard deviation is done easily enough to tell one of these from the other (in fact comparing the number of pixels with grey level at 50% with the number of pixels with grey level at black is enough to distinguish them). This permits a display only of the viewgraphs or only of the speaker. Similar techniques are used at Carnegie Mellon to take a TV news program and sort the studio scenes from the on-location photography (Stevens, Christel, and Wactlar 1994).

Segmentation in this way works; the problem is that it is not enough for a modern film. In the 1930s or 1940s, a Hollywood movie would have had scenes of a minute or two in length, and so a 90-minute movie would have had 50 or 75 scenes, a feasible number of images for a viewer to browse through. Today a movie will have scenes of one or two seconds in length; it is not uncommon for a two-hour movie to have 4000 cuts. Viewers can't usefully browse that many scenes. Heuristic techniques can select the ones deemed most important.

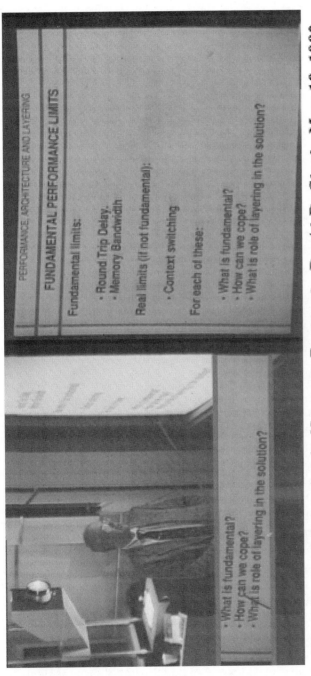

Figure 4.6   Video segmentation

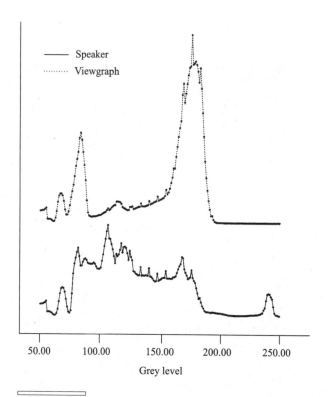

Figure 4.7   Density distributions for Speaker and Viewgraphs

Another technique that can produce amazing results is the use of the closed-captioning track that comes with many television programs. Television signals are transmitted with gaps to permit the traditional television set electronics time to move the CRT beam back to the beginning of each scanline and then to move the beam back to the top of the screen after each field. The data in TV fields do not follow immediately after each other; there is a time interval between the last pixel of one field and the first pixel of the next field. This interval is visible as a black bar between frames when the vertical hold on a TV is badly adjusted. On PAL sets, for example, with 625 lines, 580 are used for a picture and 45 lines are left unused. The gap between frames (the vertical blanking interval) made television sets easier and cheaper to build when electronics was less advanced. Now it provides opportunities to conceal additional information in the television signal.

As a service to the deaf, many television programs transmit, in line 21 of the frame gap, an ASCII version of the dialog of the program. This closed caption-ing is detected and displayed by modern television sets. It can also be captured by computers and used to search or index the material being shown, as demonstrated by Tom Landauer (1995a) and Howard Wactlar (Wactlar et al. 1996). Closed captioning does not track the actual voice display perfectly, and it sometimes contains spelling errors, but it is an enormous advantage in trying to access television programs. Unfortunately, it is only present on broadcast television (not usually in films on video), and even then only on some programs (although these are the informational programs most likely to be of interest to libraries). The vertical blanking interval can also be used for data services and will be used, for example, to transmit rating information for sex and violence on TV shows, so that the V-chip can limit which programs are watched.

Howard Wactlar at CMU, for example, has used closed captioning to accumulate a set of pictures of individual faces (Christel et al. 1995). They look through the closed captioning for names, and then try to link these with faces that they find in the video (faces can be identified by flesh tones). They identify the studio scenes so that they do not constantly get the newscaster's face for each picture. Since the closed captioning does not track the sound perfectly, and even the broadcast sound may not line up exactly with the image that one wants (as when the newscaster says, "and now we will talk to Alan Greenspan in our Washington studio" before the video cuts to the actual scene), some empirical scanning is necessary to find the right face. CMU claims to identify faces (pick the right name from a transcript to put on the image) about half the time. Wilensky at Berkeley has also been able to find pictures of people or horses in static images (U.C. Berkeley 1995). Thus, it is possible to make a database of faces from many sources. As an example of this work, Alexander Pentland at the MIT Media Lab has software that finds and recognizes faces, identifying the correct face from a population of several hundred with 99% accuracy (Pentland 1996). Thus, we can easily imagine looking through not just newscasts but also ordinary films looking for particular people.

What of programs with no closed captioning? CMU has used their Sphinx voice recognition software to prepare automatic transcripts. This is a much less accurate transcription than the closed captioning, although it does have the advantage of better linkage to the actual sound track (although again the sound track does not follow the video perfectly). Fortunately, if you wish to index important topics in the video, it is likely that each topic will be mentioned more than once, giving the voice recognizer several tries at it.

4.6 *Summary*

This chapter has described indexing of multimedia. Today this technology is still experimental. We can classify pictures very roughly by color, texture, and shape; this is not enough to deal with collections of millions of photographs. We can do speech recognition well enough to be of some use in analysis of voice recordings; we have little technology for searching music. We have various tricks for compressing and browsing video but only limited technology for searching it.

We can try to rely on browsing. For images, the human eye is extremely good at looking at large numbers of images quickly, so the provision of thumbnail-size images that can be rapidly scanned is a practical alternative to more detailed searching systems. For sound, unfortunately, this is less helpful; it is hard to scan sounds as quickly as we can deal with pictures. Browsing video is a current subject of research but has not yet led to solutions the typical library can install easily.

To review the last few chapters, we know how to store and search ASCII text. We know how to store, if not necessarily search, pictures and sounds. We can just barely cope with storage of video. Active research in indexing pictures, sounds, and video, however, is likely to produce methods we can use to handle more advanced material in a few years. The practical digital librarian, however, might choose to focus effort on the collections that can be used immediately and look forward to handling multimedia in the future.

Knowledge Representation Methods

THE QUANTITIES OF material stored in digital libraries pose the problem of finding what you want (as in all libraries). In some collections of information, the user is simply overwhelmed. Queries return either nothing or thousands of answers, and the users are often baffled about what to do. Attempts have been made over the years to provide a way for people to find information, often based on the idea of organizing everything by subject. Often, this was a by-product of the need to put books on shelves. On disk drives the physical location of any particular byte is irrelevant to the librarian, but the intellectual organization of the collection still matters. This chapter will describe the ways that people have tried to organize and arrange knowledge, with the idea of making searching simple.

If we had a single knowledge representation scheme that let us put each idea in one place, and if the users knew this scheme and could place each of their queries in it, subject retrieval would be straightforward. There would still be a need for items at different levels of sophistication and a need for quality checking, but we could imagine that we could at least solve the problem of locating items on a given subject. Is this practical?

Whether knowledge representation can be discussed outside of language processing is unclear. Two famous linguists, Edward Sapir and Benjamin Lee Whorf, proposed what is now known as the Sapir-Whorf hypothesis, which says that language constrains thought (Sapir 1949). They suggested that there would be cultural differences in the way that different peoples thought about things based on their languages. For example, they felt that the Hopi language would lend itself particularly well to modern quantum physics because of the way it discusses time. In this view, there is no independent representation of abstract thought other than a linguistic expression. Most artificial intelligence researchers reject the Sapir-Whorf hypothesis. They believe that there is some kind of abstract knowledge representation in the brain, which is translated to linguistic form when we talk or write, but which could be represented directly in the right mathematical structure. Finding that one best structure is the Holy Grail of knowledge representation.

Evidence for abstract knowledge structures comes partly from the study of aphasia, the loss of communications ability, particularly as the result of head injuries. For about a century (this research started with studies of battlefield casualties in the Franco-Prussian War of 1870), medicine has noticed a distinction between two kinds of aphasia caused by injuries to parts of the brain named Broca's area and Wernicke's area. Broca's aphasics seem to lack syntactic function; they struggle to produce words and have great difficulty arranging the words into sentences of any length or complexity. Wernicke's aphasics, in contrast, lack semantics. They produce "word salad" with great fluency and speed but cannot produce rhetorically sensible arguments. As these two kinds of aphasia are caused by damage to different parts of the brain, it is tempting to think that "meaning" is somehow formed in Wernicke's area and then formed into "language" in Broca's area, implying that they are distinct. But this does not guide us to the form and structure of whatever meaning representation the brain might use.

In practice, it seems unlikely that any single knowledge representation scheme will serve all purposes. The more detailed such a scheme is, the less likely it is that two different people will come up with the same place in it for the same document. And the less detailed it is, the less resolving power it has and the less use it is. Tom Landauer and associates did a number of experiments on the ability of people to give names to concepts (Furnas et al. 1983). They would ask people to associate a single word with a picture or a concept—for example, the idea of a command that tells you how much money you have spent in some computer system. In Landauer's experiments, people generated so many different words as answers to tasks like this that in order to get 85% coverage of the answers you need six different words. Of course, many of those words are also answers to different tasks. Thus, asking people to label concepts does not produce unique and reliable answers. Even professional indexers do not produce entirely reproducible results. Humphrey (1992) reports that interindexer consistency in Medline (selecting terms from the MeSH-controlled vocabulary) is under 49%.

The dream of perfect vocabulary is an old one, although it originated with a slightly different problem. Until the Renaissance most scholars in Europe wrote in Latin, and they could all read one another's books. With the rise of vernacular literature, scholars became unhappy about their inability to read anything they wanted. Since Latin had been abandoned, some of them thought that perhaps an artificial language would succeed as a common language for all serious thought. An example is the 1668 *Essay Towards a Real Character and Philosophical Language* of Bishop Wilkins. There were others, such as Leibniz, who even predated Wilkins in this effort.

5.1 *Library Classification*

Perhaps, however, knowledge labeling could be done consistently if it were done by trained librarians. The first step would be to define a formal list of substantives (nouns) describing all subjects. Again, this goes back to Aristotle; we still have courses with names like Rhetoric, Physics, and Politics because these are the titles of his books.

Here, for example, are the headings in some early systems. As shown in Table 5.1, the Library of Congress used a system based on the work of Bacon until 1812 and then switched to one designed by Jefferson himself. The British Museum Library used 14 headings until 1808 (see Table 5.2), some of which still reflected the source of the books rather than their content (Alston 1986). This was then followed under Antonio Panizzi by an extremely idiosyncratic system in which there were category headings such as "Evidences for and against Christianity," "Total abstinence from liquor," and "Marriage—female suffrage." Perhaps the strangest category was "Morality of war, cruelty to animals, dueling." The top-level categories are shown in Table 5.3.

Table 5.1

	To 1812 (Based on Bacon)		From 1814 on (Jefferson)
1.	Sacred history	1.	History, ancient
2.	Ecclesiastical history	2.	Modern history except UK, US
3.	Civil history	3.	Modern history, British Isles
4.	Geography, travels	4.	Modern history, America
5.	Law	5.	History, ecclesiastical
6.	Ethics	6.	Physics, natural philosophy
7.	Logic, rhetoric, criticism	7.	Agriculture
8.	Dictionaries, grammars	8.	Chemistry
9.	Politics	9.	Surgery
10.	Trade & commerce	10.	Medicine
11.	Military & naval tactics	11.	Anatomy

Table 5.1   *(Continued)*

To 1812 *(Based on Bacon)*	*From 1814 on* *(Jefferson)*
12. Agriculture	12. Zoology
13. Natural history	13. Botany
14. Medicine, surgery, chemistry	14. Mineralogy
15. Poetry and drama, fiction	15. Technical arts
16. Arts & sciences & miscellaneous	16. Ethics
17. Gazettes (newspapers)	17. Religion
18. Maps	18. Equity (law)
	19. Common law
	20. Commercial law
	21. Maritime law
	22. Ecclesiastical law
	23. Foreign laws
	24. Politics
	25. Arithmetic
	26. Geometry
	27. Mathematical physics: mechanics, optics
	28. Astronomy
	29. Geography
	30. Fine arts, architecture
	31. Gardening, painting, sculpture
	32. Music
	33. Poetry, epic
	34. Romance, fables
	35. Pastorals, odes
	36. Didactic
	37. Tragedy
	38. Comedy
	39. Dialogue (epistolary)
	40. Logic, rhetoric
	41. Criticism, theory
	42. Criticism, bibliography
	43. Criticism, languages
	44. Polygraphical

Table 5.2

1. Philology, Memoirs of Academies, Classics
2. Cracherode Library
3. Poetry, Novels, Letters, Polygraphy
4. History (ancient), Geography, Travels
5. Modern History
6. Modern History, Biography, Diplomacy, Heraldry, Archaeology, Numismatics, Bibliography
7. Medicine, Surgery, Trade & Commerce, Arts, Mathematics, Astronomy
8. Medicine, Natural History
9. Politics, Philosophy, Chemistry, Natural History
10. Ecclesiastical History, Jurisprudence, Divinity
11. Divinity
12. Sermons, Political tracts, King's pamphlets
13. Acta Sanctorum, Musgrave Biographical Collection, Music
14. Parliamentary records, Gazettes, Newspapers

Table 5.3

1. Theology
2. Jurisprudence
3. Natural history & medicine
4. Archaeology & arts
5. Philosophy
6. History
7. Geography
8. Biography
9. Belles lettres
10. Philology

At the end of the 19th century, however, the major classification systems now in use were started. These are the Dewey system by Melvil Dewey (founder of the now-defunct Columbia University library school), first published in 1876, and the new Library of Congress classification based on previous work by Charles Cutter (replacing the classification designed by Thomas Jefferson), which appeared between 1898 and 1920. These systems are well known; the top-level headings of each are shown in Table 5.4. Note that each book must be put in only one category

Table 5.4

Dewey		Library of Congress			
000	Generalities	A	General works	M	Music
100	Philosophy	B	Philosophy & Religion	N	Arts
200	Religion	C	History: Auxiliary	P	Language & Literature
300	Social Sciences	D	History: Old World	Q	Science
400	Language	EF	American History	R	Medicine
500	Science	G	Geography	S	Agriculture
600	Technology	H	Social Sciences	T	Technology
700	Arts	J	Political Science	U	Military Science
800	Literature	K	Law	V	Naval Science
900	Geography & History	L	Education	Z	Bibliography

in each system, since the shelf location is determined by the class number. This is the classification function known as "mark and park." Even if the library owns two copies of a book, it is important for both to be in the same place on the shelf (or the users will get annoyed at having to look in two places to find the book). There may be multiple subject headings, but that does not help the user trying to browse the shelves.

Of course, different classifiers looking at the same book may make different decisions about its primary topic. For example, consider a book of songs about railway accidents, entitled *Scalded to Death by the Steam* and published in both the United Kingdom and the United States. The primary subject cataloging in the United States is as a book of songs, subcategory railways (Library of Congress [LC] category number ML3551.L94, Dewey 784.6); the primary subject cataloging in the United Kingdom is as a book about railways, subcategory music (LC HE1780, Dewey 363.1). In practice, the necessary decisions to select categories involve enough choices that they will not be made the same way by two different people. A book, *Selling Mothers' Milk: The Wet-Nursing Business in France, 1715–1914*, that was clearly intended by the author as social and economic history has wound up (in the United States) being classified under infant nutrition.

Figure 5.1 shows the relative number of books in each of the main Dewey and LC headings, from a sample of over half a million English-language books from the 1970s and 1980s at the Online Computer Library Center (OCLC). The major reason for the larger number of books in the language and literature class (P) in LC than in Dewey are the large number of fictional works; novels are not classed in Dewey but are classed as literature in LC.

In general, it has been found that Dewey is preferred by public libraries and LC by research libraries. Dewey is perceived as simpler and better suited to smaller

Books in Dewey classes

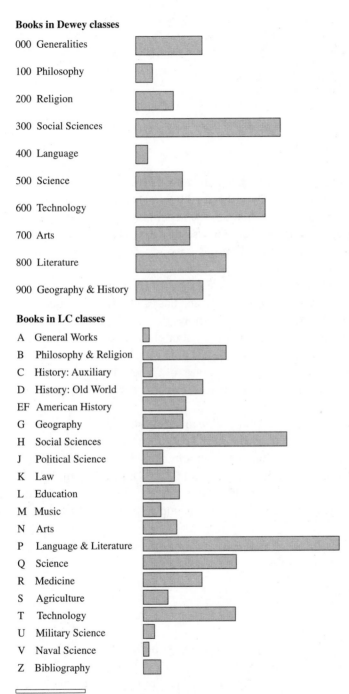

Books in LC classes

Figure 5.1   Dewey and LC frequencies

Figure 5.2   Yahoo classification

collections, while LC provides more detail, which is needed in a very large library. In Europe it is more common to use UDC (Universal Decimal Classification), which resembles Dewey in many ways but is maintained separately. At one point many large libraries maintained unique classification systems (e.g., Harvard or the New York Public Library), but nearly all such libraries have given up their schemes as shared cataloging has become common.

Several Web search systems have also made classifications of the pages they find on the Web. Figure 5.2 is the top level of Yahoo, which has categorized 200,000 Web sites under 20,000 category headings. Table 5.5 shows the top categories from several of the Web-classifying systems. Note that a number of Aristotle's labels are still with us. In particular, we still have the same general kind of subject classification, as opposed to classifying items by reading level, genre, document format, or source. The only new element in the online classification is a categorization by purpose: employment, hobbies, and so on.

In addition to hierarchical classifications, there are also lists of subject headings, not organized into a structure. Perhaps the best known set of subject categories is that produced by the Library of Congress, not the classification hierarchy (as described above) but their List of Subject Headings (LCSH). This multivolume book contains a list of acceptable headings that librarians can use to index books. Many library users are familiar with these headings. For example:

Railroads—Accidents

Railroads—History—Great Britain

Railroads—History—United States

Railroads—History—United States—New York

Railroads—Subways

This kind of classification is clearly not enough. Although it is a long list of unambiguous subjects, it does not include an adequate way to indicate the relationships between them. A book with the subject headings for armor plate and transport could be about the building of armored railway trains or about the shipment of steel plate. Nor is there a procedure for indicating the relative importance of different subjects. If a primary and secondary subject heading are indicated, the

Table 5.5

Yahoo	Excite	Magellan
Arts	Arts	Arts
Business	Business	Business
		Communications
Computers	Computing	Computing
		Daily Living
		Economics
Education	Education	Education
		Employment
Entertainment	Entertainment	Entertainment
		Environment
		Food
Government		
Health	Health & Medicine	Health
	Hobbies	
		Humanities
Internet		Internet
		Kid Zone
		Law
	Life & Style	
		Mathematics
	Money	
		Music
News	News & Reference	News
	Personal Pages	
	Politics & Law	Politics
		Pop Culture
Recreation		
Reference		
Regional	Regional	
Science	Science	Science
	Shopping	
Social Science		
Society & Culture		
		Spirituality
Sports	Sports	Sports
		Technology
		Travel

second could be 40% of the book or 5%. Finally, as with assignment to a particular classed category, different readers of the same book could easily decide that different subjects predominated. However, the LCSH scheme does have the advantage that, unlike classification, a book can have many headings. The classifier must choose whether a book on the history of British education belongs primarily under history, Britain, or education; the subject headings can reflect all three subjects.

The other side of this freedom to assign multiple subject headings is less pleasant. There is no particular need for each topic to appear only once in LCSH. You may ask, "If half the users wishing to look up *refrigerators* call them *iceboxes*, why not index all books on the subject with both terms?" The answer is not only that it would double the length of the index. It also means that you cannot distinguish between mechanical refrigeration and iceboxes if you really need to do so. But in a subject heading world, it is tempting to allow multiple names for the same concept.

Efforts have been made to do very precise subject headings. It is possible to indicate relationships between them and to have enormous numbers of subdivisions. Perhaps the most ambitious scheme for extreme precision in this area was the PRECIS system of Derek Austin (Broxis 1976). PRECIS was so named because it was, in effect, a small abstract, formally described. Each term in a subject indexing entry had a unique meaning, and its role with respect to other terms was formally coded. The roles followed syntactic relationships with such roles as "action," "object," "agent," and "location." However, even with careful supervision of the indexers, the more detail that each indexer must provide for the indexed documents, the more likely it is that two indexers handling the same document will disagree somewhere.

5.2   *Indexing Words and Thesauri*

Is it adequate simply to rely on ordinary words for the description of content? This is what most systems do today, and it seems adequate for many tasks. But words fail in two respects. First, there are often many words used to describe the same idea; users looking for *scanning* may not search for *facsimile* or *imaging*. This produces *recall failures*: material that should be found is not. Second, the same word can mean two different things in different contexts. Users typing *grain* at a search system prompt might get articles about wheat and articles about wood grain, and it is unlikely that they wanted both.

Sometimes it is possible to sort out the meanings by knowing the part of speech of the word. "Time flies like an arrow" cannot be about houseflies if *time* is a noun and *flies* is a verb. It is possible to guess part of speech fairly accurately without doing a complete syntactic analysis. Geoffrey Sampson and coworkers at Leeds and

Lancaster Universities developed statistical methods based on the probabilities of certain word sequences. They started with two kinds of information:

1. A dictionary giving for each word the possible parts of speech it might have. Thus *fly* may be either a noun or a verb; *fat* may be either an adjective or a noun.

2. A corpus of parsed English giving the parts of speech of each word, from which probabilities of different sequences could be computed. Thus *adjective-verb* is impossible while *pronoun-verb* is very common.

Then, given a sentence, they would make a list of the possible choices for each word and look for the selection that would give the best overall probability for the sentence. Garside, Leech, and Sampson (1987) worked with pairs of words at a time; Ken Church (1988) got better results later by working with trigrams. Church used the Brown corpus (1 million words of tagged English) as a base and then tagged 15 million words of wire service text, claiming better accuracy than any other tagging system. A similar program is now available at HarperCollins Publishers that will tag anything sent in email. Sampson (Sampson, Haigh, and Atwell 1989; Haigh, Sampson, and Atwell 1988) later extended this kind of work to an entire parser that used statistical techniques to assign structures to sentences.

Sometimes knowing the part of speech of a word is enough to settle some question regarding it. But many of the semantic ambiguities are still there even if the part of speech is known. If *wing* is a noun, it will not usually mean *to try* but it can still be either part of a bird, a plane, or a building. Are there similar statistical tricks for deciding on the meaning of a word within one part of speech? One possibility is simply average statistics across a document. Knowing whether a document is about astronomy or Hollywood will probably tell you the meaning of *star.* This can be handled by looking up each word in a thesaurus and counting the category occurrences; whatever category is most frequent in the document as a whole is the best choice for a word that could be in more than one category (Amsler and Walker 1985). Is it possible to do something more precise? One answer is to use a dictionary, rather than a thesaurus or a grammar, and to count overlaps between the definitions of different senses of nearby words (Lesk 1986).

Consider, for example, the problem of knowing what the words in the phrase *pine cone* mean, and distinguishing them from the meanings in phrases like *ice cream cone.* Look at the definition of *pine* in the *Oxford Advanced Learner's Dictionary of Current English.* There are two major senses: "kind of evergreen tree with needle-shaped leaves" and "waste away through sorrow or illness." And *cone* has three separate definitions: "solid body which narrows to a point," "something of this shape whether solid or hollow," and "fruit of certain evergreen trees." Note that both *evergreen* and *tree* are common to two of the sense definitions; thus, a program could guess that if the two words *pine cone* appear together, the likely senses are those of the tree and its fruit. Here is the output:

```
Word Sense Count       Sense Definition
pine   1*     7    kinds of evergreen tree with needle-shaped
                      evergreen(1) tree(6)

       2      1    pine/ ~
                      pine(1)

       3      0    waste away through sorrow or illness:

       4      0    / pine for sth; pine to do sth, /  have a

cone   1      0    solid body which narrows to a point from a

       2      0    sth of this shape whether solid or hollow,

       3*     8    fruit of certain evergreen trees (fir, pine,
                      evergreen(1) tree(6) pine(1)
```

What are the advantages of this technique? It is nonsyntactic and thus a useful supplement to syntactically based resolution. Syntax can distinguish *foot* in "foot the bill" and "one foot six inches," but there are many different meanings of *mole* as a noun, for example: "I have a mole on my skin"; "there is a mole tunnelling in my lawn"; and "they built a mole to stop the waves." This technique successfully finds the correct meaning in each of these sentences.

Another major advantage is that it is not dependent on global information. Here is a sentence from *Moby Dick* (with only the pertinent sense definitions listed):

```
There              ---
now                ---
is                 ---
your               ---
insular    1*  4   of or like islanders; narrow-minded:
city       2*  9   (attrib): / city centre/ central area
of                 ---
the                ---
Manhattoes     ???
belted     2* 86   any wide strip or band, surrounding
round      4* 28   (compounds) / round-arm / ~  adj, adv
by                 ---
wharfs     0*  1   (or wharves) wooden or stone structure
as                 ---
Indian     2* 16   (various uses) / Indian club, /
```

```
isles     0*  3 island (not much used in prose, except
by            ---
coral     0* 15  hard, red, pink or white substance
reefs     1*  9 ridge of rock, shingle etc just below
commerce  0*  1 trade (esp between countries); the
surrounds 0*  0 be, go, all round, shut in on all sides
it            ---
with          ---
her           ---
surf      0*  5 waves breaking in white foam on the
```

Note that it got the correct meaning of *reef*; the alternative meaning is "all hands to reef topsails." If you depended on global information, you would conclude that since *reef* appears nine times in *Moby Dick* and seven of those are related to sails, that should be the meaning chosen, and the two instances of *coral reef* would be mistakes.

On average this technique seems to be about 50% accurate in finding word senses. It is difficult to measure this, since there is no agreement among dictionaries as to the possible meanings of each word. Furthermore, although the examples here are chosen from words with widely varying meanings, many of the sense definitions in a dictionary are very close together, and retrieving one when another was intended might not be a serious mistake.

Just as some syntactic ambiguities cannot be resolved because the speaker or author did not provide enough information, there are some semantic ambiguities that must be left unsettled. In the above sentence from *Moby Dick*, when Melville wrote "your insular city of the Manhattoes," did he write *insular* to mean that Manhattan was "surrounded by water" or to mean that its inhabitants were "narrow-minded"? Of course he meant both.

Many systems, in processing texts, apply a *stoplist* of words that are not significant for semantics, such as the syntactic function words like *the* or *and*. More generally, words may be weighted according to patterns of appearance. The most common weighting is *inverse document frequency* and views that a word is more important if it appears in few documents. This reflects the tendency of vague words to appear in a great many documents. In classified collections, systems can even distinguish between words that appear mostly in one part of the collection and words that appear evenly distributed across all subject areas, assigning lower weight to the evenly distributed terms.

If words, whether from the original document or from subject headings, are not enough, what about thesauri? The use of thesauri for indexing has been described in Section 2.7. An indexer in a traditional thesaurus-run system has two tasks. One is to identify which topics in the document are important enough to index. The other is to assign the thesaurus entries for each of these topics.

Thesauri, unlike subject headings, do try to have only one place to put a single item. In *Medical Subject Headings* (MeSH), as an example, the term *cancer* is normally called *neoplasm*. There is an *entry vocabulary* to tell you about this synonym. The ideal thesaurus would have one term for each concept and one concept for each term, and there would be minimal overlap between the concepts. This is the mathematical idea of *orthogonality*—a set of dimensions, none of which can be expressed in terms of any of the others. For example, maps have scale, location, and features shown. Any of the choices

scale: 1:24,000 or 1:62,500 or 1:250,000

location: any point in the United States

features shown: roads, land cover, topography, buildings

make a sensible map. None can be deduced from the others. Ideally indexing of documents could be like this, but language is not so neatly laid out.

In addition, there can be ways to express relationships between the terms. In MeSH, for example, it is necessary to distinguish between tamoxifen as a treatment for breast cancer and a cause for ovarian cancer. This would be expressed as *Tamoxifen—Therapeutic Use* for the treatment and *Tamoxifen—Adverse Effects* for the possible carcinogenic role.

Although thesauri such as MeSH are used by trained indexers, that does not mean that everyone agrees on how to index documents. The National Library of Medicine (which produces MeSH) keeps track of interindexer consistency as part of their quality maintenance program and accepts that 50% agreement is a practical measurement. This means that half the time the indexers disagree on which term to assign. This is a lot better than the 85% or so that Landauer would expect for disagreement among novice indexers, but it is certainly not perfect (Furnas et al. 1983).

Indexing thesauri are not the whole answer to any of these problems, largely because they require trained searchers and indexers. But they anticipate many of the suggestions for complex knowledge representation languages, and they actually do support large, operating information retrieval systems.

5.3 *Artificial Intelligence Structures*

Artificial intelligence researchers have attempted to define formal knowledge languages, with the goal of permitting knowledge to be expressed with such detail that it can be manipulated automatically. As in indexing thesauri, a typical knowledge representation language will have a hierarchy of concepts and then store relationships between them. For example, animals might be grouped into the traditional Linnean hierarchy:

animal $\longrightarrow$ mammal $\longrightarrow$ carnivore $\longrightarrow$ dog $\longrightarrow$ Fido

The relationship between "Fido" and "dog" is not really the same as that between "dog" and "mammal," so they wind up getting slightly different relationships ("isa" and "subset" are typical names).

The relationships between items can be of varying degrees of complexity. Once you get beyond the defining hierarchy, there are many obvious relationships that can be used in writing down information. To understand the use of such relationships, remember the relationships in MeSH. If you wish to distinguish not just the question of whether a particular substance causes or cures a particular disease, but all possible relationships between nouns, a great many relationships might be needed. Virtually every verb in the language might be needed as a link name between substantives. Normally a somewhat smaller set is used, since a knowledge representation structure is supposed to be something more systematized than a parse tree. Often they seem similar to the cases used in linguistics: agent, object, location, and so on.

By organizing the nodes of an AI language into a hierarchy, each fact can be stored at an appropriate level. The statement that canaries are yellow is stored with "canary," that they fly is taken from a statement about birds, and that they breathe from a statement about all animals. Of course, life is not always so simple. We could easily write in a knowledge representation language "all cats have a tail." But what about Manx cats? Does the node for "cat" have to be divided into "Manx" and "non-Manx" cats? Pretty soon there will be so many divisions that the gain from having hierarchies disappears.

Something more tractable is the use of *frames*. Frames were invented by Marvin Minsky and represent specific lists of attributes ("slots") to be filled in for specific nodes, so that everything is not linked to everything else (Minsky 1975). Thus a frame for describing a cat might have slots for weight, color, sex, and so on, while a frame describing a theatrical performance would have slots for playwright, director, cast, and so on.

This is more reasonable for a large knowledge area. For example, Susanne Humphrey has built a system named MedIndEx that uses frame structures to provide aids to medical indexers (Humphrey 1989). The frames encode information about what medical subject headings can be used in which parts of the index entries. For example, the site of a disease must be coded with a term that comes from the anatomical structures part of the MeSH hierarchy. The location of some conditions is even more restricted; a bone neoplasm, for example, must be coded with a term from the skeletal section of the hierarchy. And the frames can make use of the slots that are filled to improve the indexing; Humphrey explains, for example, that if an indexer codes *Bone Neoplasm/Anatomical Structure/Femur* the system will suggest that the top-level term should be *Femoral Neoplasm*. This system is very detailed, encodes a great deal of medical knowledge, and is now being tested to see how much improvement in indexing results from its use. It is unusual in the breadth of its coverage.

Translating all written English into a knowledge representation language requires, in principle, the need to disambiguate every ambiguity in the original text. This is not practical. For many ambiguous sentences, the speaker has been willing to say something with an ambiguity because it is not worth the trouble to resolve it; it will make no difference to the listener. We are accustomed to ambiguity both that can be resolved and that cannot be resolved. The sentence "John drove away in a fury" could mean either "John drove away angry" (John was angry) or "John drove away angrily" (the manner of his driving displayed anger). This does not bother a listener since the meaning is basically the same in either case, and unless John then got into an automobile accident, it is probably not important which was meant. The work of disambiguating each such possibility is totally impractical. And things get worse if translation is the goal. Martin Kay of Stanford mentions that when you board a bus in Switzerland, you put your ticket into a machine that, in the French parts of the country, validates it (*valider*), but in the German parts of the country, invalidates it (*entwerten*). There are many stories about widely hyped systems making mistakes such as translating the name of the late Israeli prime minister Menachem Begin as Monsieur Commencer.

However, the designers of AI systems do not necessarily need to imagine converting all of an English text into a knowledge representation language. Two other choices are converting some of the knowledge of a text into the formal language, and writing the knowledge directly in the language instead of in English.

The conversion idea was perhaps pursued most ambitiously by Roger Schank at Yale and his students (Schank 1973). They worked on what were first called "scripts" and then called "MOPs" (memory organization processes) and which represented certain standard scenarios for common situations. For example, there was a "restaurant script" involving the standard actions of seeing a menu, placing an order, getting food, eating food, and then paying the bill. Another was the "natural disaster script" of an earthquake or hurricane; something happened, at some place and time, and caused a certain number of deaths and injuries. Schank produced programs that went through the United Press news wire and tried to list the basic elements from each story that matched one of the scripts. In some ways this was a basic data extraction task, to take a text that contains specific data elements and pull them out for a database.

The most elaborate attempt to produce an enormous body of codified knowledge is the CYC project of Doug Lenat in Austin, first at MCC and now at Cycorp (Lenat and Guha 1990). Lenat set himself the goal of writing down all common-sense knowledge in a formal way. He suggested that the problem with machine learning was that computers lacked the more elementary parts of the knowledge that people have. Over a period of a decade, Lenat and his associates attempted to encode everything from elementary biology to time series. They used 100,000 concepts and wrote down 1 million rules. They ran into several practical difficulties. One was that a great deal of skill in logic was needed to enter the knowledge; despite a goal of entering very simple knowledge, it was not possible as originally hoped to use high school students to do it. Another difficulty was that different people entering similar concepts would choose different ways to do it, as has happened in other experiments of this sort. Most serious was Lenat's discovery time and again that the basic principles of CYCL, the CYC knowledge representation language, had to be adjusted as new areas of knowledge were studied. Initially, for example, Lenat tried to assign probabilities to each rule to indicate degrees of certainty, but he was unable to do this in a consistent way.

CYC has no unifying overall ontology, since CYC is broken down into a number of "microtheories," each of which is created specially for its domain. Time will have to tell whether CYC will ever achieve its goals of having the common-sense knowledge of a human being (Stipp 1995).

5.4 *Hypertext*

If it is not going to be easy to translate all text manually into formal language, is it possible to rely on specific links for specific document-to-document queries? This is the model of "trails" suggested by Vannevar Bush in 1945. Theodor (Ted) Nelson, now at Autodesk Corp., rejuvenated this idea in 1960 and coined the name *hypertext* for it. In a hypertext document collection, there are pointers from one place in the text to another. Hypertext links, as commonly used, are asymmetrical: there does not need to be a link in the reverse direction for each forward link. They are also modeless: all links are the same kind of link, rather than being labeled with types.

There were various experiments with hypertext systems in the 1970s and 1980s. Perhaps the best known are the system at Brown University (IRIS), which attempted to use hypertext for teaching courses, and the programming systems like Hypercard (Apple) and Notecards (Xerox). In these experiments it was found that hypertext was frustrating both to write and to read. In terms of writing, the author has great difficulties writing something if the user need not have read the paragraph immediately preceding the one being written. A world in which readers jump from one place to another is one in which the author never knows what the reader already knows, and it becomes difficult to carry through a logical argument. Brown found it very time-consuming to create their hypertext courses, and the students in the courses contributed less than they expected.

The readers have the converse problem. They can easily get lost and not know how to get back to something they have read. "Navigation" quickly became the big problem in hypertext, and it became commonplace for each hypertext document to have one page that functioned like a traditional table of contents or index, providing pointers to every place in the hypertext and being pointed to by every page as well. That way, users always had a place to which they could return and from which they could find any other point in the text.

Several evaluation studies of hypertext, in fact, found that it was more difficult for people to deal with than traditional paper texts. Gordon et al. (1988) at the University of Idaho, for example, converted four short magazine articles into a hypertext system and tested students on what they learned from the articles. Half the articles were general interest and half were technical. Both the linear (traditional) and hypertext versions of the articles were read on the same computer screens. The students remembered more of what they read in a linear format, although the time taken to read either version was about the same. The students also preferred the linear version. Similarly Shneiderman (1987) compared the ability of people to answer questions from a 138-page set of articles that was available both on paper and in his system Hyperties. For information at the start of an article, paper was better; for information buried in an article or requiring references to more than one article, the formats were equivalent. A more dramatic instance was an experiment done by McKnight, Dillon, and Richardson (1991), in which the text used came originally from hypertext format rather than paper. Again, the results failed to show an advantage for hypertext.

Despite these early difficulties (Nielsen 1990), hypertext has now exploded on the world. Today's famous hypertext system, of course, is the Web. Created by Tim Berners-Lee at CERN in 1990 (Berners-Lee et al. 1992), the Web as of April 1996 contained about 180 GB of material in 12 million documents, with perhaps 30 pointers on each Web page, or a total of 360 million hypertext links. Much of the Web consists of organizations of other people's pages; there are innumerable hot lists, bookmarks, and other ways of keeping track of what has been seen. There are also, of course, the search engines, and finding things on the Web is partly handled by search engines and partly by the hypertext links.

Part of both the glory and the frustration of the Web is that it has no maintenance organization whatever. Individuals add and delete things at will, making it easy for material to appear but also for it to disappear. The ability of individuals to place what they want in the Web has also produced problems since some of the people on the Web want attention for their pages and do things like place irrelevant words on their page to attract the attention of some search engines. Libraries will have to try to decide which items are relevant and useful and which are not.

Web pages not only can appear without any organizational approval, but also can and do disappear. As of April 1996 the average life of a uniform resource locator (URL) was 45 days, so that the Web is full of pointers to files that no longer exist (Chankhunthod et al. 1996). This means that somebody who sees something good on the Web must make a judgment as to whether it is likely to still be there if it is wanted again. If it does not appear to be from a source such as a university library or other permanent organization, the only safe thing to do will be to copy it, given permission.

Whether in the long run libraries can rely on hypertext links as a way of accessing information is doubtful. Unorganized and amateur indexing has been tried in the past with author-assigned keywords and such proposals, and has been inadequate. Relying simply on citations in known papers is effective but inadequate for complete coverage; a surprising fraction of published papers are never cited at all. Thus, sole reliance on volunteer-built hypertext may not be an adequate method of achieving general library coverage.

5.5   *Vector Models*

If reliance on manual methods is not going to be enough for digital libraries, what can be done mechanically? In the SMART project, Gerard Salton introduced the idea of the "vector space" as a way of handling documents in retrieval systems (Salton 1968). In vector space mathematics, each different word in a document can be viewed as a direction in a very high-dimensional space. The number of dimensions is equal to the number of different words in the document collection. The strength of the vector in each direction is the number of times that word (since each word is one dimension) appeared in the document. Thus, each document can be viewed as a vector in this high-dimensional space, and the similarity of two documents can be judged by looking at the angle between the vectors. Documents on very similar subjects should have a small angle between their vectors; very dissimilar documents should have a large angle between their vectors.

Salton also considered the use of a thesaurus in this model (Salton 1968). In this case, each word was replaced with the thesaurus category to which it belonged, and the number of dimensions was the number of categories rather than the number of different words. This still leaves, however, an enormous number of dimensions. And that large number of dimensions means that it is often going to be the case that a particular document will not be found in a search for a particular concept because a related concept was used to describe the document. A document relevant to *dogs* might be missed because it used the word *canine* or *pet*, for example.

Attempts were made over the years, beginning with Vince Guiliano in 1961, to identify related terms on the basis of their overlaps in documents (Guiliano and Jones 1963). Statistical methods for word associations looked for words that appeared together. In fact, early suggestions were that one should look not for words that actually occurred together, but that occurred with similar word neighborhoods.

For example, if we imagine that all documents are spelled with either consistent British or American spelling, the words *airplane* and *aeroplane* will not appear together, and their synonymy will be missed; a searcher who only asks for one word will not find documents containing the other one. But both of these words will appear in documents containing words such as *jet, propeller, wing, rudder, cockpit, APEX*, or *carry-on*. Thus, their relationship could be detected. The irregularities of word statistics in small collections, however, caused most such experiments on small test databases in the 1960s to yield unsatisfactory results. And most examples of synonymy are much less clear-cut than this one.

Scott Deerwester, Sue Dumais, George Furnas, Tom Landauer, and Richard Harshman of Bellcore thought of trying to mechanically condense the vector space into a space of fewer dimensions using standard mathematical techniques (singular value decomposition). They called this technique Latent Semantic Indexing (Deerwester et al. 1990). LSI operates on a term-document matrix for a text collection, which has rows and columns labeled, respectively, with each word that appears in the collection and each document that is in the collection. The value of the element at any position in the matrix is the number of occurrences of that word in that document. Thus, given a collection of 10,000 documents with 50,000 words appearing in them, the matrix would have 500 million cells. This might seem much too large for any kind of practical manipulation, but fortunately the matrix is very sparse (the average word does not appear in the average document). Thus, special matrix techniques can be used to accelerate the calculations. What LSI does is to find a smaller set of dimensions and values that can be used to substitute for the original matrix. Instead of a document being represented by a vector in a 50,000-dimensional space with almost all elements zero and little chance of finding overlaps, it is represented by perhaps a 100-dimensional vector in which it is likely to have *some* weight on each element.

Imagine two groups of documents, one set about mathematical theory and another about human factors. Terms such as "interface" and "ergonomics" might not appear in the same document, but as long as they both appear with terms such as "display" or "format," they will be connected by the process. Thus, LSI can make significant improvements in recall as well as precision.

Tom Landauer and Michael Littman also used LSI to do cross-language retrieval. Earlier, Salton had done cross-language retrieval by creating a bilingual thesaurus, in which words in both languages were mapped into one concept space (Salton 1970). Landauer and Littman (1990) realized that by obtaining a collection of documents in two languages and performing the term/document overlaps using both languages, they could make vector spaces into which terms from each language could be mapped. This eliminated the need for manual construction of a bilingual concept thesaurus, although a translated collection was still needed to start the process. For example, here is a passage from the Canadian *Hansard* (Parliamentary proceedings) in English and French for May 12, 1988:

Mr. Speaker, during the 1980 election campaign the Rhinoceros Party promised Canadians that if elected they would make us drive on the left hand side of the road instead of the right hand side, and that this new system would be phased in starting with buses in the first year, followed by trucks in the second year, and cars later.

Monsieur le Président, pendant la campagne électorale de 1980 le parti rhinocéros avait promis, que s'il était élu, il nous obligerait à conduire du côté gauche de la chaussée plutôt que du côté droit, ajoutant que ce nouveau système serait appliqué graduellement, en commençant par les autobus la première année, les camions la deuxième année, et les voitures par la suite.

(The speaker was, of course, not endorsing the Rhino platform but complaining that some actual traffic regulation was almost as ridiculous.) By treating these paragraphs (and all other translated pairs) as the same document for purposes of building the vector space, the words that are consistently paired will be found to be related. Thus, in this case, if *camion* and *truck* usually appear together, they will get very similar representations in the LSI space, and a search for either word will retrieve the same documents.

The word relationships found are not necessarily those you would find in a dictionary, since they combine aspects of the basic word meaning with the context. In the Canadian *Hansard*, for example, the word *house* is most closely related to *chambre*, because the contexts for these words are typically *House of Commons* and *Chambre de Communes*. If one is doing a search in *Hansard* on a topic like "What did the House say about traffic in Ottawa?" the word *chambre* is indeed the most useful translation.

Landauer and Littman (1990) in an early experiment used a sample of 2482 translated paragraphs with at least five lines in both French and English. They trained the LSI system on 900 such paragraphs and computed a 100-dimensional space. Then, using other monolingual paragraphs as queries, they would find the translation as the best document over 90% of the time, as one would hope. LSI cross-language works extremely well in assigning these documents to the same positions, despite imperfections in either the translations or LSI and despite the great similarities between many speeches.

An interesting subquestion is the determination of *which* language an unknown text is written in, so that a system can decide what software to put it through. You would not wish to index French or German under the misunderstanding that they were English. There are various techniques to solve this, by looking for specific words that are very frequent in a particular language or looking at the letter frequencies in the language. A short text in any language, however, may be missing particular cue words. However, there is a cheap trick that works well: given known samples of the different languages, append the unknown text to each sample and run any standard compression algorithm that detects repeated strings on the combination. The one that compresses best is the right language. The compression program will do all the statistics for you.

5.6 *History-Based Information Resources*

Another technique for finding information is based on what has been used before. There is strong clustering in citations, in photocopy requests, and in library circulation. Digitally, it will become much easier to gather such information and use it.

Clustering phenomena in library usage are well known. A few items get heavy use, and many more are not used at all. The average item in a large research library does not circulate in an average year; it is probably not even touched (Burrell 1985). Approximately 80% of the circulation of books comes from 20% of the titles. Can the bunching of requests be used as a way of helping retrieve information? Some years ago in an experiment at Bell Labs, the usage of an Associated Press wire service was tracked (Geller and Lesk 1983). The screen display of stories is shown in Figure 5.3.

At the top is the list of stories, identified by their "slug" (the two hyphenated phrases); picking a number gives that story. The system doled out the actual stories in 10-line screens. It tracked the number of such segments that people read. The number to the right of each identifying phrase is the average number of screens that people who have read this story have gone through (up to 5). So a story with 4 or 5 to its right is one that the average reader has read 40 or 50 lines of; while a story with a 1 is a story that readers have stopped reading immediately, and a story

```
 1: (f0055) Indexes [1]           11: (f0050) TimeWarner-Turner
 2: (a9510) WEA--USTempsSN.usw10  12: (a0550) China-Fire [5]
 3: (a0554) TourdeFrance-Basques [3] 13: (f0049) Austria-Supermarkets [1]
 4: (f0054) Transactions [1]      14: (f0048) Austria-Supermarkets [1]
 5: (f0053) DJ10 [1]              15: (a0549) Lite-WifeWanted [2]
 6: (f0052) Sema-Olivetti [1]     16: (a0548) TimeWarner-Turner [2]
 7: (a0553) UN-GlobalWarming [3]  17: (f0047) LateNewsAdvisory [1]
 8: (a0552) TimeWarner-Turner [1] 18: (f0046) TimeWarner-Turner [1]
 9: (f0051) Earns-Ford [1]        19: (a0547) Breast-feedingSwitch [5]
10: (a0551) Pint-SizedSpeedster [3] 20: (f0045) OddLots [1]
3

r i PM-TourdeFrance-Basques     07-17 0231
^PM-Tour de France-Basques,0234<
^Basque Separatists Harass Riders, Protest as Race Enters Spain<
        PAMPLONA, Spain (AP) _ Basque separatist protesters walked onto
the path of cyclists in the Tour de France race today, forcing the
riders to slow almost to a stop as they climbed a steep ascent.
        About a dozen protesters held a Basque-language banner and
yelled slogans at Tour leader Bjarne Riis and several other
cyclists on the highway in France, about 15 miles from the Spanish
border.
        The Tour cyclists today were entering Pamplona in the Navarre
region of northern Spain.
        The armed Basque separatist group ETA, which wants Navarre and
six other provinces in Spain and France to be united as an
```

Figure 5.3 News story presentation

with no number next to it has not been read by anyone. Thus, a story like number 12, "China-Fire," with a 5 rating, is one that somebody has read through, whereas nobody has looked at story number 11. In this particular display, the user picked story 3, on the Tour de France, and the first 11 lines are shown in the figure.

Given this data, you could search for stories that had ratings of 3 or above, for example, producing a set of stories that other people found interesting. In practice, this would in fact distinguish stories in a useful way (it suppressed, for example, all stories about revolutions in Central America). With no names attached, this did not cause a worry about invasion of privacy.

Another possibility, of course, is citation indexing. For some years, *Science Citation Index* (from the Institute for Scientific Information, Philadelphia) has indexed papers based on the other papers they reference. As an alternative to keyword-based indexing, this can often turn up quite different documents. On the Web, it is similarly possible to track through hypertext links to a given page.

Don Swanson has done some particularly provocative work on the results of studying term and citation networks (Swanson 1987, 1991). He hypothesized that if topic A and topic B are not connected by citations, but topic C is strongly connected to both, it is worth considering whether A and B should be related. In the important example he gave, he found 25 articles arguing that fish oil causes certain blood changes and 34 articles showing how the same blood changes would alleviate the problems of Reynaud's disease, but no articles discussing fish oil and Reynaud's disease. And, indeed, later experiments showed that fish oil appears to be of some use in treating Reynaud's disease. Similarly, he found that there is considerable literature about migraine and epilepsy, and about epilepsy and magnesium deficiency, but no papers about dietary magnesium and migraine. Since Swanson's publication, several papers have appeared with evidence that magnesium alleviates migraine.

Will usage-based searching be important in digital libraries as well? Digitally, it is much easier to track usage of different items. As yet, there are no systems that say, "Show me things lots of people have liked" or systems that say, "Show me things other people have overlooked."

5.7 *New Information Techniques*

Another possibility is so-called community-rated information. The idea here is that you could model the search you wanted to do by looking at what other people have done. This is the logic of "anything Joe recommends I will like" done mathematically and with a large set of people.

An early example was the video recommender of Will Hill and Mark Rosenstein at Bellcore (Hill et al. 1995). They set up an email address that asked people to

Table 5.6

Correlation	Method
0.16	Choosing movies at random
0.22	Using recommendations of published movie critics
0.62	Community rating as described

rate movies from one to ten. They sent out a list of 500 movies; amazingly, the average person who returned this list rated about 200 movies. They wound up with a database of about 25,000 ratings. When a new person entered ratings, the database was searched to find the 10 people with the closest agreement. This new person could then be modeled as a linear combination of the best 10 matching people. Given this way of modeling the person, the system could then suggest movies that the model predicted the user would like but that the user had not rated (and presumably not seen).

Tests showed that this was a very effective way of recommending movies. Table 5.6 shows different methods of suggesting what videotapes you might want to rent. The correlation coefficient is between the actual rating and the rating predicted by the method given. Similar work has been done for audio (popular music CDs) by Patti Maes and her group at the MIT Media Lab (Shardanand and Maes 1995).

Whether this can be generalized to other domains is not so clear. The system depends on having a large number of items that many people have seen. For rarely read scientific papers, for example, it might be hard to find any data since nobody would be prepared to rate them. Movies and TV series have the property that a surprisingly large fraction of your friends and colleagues have seen the same programs; there is not the same shared experience for most books and certainly not for scientific journal articles.

5.8 *Summary*

What should librarians in digital libraries do for knowledge representation? This chapter has reviewed several possibilities. The first four choices offered were manual. Three of these forms of knowledge organization are typically created by paid experts: library catalog headings, thesauri, and artificial languages. Cataloging requires the least manual work; the use of thesauri or artificial languages requires more work in exchange for more detailed representations. Since even manual cataloging is fairly expensive at $17 per book (Wilhoit 1994), it is unlikely to be used for the majority of small Web documents. Hypertext is a manual method that spreads the work around a great many unpaid volunteers and is thus more practical although less reliable.

More mechanical possibilities than these first four involve vector models, retrieval histories, and community rating. These all seem to work, and vector models are widely used today. But the history and community techniques rely on enough people seeing each item to obtain useful judgments, which may not be the case.

Compared with all of these methods for organizing information, it seems likely that text searching will be the major method of accessing materials in digital libraries. Text searching, however, works best with items with particularly precise word definitions, such as unusual author names. If we want searching by concepts, or browsing in general subject areas, there may be a place for classifications and conceptual representations. They may also be valuable as a way to help with collections in multiple languages. Research is needed on the most effective ways of using representation languages and on their applications to digital libraries. Research is also needed on the ways to combine information on genre (e.g., works aimed at children) or quality (e.g., refereeing) with cataloging. The biggest technical problem is extending any of the automatic search methods to sounds and images; as shown above, some of this is being done, but the selectivity is still primitive compared with text searching.

Ideally, we would be able to combine information derived from classification, from hypertext links, from text and image searching, and from users. We use all of these sources in today's libraries, albeit informally, and we would like to be able to continue using them in the more mechanized future.

6

Distribution

T HE LAST FEW CHAPTERS have covered how the contents of a digital library are stored and organized. This chapter asks how those contents get to the readers. How is information to be moved from creators to receivers? Originally, it came via direct physical transmission: one person talked to another. This kind of transmission has advantages and disadvantages. It can be tailored to the individual listener, for example. It offers the chance for the listener to ask clarifying questions. But it doesn't travel very far, nor can it reach many people at once (the best opera singers without amplification fill a hall of 3000 people). The listener can't back up (without asking the speaker), there is no permanent record, the speaker has limited ability to use aids such as pictures or sound recordings, and the listener and speaker must be present at the same time in the same place.

6.1 *Physical Objects: Books and CD-ROMs*

Writing made it possible to have a permanent version of information, and writing on papyrus, paper, or parchment (rather than carving on stone walls) made it possible to move texts from place to place. In the Middle Ages there was an active market in copying manuscripts and selling them; this market was taken over by printed books when they arrived.

In the preparation of a $20 book today, the costs are distributed as follows (Rothman 1992):

Printing	$3
Wholesaler	$3
Retailer	$8
Office expenses	$4
Author royalties	$2

The economies of scale in modern publishing are such that it is difficult to issue a book today in a small press run. University presses, for example, which print 16% of the titles in the United States but take in only 2% of the revenue (Meyer and Phillabaum 1996), are all seeing economic difficulties. They are pressured by authors who wish to see their books in print, in order to get tenure, but their main market is university libraries, none of whom have budget increases adequate to keep up with the inflation in book prices. Since so many of the costs of printing a book are incurred before the first copy comes off the press, a small press run means high costs and thus high prices (which further cause libraries to drop purchases).

Scholarly journals are even more affected by the push by authors to see their names in print. Their prices have been raised to levels that no one could have imagined 30 years ago; today a journal subscription can cost as much as a new car. Since the authors are not being paid for their contributions, and since journals do not carry a retailer's markup, these prices reflect the very small number of libraries that are still willing to subscribe. Ann Okerson reports that book purchases dropped 15% in the five years prior to 1991, and journal purchases per faculty member in universities went from 14 to 12 in the same period (Okerson and Stubbs 1992). She projected her numbers to suggest that by 2017, libraries would buy nothing at all. The publishers react to statistics on the increases in costs facing libraries by pointing to the general consumer price index increase plus the increase in the number of pages per journal issue; together these effects dominate the journal price increases. The libraries, however, have no way of enforcing greater selectivity on the publishers to keep the sizes down, and there is a residual increase in inflation-adjusted price per page, especially for non-U.S. publishers (Marks et al. 1991).

Traditional publishing and distribution have accelerated substantially in recent years. Time-to-market is everything on instant books such as those published during the O. J. Simpson trial, and publishers have learned to speed up printing and distribution even for ordinary books. Libraries wishing to exchange items can take advantage of a wide array of new delivery services specializing in overnight package handling, and of course the fax machine has made interlibrary copying of journal articles a very rapid process.

CD-ROMs share many distribution properties with books. The CD-manufacturing process, like the book-publishing process, is most economic at large pro-

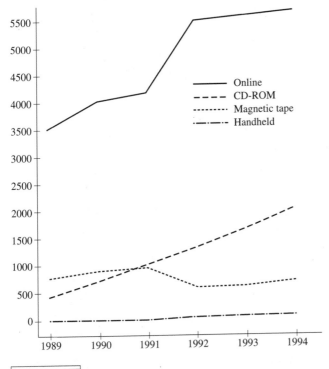

Figure 6.1 Media for electronic databases

duction runs. It was designed for high-run popular music disks, and the signal can be read as digital or converted to analog sound. CD-ROMs cost, in quantity, $1 to $2 for incremental costs, even less than a book. CD-ROM distribution began in the mid-1980s, some half dozen years after the audio CD started. Through the late 1980s most libraries bought CD-ROM drives and began to purchase CD-ROM versions of the abstracting and indexing journals. These purchases displaced online searching on a pay-per-minute basis; libraries realized that if they were spending large amounts of money on online searching, they could save money by purchasing the same database on CD-ROM.

There has been a considerable shift toward CD-ROM distribution of databases, away from magnetic tape, for example. Figure 6.1 shows the number of databases distributed in different forms. It does not quite go far enough in time to cover the Web. Note the low but noticeable presence of handheld gadgets; many dictionary sales, for example, are now in this format. CD-ROM and online are gaining, to some extent at the expense of magnetic tape and batch services.

In the early 1990s the individual CD-ROM business exploded. CD-ROM drives dropped in price to $100 at the same time that software distributors realized they wanted to distribute much larger programs. When PC computer RAM memory was

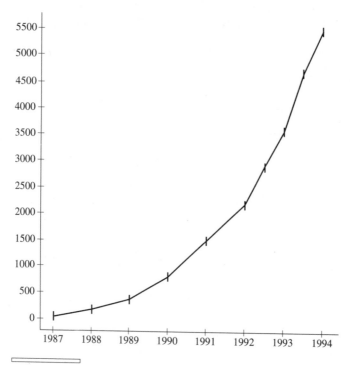

Figure 6.2   Number of CD-ROMs published

limited to 640 KB, a 1.4-MB diskette was an adequate distribution mechanism. Now that PCs with 40 MB of internal memory are common and software comes with manuals, options, and elaborate background images, it is inconvenient to have to deliver software in units of 1.4 MB. Many CD-ROMs came onto the market, with the market doubling every year up to early 1995; see Figure 6.2 (Finlay 1993).

The home reference CD-ROM market was part of this explosion. CD-ROM encyclopedias, for example, have greatly reduced the market for traditional paper encyclopedias. Other important categories of reference CD-ROM publishing are atlases, phone books, and educational aids for children. However, CD-ROM publishing is dominated by game programs. Of the top 15 best-selling CD-ROMs in March 1996, 9 were games (the others were TurboTax, Microsoft Windows and Encarta, and three print programs). There was a sudden slackening in CD-ROM sales in late 1995; many wondered if the CD-ROM customers were surfing the Web instead. Sales in the fourth quarter of 1996 actually fell below those of a year earlier. And, in a reversal of the game trend, the hottest consumer CD-ROM at the end of 1996 was Barbie Fashion Designer.

CD-ROM publishing is unusually concentrated by the standards of normal publishing. The distribution channels are harder to break into than for books; stores sell relatively few titles and most of those are from a few major publishers (most obviously Microsoft). As a result the wide variety of titles available are unknown to most buyers or are sold in very specialized places (e.g., art museum CD-ROMs in other art museums). Unlike audiobooks, which are sold in normal bookstores, CD-ROMs are sold largely through computer stores, which don't have the same traditions of special orders and generous stocking policies.

From the viewpoint of a library, CD-ROMs are very like traditional publications; they are purchased, and generally they remain as reference works and are not lent. They are very durable, and the main worry is not physical deterioration but that the equipment that is needed to use them will become unavailable. CD-ROMs place no unusual requirements on collections policy in a library, aside from the problem of networking. Since many reference CD-ROMs are quite expensive, libraries would like to let more than one person at a time use them, or at least to be able to access them from more than one computer workstation without having to physically move the disks from one place to another (incurring a risk of theft). Publisher policies vary on permission for this. The argument is unusual: making multiple copies of a CD-ROM is cheap, and one could imagine economic pricing policies that made networked access to CD-ROMs irrelevant.

6.2 *Computer Network Technologies*

To share information between libraries, the digital world allows much faster alternatives to faxes or postal mail. Computer networks now link almost every country in the world. Of course, computers have always exchanged bits with their peripheral devices. These exchanges typically follow a master-slave protocol; it is clear which device is in charge and which is responding. A key difficulty in designing intercomputer protocols, and part of the reason why they are different from protocols used within a single computer, is that they must anticipate that the two machines are of equal status; neither can be assumed willing to just wait around for the other one. Also, of course, the longer delays involved in transmitting over distances and through phone lines means that the protocols cannot assume immediate responses to all messages. The winning network has turned out to be the Internet, running IP (the internetworking protocol). There are several basic choices to be made in network design. These include the choice of packet or circuit switching and the choice of bus or star physical arrangements.

6.2.1 *Packets vs. Circuits*

In a *packet network*, each batch of information is handled separately. The analogy is letter mail or the telegram; in fact, packets are often called datagrams. Packet networks are like adding sand to your garden, bucket by bucket. In a *circuit network*, there is a preliminary negotiation to set up a route and then information flows along it. An analogy is the telephone system or the way that water flows along a hose; the faucets are turned and then the water moves. Roughly speaking, a circuit network involves overhead to arrange a path but may recover the cost of the arrangements by being able to move information faster. A packet network is simpler since each packet is completely independent, but there is no opportunity to save routing arrangements that have been set up for one packet to use for future ones.

6.2.2 Stars vs. Buses

To run wires around a building, two different topologies can be used. One wire can be threaded through each place that needs one, and everything hung off that wire, like the lights on a Christmas tree. This is called *bus* wiring: one wire passes every place that needs service. The alternative is to have each spot that needs a wire connected to a central location (e.g., a fusebox). This is called *star* wiring since a map of the wires looks like a star, with lines going from one central point to each spot that needs service.

Bus wiring requires less total wire but requires everybody to share the same wire. It is thus appropriate for a system in which expensive but high-capacity wire is used. Some early computer networks relied on coaxial cable and leaned toward this kind of system. However, bus wiring creates some administrative problems. Since everyone is sharing the same physical cable, if one machine on the cable malfunctions, everyone may suffer loss of service. Similarly a cable break necessarily affects a great many users. Thus, there has been a tendency to use star wiring, made of cheaper wires, but each machine has its own connection to some kind of data closet or local switch. This kind of system is easier to manage and usually cheaper to install, and in the form of the 10-base-T standard using twisted pairs of copper wire has replaced the thick coaxial cable Ethernet. It also simplifies administration of the network since users are less likely to interfere with each other.

6.2.3 Ethernet

Originally, different vendors developed different computer network systems and protocols. IBM was known for its SNA (system network architecture) linkages between machines, while Digital had DECNet. The most important development, however, was that of Ethernet at Xerox PARC, invented in 1976 by Robert Metcalfe and David Boggs. The basic idea of an early network of this type was the Alohanet protocol: any system that wishes to transmit simply puts out a packet on the bus with a header saying from whom it has come and at whom it is aimed. Each system listens on the bus and picks up all packets meant for it. Any system wishing to send merely sends a packet and hopes nobody else is doing so at the same time.

This extremely simple Aloha protocol cannot use much of the bus throughput, since as usage increases the chance increases that two computers will transmit at once. One improvement was the slotted Aloha, in which instead of transmitting anytime one wishes, the computers only transmit at fixed intervals. Ethernet improved this further while retaining the passive medium of Aloha. The Ethernet fabric is a plain coaxial cable with no active parts and thus fewer chances to fail. As in Alohanet, machines communicate by putting addressed packets on the bus fabric. What Ethernet adds is the idea that machines listen as they are transmitting. If, before it starts sending, a computer hears some other machine transmitting, it does not transmit. And, should two machines start transmitting so closely together in time that neither hears the other before starting to send, they both stop as soon as they detect the collision. Each then waits a random time before trying again, so that the next try will not produce a collision. This is why Ethernet is called CSMA/CD (carrier sense multiple access, collision detection). It is still not possible to use all the capacity of the cable, but it is a great improvement over the original Alohanet. In the Ethernet protocol, each machine needs to be able to hear every other machine in a time shorter than the time required to transmit an entire packet. This limits a single Ethernet to perhaps 100 meters, depending on the transmission speed on the cable.

The simplicities of the basic Ethernet idea are sometimes disadvantages. Every machine can see every packet on the cable, no matter to whom it is addressed. Unless packets are encrypted, sniffing machines can cheat and pick up all sorts of information not intended for them. Also, there are no constraints on the ability of an individual machine to transmit. If a machine on the cable goes haywire and starts transmitting constantly, ignoring all collisions and all other machines, there is nothing the other machines can do. Fortunately, a single Ethernet is limited in length and is likely to be contained within a singly administered domain, so something can be done to bring pressure on the operator of the haywire machine to fix it or at least shut it down.

Since a single Ethernet is only 100 meters long, to build larger networks Ethernets have to be connected. At first this can be done by *bridges*, which simply sit between two cables and copy every packet from one of them onto the other one. This approach doubles the traffic on the cables, however, and is not an adequate answer for large networks. Larger networks need *routers*. A router is a device that sits between two networks and, like a bridge, moves packets from one to another. But a router does not move every packet across the network. It knows which addresses are on which side. In the simple one-bus Ethernet, machines can be very sloppy about addresses; so long as each sender and receiver know who they are, it doesn't matter if any other machine does. Once routers are introduced, however, addressing matters. Each router looks at each packet address and decides whether it belongs only on the cable it came from or should be sent to a different cable.

What does a router do if it wants to put a packet on an Ethernet cable but suffers a collision? It must wait and try again, just like a normal computer. And this means it must have some memory to save up packets that it has to retransmit. Packet networks with routers are thus store-and-forward networks in which information flows with somewhat unpredictable timings toward the destination. And, packet networks need some way of sending back to the originator a message of the form "Your packets are coming too fast; please stop sending."

Of course, a network with routers in it is no longer totally passive. However, the basic idea that computer networks have a cheap dumb fabric and intelligent devices remains, and contrasts with the idea of the telephone network, which contains expensive switches and dumb telephones as peripheral devices. For example, in 1996 a digital telephone switch cost about $200 per line (world average price), and the phones could be bought for $10. Hubs and routers connect $2000 computers, with even the Ethernet interface card costing $150, but the cost of the hubs and routers is about $10–20 per line. The central cost of the traditional telephony service is much higher than that for data switching; the distributed cost of the data switching is higher. Stringing the wire, nowadays the same unshielded twisted pair for either voice or data, is more expensive; wiring may cost $350 per line within a typical building.

Table 6.1 shows the conventional transmission speeds found in computer networks. Above 155 Mbits per second there have been experiments, such as the gigabit experiments run by the U.S. government (running at 600 Mbits per second) and some use of telephone services (running at 1600 and 3200 Mbits per second) under the name SONET (Synchronous Optical Networking). There is enormous basic transmission capacity available on fiber, which has raw transmission capacities well into the gigabits and is commonly laid in batches of at least 12 fibers at once.

6.2.4   *Arpanet and Addressing*

The real precursor of the networks we have today was the Arpanet, started in 1969 by Larry Roberts. Arpanet was a connection between computers doing military research and provided to these sites by the Department of Defense. ARPA was then and is now the Advanced Research Projects Agency of the Department of Defense; for most of the 1980s it was called DARPA, with Defense added to the acronym. The Arpanet was high speed; it started with 56 Kbits per second lines at a time when 300 baud modems were still standard. Arpanet was intended from the beginning to be real time, since it was to support remote computing facilities, so that users at RAND could log into computers at MIT or at military bases (for example).

The Arpanet introduced a protocol and addressing system for a worldwide computer network. On the networks today, each machine has a 4-byte address, with each byte representing a separate parsing step in the routing. For example, a machine address might be 128.253.78.249, in which 128.253.78 specifies a particular Ethernet at Cornell, and 249 is the address of the particular workstation. Nor-

Table 6.1   Transmission speeds (bits per second)

Speed	Device and Comments
110	Traditional model 33 teletype, 1950s
150	Model 37 teletype, 1969
300	Many modems in the 1970s
1200	Common modem around 1980
2400	
4800	
9600	
14.4 Kbits	
19.2 Kbits	
28.8 Kbits	
33.6 Kbits	
56 Kbits	Latest modem (1997) Below this point analog dial-up telephone lines cannot be used; some special service must be ordered from the telephone network or some special engineering used.
56 Kbits	Lowest speed special digital circuit, leased audio line configured for digital
128 Kbits	ISDN (Integrated Services Digital Network)
1.54 Mbits	DS-1 (Digital Services-1 protocol)
45 Mbits	DS-3
155 Mbits	ATM (Asynchronous Transmission Mode)

mally such addresses are given symbolically. In this case the machine is named `woop.mannlib.cornell.edu`, which is interpreted from right to left, like a post office address (from general to specific locations). The `edu` string is the *domain* of educational institutions in the United States; alternatives include `com` (commercial), `gov` (U.S. government), `org` (organizations), and `net` (miscellaneous). So, for example, in addition to `cornell.edu` we have universities such as `princeton.edu` or `umich.edu`, companies such as `ibm.com` or `bellcore.com`, government agencies such as `loc.gov` (the Library of Congress) or `nasa.gov`, and miscellaneous organizations such as `acm.org` (Association for Computing Machinery) or `npr.org` (National Public Radio). Non-U.S. addresses normally end with the two-letter country code—thus `inria.fr` (the French research organization INRIA) or `ox.ac.uk` (Oxford University, academic, United Kingdom). Before the domain name come other names describing a location within an institution; thus `mannlib.cornell.edu` is the Albert Mann Library at Cornell and is distinct from `cit.cornell.edu`, which is the Computing and Information Technologies organization at Cornell. Finally, `woop`

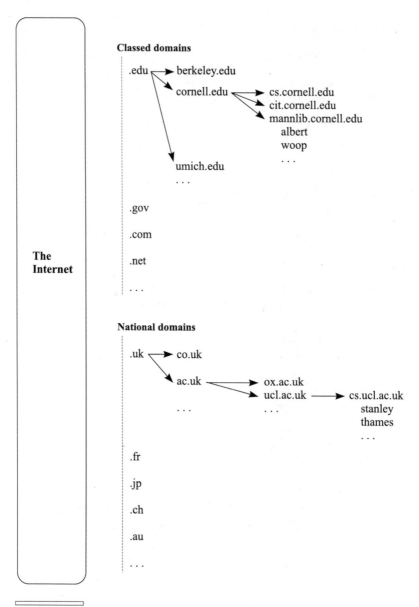

Figure 6.3 Domain names

is a particular computer in the Mann library. Figure 6.3 shows some of this, partially expanding out the sections for Cornell and University College London (ucl.ac.uk).

Over the years, more and more machines joined the Arpanet. Fewer and fewer of the institutions running these machines had military research as their primary purpose; at the same time, the military was starting to use the Arpanet for more critical applications than research and became less comfortable about sharing the Net with other users. In the mid-1980s the Arpanet was split and divided into MILNET, a purely military set of machines, and the civilian machines. NSF took over the administrative and funding responsibility for the backbone of the civilian networks, called NSFNet. NSFNet connected the key supercomputer centers and other users bridged into those centers. The funding NSF provided was relatively small ($10 million per year) but enabled the backbone to stay up without complex ways of allocating its costs. Users paid much more (perhaps $600 million in 1993) to buy computers and connect them to the backbone.

Since many of the people now wishing to connect to the network had nothing to do with the United States, let alone U.S. military research, other ways of constructing the network were needed. Commercial and semicommercial nonprofit groups started building regional networks, which then linked up through the internetworking protocol (IP) designed for the Arpanet. This gave rise to the name "Internet": a network that connects other networks. For example, Bellcore has several internal networks, as do many other corporations. There are various regional networks that link places like Bellcore or universities, including JvNCnet (based at the John von Neumann Center at Princeton), NYSERNet (New York State Educational Resources Network), and many others at other places around the country and the world. In the United Kingdom the British established JANET (Joint Academic Network) to connect their universities. All of these machines were linked to the NSFNet backbone at various places (for example, although the U.S. NSFNet node geographically closest to the United Kingdom was at MIT, the JANET connection came into the University of Maryland, which was less congested).

As traffic on the Internet exploded in 1994 and 1995, more and more commercial companies started connecting customers to the NSFNet backbone. Since NSF had a goal of supporting university research, and for years maintained an "acceptable use policy" that limited what the commercial organizations were allowed to do on the Net, the commercial organizations began building their own backbones, and as a result the Internet is no longer actually dependent on NSF for anything. This change has been transparent to most users, as the commercial companies will carry traffic among themselves without regard to originating point.

Many libraries are now connected to the Net. In fact, the United States has set a national goal of linking every library, school, and hospital to the Net, reiterated by President Clinton in a speech on August 27, 1996. Many states are implementing this goal; Maine, for example, announced in July 1996 a five-year plan to link every school in the state to the Internet. The cable TV industry offered to wire every school in the U.S. to the Internet. As the costs of Internet connection decline, the actual connection will be much less of a question than the need for computing facilities in the library and the need for staff that knows what to do with them. Libraries are also, in some communities, seeking the role of providing Internet access to people who do not have their own connection at home. Whether such services should be provided, and whether they should be provided free, are new questions for library services that are not yet resolved.

Since the Internet is growing so rapidly, people ask when it will be as large as the voice telephone network. The question can be defined in ways that suggest it is already bigger: for example, many businesses have local networks that carry more traffic than their internal phone network (partly because of the widespread use of remote file servers for computer workstations). The Internet makes more switching decisions than the telephone network, since the Internet switches each packet, typically about 50 bytes long, while the voice network switches only each call, and a phone call is typically 3 minutes long (which represents 1.2 MB at normal digitization rates). The normal definition is in terms of quantity of traffic. The inter-LATA (long distance) U.S. voice telephone network carried about 500 billion call-minutes per year in 1994, or an average load of approximately 50 Gbits per second. The Internet is harder to estimate since there are many backbone carriers, but a guess from an expert was 1 Gbit per second average load (Sincoskie 1996). (In 1994, when NSFNet was the primary backbone, the traffic on it was about 50 Mbits per second.) In any case, given that the Internet doubles every year, it would pass voice telephony (assuming it has not taken it over) in about 2004. For comparison, estimates by Roger Hough in 1970 and A. Michael Noll in 1991 suggested that voice telephony will dominate into the indefinite future (Hough 1970; Noll 1991). Noll assumes that a computer user might get 20 MB per day of data (this might, for example, be 1000 images at 20 KB each from the Web) but that there would only be 20 million computers in the United States; this number is already too low.

Given the Internet, how is information provided on it to be made available? The two original services were remote login and file transfer. These have then been encapsulated so that the user does not perceive what is being done, but the basic rules are the same: a user connects to a machine (called a server), and then bits are transferred to the user's remote machine (the client).

The earliest service was remote login. Users would make a remote connection to a machine as if they were going to log in, using the telnet command, but would connect to a particular program that, for example, might provide a library catalog. To protect the server machine, the particular program would provide no service other than the library catalog. In fact, there are still many catalogs on the Net that operate this way; the user does a telnet command, and instead of logging in with a general user login that would permit executing arbitrary commands, gives a user ID (such as `library`) that prevents the user from doing anything other than accessing a catalog. On some of these systems, the user even has to type a password, albeit one that is publicly posted, to deal with administrative restrictions on the server machine that require every account to have a password.

Using remote login, all the computing and data are actually on the server machine. Effectively, the client machine is merely a remote terminal. It has no computing to do other than to provide the screen display, and it need have no copies of the data being transmitted. Often, however, the user wishes to obtain actual data files from the server machine and keep these. For example, the server may not be providing catalog access, but may be providing a library of freeware—software or freely available text that users are welcome to download.

For file transfers, the standard protocol was ftp (file transfer protocol). Quite large arrays of information became available on some servers using ftp, including, for example, the literature texts held by Project Gutenberg, the software distributions at many sites, collections of images posted by people, and many other kinds of information. To deal with security restrictions, the convention arose that the login anonymous (or ftp on newer software) meant that only public access files could be retrieved. Inherently, the ftp idea involves people making copies of files, resulting in problems distributing updates, and old versions proliferating around the world.

The ftp archives, scattered over a great many machines, became quite large, and a searching system called archie began as a way of finding particular files. The archie system relied on searching file names and directory titles, since most of the material on ftp was not suitable for free-text search (computer programs and binary images). Various systems run servers for archie and accept queries to which they reply with suggested site names and files.

Although ftp and telnet worked, they are inconvenient interfaces for many purposes. Each requires some dialog and too much computer-expert stuff. For example, when retrieving files with ftp, the user needs to know whether the information is ASCII or non-ASCII and, if it is not ASCII, to type a command (usually bin or image) to specify an 8-bit-wide rather than a 7-bit-wide path to the data. More seriously, the constant need to know addresses (remembering that the University of California library was 31.1.0.1) was not convenient for novices or the impatient. The need to organize the information in these remotely accessible archives so that they could be found in an organized way stimulated the development of newer interfaces.

The first interface that achieved really widespread acceptance for remote access to free information was gopher, from the University of Minnesota. The gopher interface was based on the concept of hierarchical menus and was text only. It is now being supplanted almost entirely by Mosaic, which has now overrun not only gopher but almost every other use of the Internet. The Mosaic interface, based on the Web protocol, was designed by Marc Andreesen, then at the National Center for Supercomputer Applications at the University of Illinois, and now one of the founders of Netscape Corporation.

Both gopher and Mosaic work by allocating specific ports for access using particular protocols. Although only one wire may connect a computer to the network, it is desirable to have multiple conversations on that wire. Thus, computers usually support a range of subsidiary addresses, called ports, each of which can handle a logically separate connection. When a network connection is made to a given machine, the packets are addressed to a particular port number on the machine. This permits more than one conversation at once to be going on, and also lets the conversation choose what kind of high-level protocol is to be executed. For example, telnet requests come on port 60, and ftp uses ports 20 and 21 (one port is the control requests and the other handles the actual data). By convention, a request on port 70 is a request for a gopher connection; port 80 is http, the protocol used by Mosaic and Netscape. The name "http" stands for *hypertext transfer protocol* and signals one of the main differences between gopher and Mosaic; gopher is a purely hierarchical structure, while Mosaic is a hypertext network. To access library catalogs, the user clicks through a set of menus until finally getting a list of libraries. Gopher is still widely used for remote access to library catalogs.

The Mosaic program does not rely on a strictly hierarchical organization. Instead, hypertext links stored anywhere within a document can link to any other place on the Web. Here is an example of a bit of text set up for Mosaic use:

```
Click for information on
<a href=http://www.seagate.com>Seagate disk drives</a>.
```

When displayed, this will appear as follows:

Click for information on <u>Seagate disk drives.</u>

The underlining (and on color displays a color change) indicates that the words "Seagate disk drives" represent a link. The phrase representing the link is shown within <a> . . . </a> brackets, as in SGML syntax. The href= . . . string within the opening <a> denotes the location to which the browser should go if this item is clicked. In this case, the location, called a *URL* (uniform resource locator), is http://www.seagate.com, which is interpreted as (1) http signals that this is a file that is to be interpreted as http protocol (as opposed to locations that might begin gopher: or ftp:); (2) the double slash, which indicates that what follows is a machine name rather than the name of a file on this machine; and (3) the machine name www.seagate.com, which is the name of a computer on the Web, to which the http request should be addressed. There can also be a following file name; for example, the URL http://www.cs.ucl.ac.uk/External/lesk asks first for the machine www.cs.ucl.ac.uk and then for the file (relative to the root of http files) named External/lesk.

The Web browsers, unlike gopher clients, can display pictures, play back sound recordings, and even show multimedia. For text, they have access to a few typesetting options, are able to display italic and bold text, and handle paragraphing and a few sizes of type. Some browsers can also do tables, and the capacity of HTML (hypertext markup language) to do typographic display is increasing. Features in HTML permit a Web page to contain enough decoration and formatting to permit attractive graphic design and thus attract users to this format.

Color Plates

(a)

(c)

(b)

(d)

Figure 4.1 Color quantization: *(a)* 7 colors, *(b)* 20 colors, *(c)* 50 colors, *(d)* 256 colors

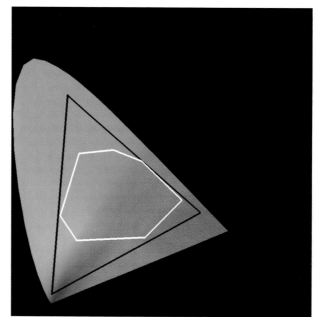

Figure 4.3 Gamut. The color space is the CIE representation of perceived colors, bounded by the spectrum. The black triangle is the limit of colors that can be displayed on a typical RGB monitor with three phosphors. The white polygon includes the colors that can be printed with a typical set of printing inks on an offset press.

Finding horses using body plans

Figure 4.5 Image retrieval of "horses"

Following the trail itself, Whispering Smith rode slowly.

Figure 7.2 Base picture

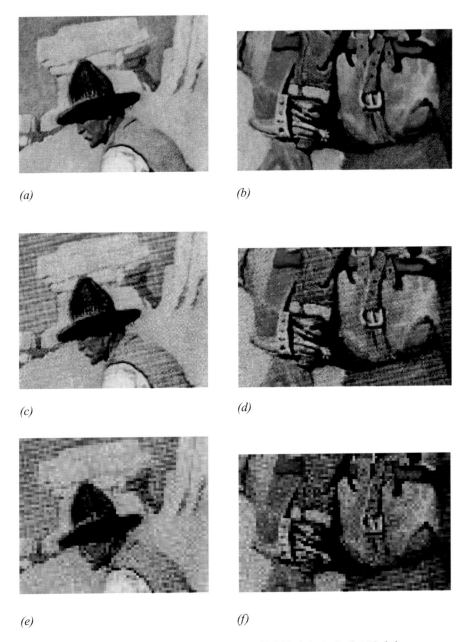

(a) *(b)*

(c) *(d)*

(e) *(f)*

Figure 7.3 Color resolution examples: *(a & b)* 300 dpi, *(c & d)* 150 dpi, *(e & f)* 75 dpi

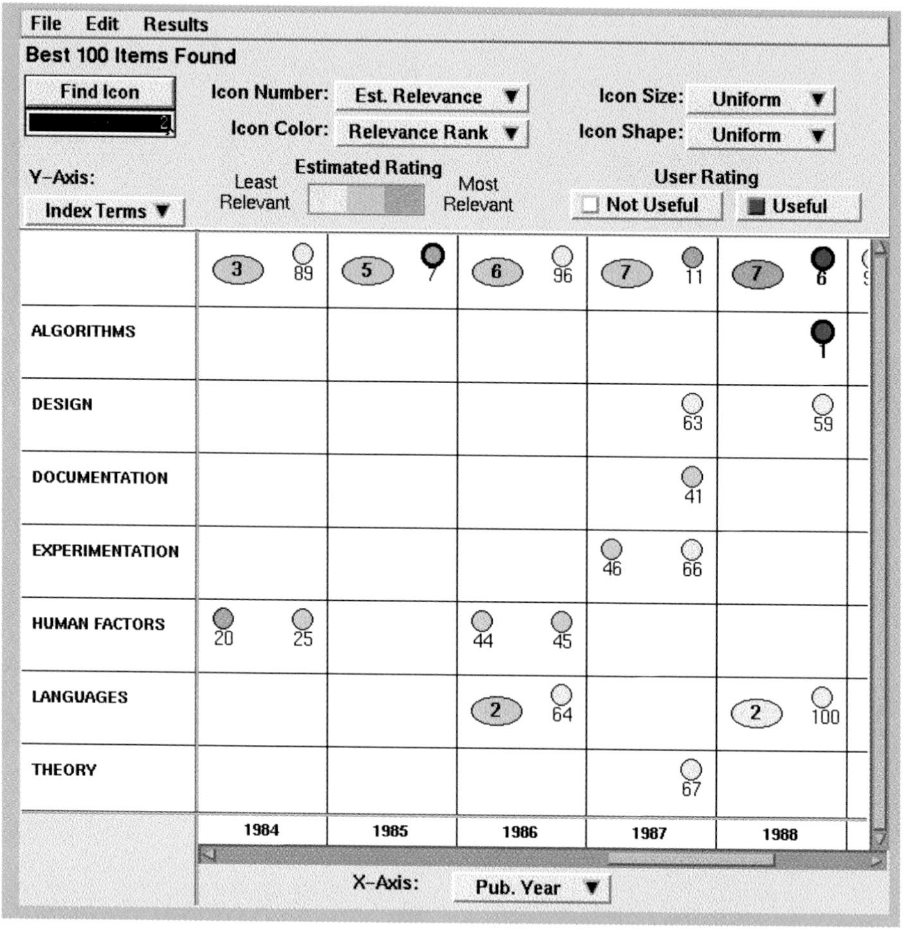

Figure 7.6 Envision

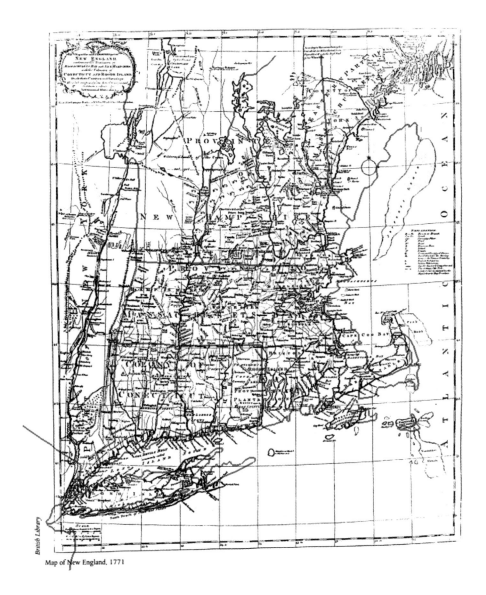

Map of New England, 1771

Figure 8.3   New and old maps

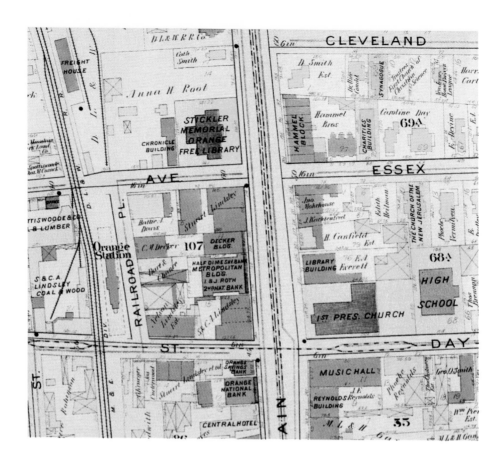

Figure 8.4   Fire insurance map

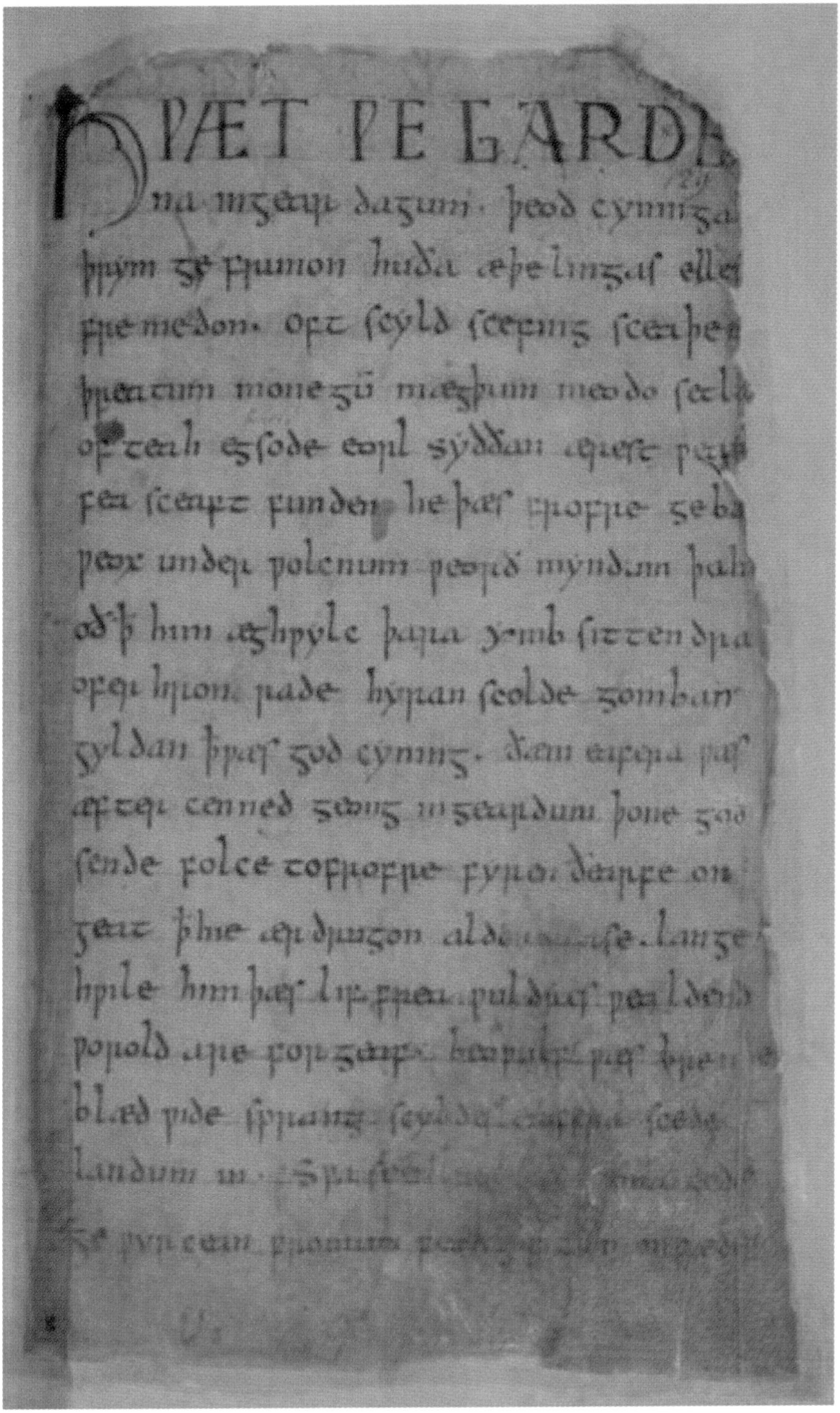

Figure 11.3 Beowolf image

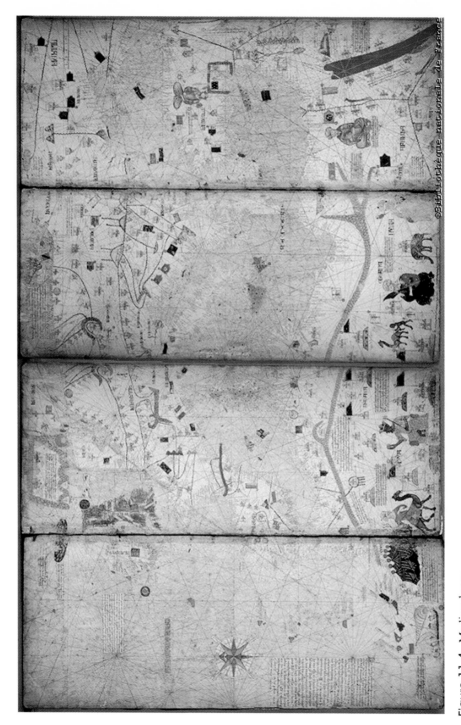

Figure 11.4 Medieval map

Figure 11.5 Aztec manuscript

Figure 11.9 Papyrus

The reader of the Web page also gets to make certain choices about appearance. HTML, as now defined, does not specify exact point sizes or type fonts. Instead, the author specifies size as normal, larger, or smaller, and type font as normal, bold, or italic. The client software in the browser chooses whether the overall type is to be small or large, and in principle could make choices about the font as well. For some publishers and authors, this is inadequate control of the format, and they push constantly to have HTML extended to support double-column text, equations, and a choice of type fonts. For some readers, on the other hand, it is convenient to have a way to enlarge the print; one advantage seen in digital libraries is the ease with which those with failing vision (or even those reading on poor-quality screens) can choose the presentation format to their taste.

The use of links in Web pages is unconstrained. As in the tradition of hypertext, anybody can put a link to anything. The collection of all such pages is called the World Wide Web, and Web pages can be found in virtually all the ways described so far:

1. There are several free-text search engines that retrieve everything on the Web at regular intervals and index it.

2. There are lists, arranged by subject, of pages on particular topics; the best known is Yahoo (yet another hierarchical organization).

3. There are hypertext pointers on most pages, creating a great chain of references that can be followed.

Most users supplement these public techniques with bookmark lists of pages they like, and sometimes with pages of their own containing lists of pages of interest.

A digital library today will have to face up to access to Web pages. Large amounts of material are being prepared and distributed in this format, and its selection, organization, preservation, and delivery will be major challenges for libraries in the future.

6.3   *Security on the Net*

Is it safe to put information on the Web? Or even to connect a computer to it? Computer viruses and computer crime have given a bad reputation to many kinds of computer connections, and the Web is no exception.

Fortunately, the standard kind of viruses that infect MS-DOS computers and are based on special file extensions on diskettes are not relevant to the Web. Contrary to a rumor that pops up regularly, merely reading ASCII electronic mail cannot infect your computer with a virus. However, the presence of servers that respond to outside commands does offer possibilities to vandals and criminals, and Web servers need to be careful about the steps taken to protect their programs. Executing software that comes attached to files or mail messages or even as macro routines to be executed by word processors can be dangerous, and users need to know that it comes from a trusted source.

There is no substitute for basic security and sensible administration on the server machines. Each user should have a password, and each password should be checked to see that it is not easily guessed (i.e., that it is not a common English word or name, or obvious string of letters). Each user should have a separate password, and each reminded to keep it private. There are many administrative decisions to be made that enforce security. For example, at one point a major workstation manufacturer was shipping machines configured so that any remote machine could log in without any authorization check. Reasonable system administrators would change this configuration before connecting the machine to the Internet.

In this context, it is important to remember that in line with the general behavior of Ethernets, it is possible for people to snoop on nets and collect packets. They can then look through these packets with programs for login and password sequences, or numbers that appear to be credit cards, and attempt to misuse them. This is not as bad as, say, cell phone conversations, where (as the British royal family has found out to its discomfort) there are so many people spending their spare time listening to scanners that perhaps half of all cell phone conversations are overheard. But it does pose risks against which server operators should protect themselves.

One obvious danger comes from the telnet connections, which allow outsiders to log in. Computer vandals regularly probe machines on the Internet looking for chances to log into the computers, trying various names and passwords that have been found by eavesdropping or by other means. Many Web servers have no need to run a telnet port, and do not; no one can log into these machines from outside the home organization.

Others use a *firewall* machine to isolate themselves from the probing vandals. A firewall machine is simply another server computer that bridges packets between the outside Net and the computers inside an organization; it is a kind of router. It decides which packets to let through based on some principles and some authorization rules. For example, it may allow only connections to the gopher and http ports, except for authorized users. The trick is to decide whether someone sending in packets is indeed an authorized user. Relatively little information comes with the packets that is of use; in particular, the identification of the sending machine cannot be relied on, since it is possible to send messages with fake identification. One feature that a firewall router should have is a little bit of knowledge about possible sources of packets, and it should reject packets that are obviously mislabeled as to their origin (e.g., they are labeled as coming from a machine inside a corporation but have appeared on the outside of the firewall).

The simplest way to verify the legitimacy of a packet source is a password. The problem with passwords that do not change is that if a vandal snoops on the Net and picks up a password today, the vandal can use it tomorrow. Attempts to print out a sequence number for each logon or the date of the last logon, hoping that the legitimate user will notice if these are wrong, are not really reliable. Thus, good systems rely on identification strings that are never used twice. Two such schemes are the SecurID cards marketed by Access Control Encryption, Inc. and the S/Key system invented at Bellcore.

The SecurID card is a credit-card-sized computer with battery, clock, and a display window that shows a six-digit number. Inside the card, an algorithm computes a new six-digit number every minute. The company supplies a program for the firewall machine that can run the same algorithm and thus know for each card what number it should be displaying at any time. A user identifies the card (not using any number printed on the outside) and enters the six digits it is displaying; the firewall compares this number with what it should be, and if they match, the user must really be in possession of that card. The cards cost about $75 each and are programmed to expire after three years.

The S/Key system is distributed as freeware. It is modeled on the one-time pad of conventional cryptography. These are pads of preprinted keys, each used for only one message and then torn off and destroyed. The user has a sequence of strings, each of which is used once. At any attempt to claim to be an authorized user, the firewall asks for the next string in sequence. As before, the firewall router has a computer program that can compute a sequence of valid strings. The user either prints out and carries around the strings or has a computer that can also generate the sequence. Each string is only transmitted once, and there is no way for an outsider to guess from one string what the next one might be. The strings are actually numbers, but to make them easier to type are conventionally converted into strings of words. For example, suppose a dictionary of 2048 short words and names is available. Then a 66-bit number can be selected by choosing six of these words, each of which gives 11 bits of the number.

Another danger of vandalism comes from the server programs themselves. As indicated before, programs like gopher and Mosaic rely on programs sitting on the server computers that execute when they receive packets. If the only thing they can do is to pick up entries from their databases and forward them as they are designed, then they are no risk. But what if one of these server programs could be persuaded to execute arbitrary programs? Then there would indeed be a risk. This was demonstrated in the case of the finger program by the Morris "worm" in 1988. The finger program was merely supposed to be a form of directory assistance; given a userid or a name, it would return the userid, name, and phone number of that person on the server machine. Robert Morris, a student at Cornell University, made use of a bug in the finger program to write a program that would try to run on as many machines as possible and collect user names and encrypted passwords. As it happened, this program generated so many copies of itself on so many machines that it effectively brought the Internet to a halt on November 2, 1988. Since that time the recognition of the danger has prompted many security improvements in Internet software.

For libraries, the danger here is that since programs like httpd (the interpreter of requests for net browsers) are much more complex than finger, it is hard to be sure that they contain no similar risks. They have been subjected to much greater scrutiny. There is now an organized group called CERT (Computer Emergency Response Team) at CMU that looks for security holes and collects and redistributes information about them. One problem, however, is to be sure that the information about the holes gets to the system administrators *before* it gets to the hacker. Regretfully, CERT sometimes has to use telephones rather than the Internet to try to keep its own communications private. No incident as serious as the 1988 problem has occurred since, however.

6.4   *Cryptography*

Computer messages come with very little context and have very little security. There is a real danger of eavesdropping on the Net, and there is also a danger of impersonation (sending messages with false indications of their origin). Thus, electronic messages are more likely to need to be enciphered than are postal service messages, which come in sealed envelopes. Electronic messages are more like postcards.

Encrypting a message requires a *key*. The key traditionally tells you how to encode or decode the message. For example, suppose the cipher system is "move n letters along in the alphabet." Then the key is the value of n. Suppose the key is 2, so that the cipher is to move two letters along; thus, *cipher* becomes *ekrjgs*, and we have an example of the Caesar cipher. It is not considered secure today, although it was apparently good enough for the Romans. Note that the decoding process is to move two letters back in the alphabet; the key for decoding is the same as the key for encoding. If two people both know a key, they can send messages to each other and read them. In fact, since the key to a Caesar cipher is always the same for encoding and decoding, anyone who can read a message can send one and vice versa.

In order to communicate safely in a single-key system like this, both sides of the conversation must have the key, and the key must be distributed in some secure fashion. For years (and it may still be going on) couriers went around carrying keys from one government to its embassies and military installations. Maintaining key security is critical to this kind of cryptography and can be quite tedious. It means that both sides to the conversation trust each other, since either side can divulge the key through either incompetence or treachery. For computer messaging systems, this is a major problem. Since we often send email to people we barely know, we can hardly use the same key all the time, but if we imagine using a separate key for every pair of correspondents, or for every day, the distribution of keys in a single-key system would be an enormous problem.

In 1976 it became publicly known that there were enciphering systems that had separate keys for encryption and decryption, and in which one key could not be found from the other. These systems are based on the idea of one-way functions; mathematical procedures that can be carried out in one direction but not reversed. To a typical fifth-grade student, for example, computing a square is a one-way function; the student knows how to multiply 15 by 15 to get 225, but has not yet been taught a method (other than trial and error) to start with 225 and discover that it is 15 squared. One-way functions permit *asymmetric cryptography*, in which I can encode messages that you can decode but where you could not have encoded the messages yourself.

Consider, for example, use of a one-way function for identification. Suppose we accept squaring a number as a one-way function, and I wish to assure you of my identity or, more precisely, assure you that a second message from me has in fact come from the same person who sent you the first message. I could send the string 361 in the first message and in the second one send you 19. You could multiply 19 times 19 and verify that it is 361. Since, in our hypothetical example, nobody can compute a square root, I must have started this process by picking 19 and squaring it to send you the 361 in the first message; no one else could have arranged to know to pick 361 as the number to send first.

In asymmetric cryptography, there are two keys, one for encryption and one for decryption. Usually, one of these keys is kept secret, and one is disclosed; thus the alternate name *public key cryptography*. Either the encryption or the decryption key may be public, leading to two different functions:

1. If I disclose my *encryption* key, then anyone can *send* messages to me, knowing that only I can read them.

2. If I disclose my *decryption* key, then anyone can *receive* messages from me and know that I had sent them.

Again, to explain this, let us assume that some simple arithmetic is not reversible. Suppose that multiplication is easy, but nobody can do division without special tricks. Let us suppose that I know something about the number 17, for example, which lets me divide by 17, but that no one else can divide by 17. I can then publish 17 as my key and ask you, whenever you wish to send me a message, to multiply it by 17 and send the result. If you wish to send me the sequence of numbers 2, 3 (which might mean that you were sending me the second letter of the alphabet followed by the third), you would send 34, 51. By hypothesis, nobody else can divide by 17, so this is perfectly safe. I can do the division, so I can recover the 2, 3 sequence. No eavesdropper is able to do this.

Conversely, I can send a message that must have come from me. Suppose I wish to send you the message 85. I divide it by 17 and send you 5. You (or anyone else) can multiply 5 by 17 and get back the original 85; but, in this imaginary world, I am the only person who could have done the division to discover the 5, and so the message must have come from me.

The actual mathematical function that is hard to reverse is factorization of integers. It is relatively easy to find that 17×19 is 323. There is no direct way to start with 323 and determine that its factors are 17 and 19; all methods for doing this involve considerable trial and error. For large enough numbers, numbers with perhaps 150 digits, it is, in practice, impossible to factor them, and yet it is relatively easy to start with two 75-digit primes and multiply them together.

The cryptographic technique that uses this method is known as RSA, after the three then-MIT professors Ron Rivest, Adi Shamir, and Leonard Adelman. The details of RSA cryptography are widely available (see, for example, Stinson 1995).

To repeat, with asymmetric cryptography, either key can be public. If my encryption key is public, then anyone can send me messages knowing that nobody else can read them (privacy); if my decryption key is public, then I can send messages that must have come from me (authentication). Both are valuable functions for different purposes. Cryptography also has other uses:

1. *Message integrity.* If the encryption key is private, no one but the sender can change the message and still send it in the correct code.

2. *Nonrepudiation.* If a message comes encoded in my private key, no one without the key can have encrypted it. Variants of cryptography are used to create *digital signatures* that can only be applied by the holder of a key (but can run faster since there is no need to recover the message from the signature).

3. *Digital cash.* Banks can send strings in exchange for money, which they are willing to change back. Again, nobody but the bank can create a valid string, although anyone can verify that the bank created it.

Asymmetric cryptography, although elegant, is about 10 times slower than private key cryptography today. There are many good algorithms for private key encryption, including most notably the standard DES (Data Encryption Standard); those too suspicious to trust the National Security Agency can use alternative cryptographic algorithms. Symmetric cryptographic systems can encrypt 3 Mbits per second on a 50-MHz 486. Since asymmetric cryptography is much slower, it is customary to use it to exchange a session key generated randomly for the next session of traffic and then send the actual traffic with the new private key.

Libraries need to worry to some extent about security both with respect to the privacy of their transactions and also with respect to any charged services they use or sell. Much more attention has been paid to security since the interest in electronic commerce has started. People wish to order across the Internet, and to do this they need to give some kind of authorization number or credit card number. In principle, you would wish to encrypt packets containing such numbers for transmission. It is difficult to agree on a method for doing this within the confines of U.S. government laws regarding cryptographic technology. Under U.S. law (as of early 1997), it is illegal to export computer software containing cryptography that uses keys more than 56 bits long. Until recently, 40 bits was the limit and is still the limit unless keys are made available to the U.S. government. Netscape implemented a 40-bit key system and it was broken, with some publicity, by some French graduate students in a matter of weeks. The laws are presently in flux. The U.S. government does realize the contradiction in the present laws, which allow export of cryptographic technology to NATO countries such as Holland, which have no laws themselves restricting the export of this technology. Other NATO countries may have even stricter laws than the United States, and in France any nongovernmental use of cryptography is illegal. Most importantly, it is becoming clear that U.S. laws will simply move the cryptography industry to Finland or Switzerland. As of early 1997, though, it is still common to see programs produced in U.S. and foreign versions, the U.S. version having adequate levels of security and the foreign one being vulnerable.

A variant on cryptography is the question of dating and notarizing electronic documents. Electronic messages lack the physical attributes that would let them be dated, and of course any date shown on them can be edited. As a result, it is not clear how to establish priorities and dates for electronic messages. Some government organizations require printed documentation instead of electronic documentation in order to be sure of the dates. The dating problem was solved by Scott Stornetta and Stuart Haber of Bellcore when they invented "digital time-stamping" as a way of running an absolutely secure electronic notary system (Haber and Stornetta 1991).

Their algorithm makes it possible for someone to operate an electronic notarizing system that is invulnerable to corruption. In a simplistic notarizing system, users send the operator messages and the operator dates them and digitally signs the message. However, this leaves open the possibility that the operator could be bribed to falsely date messages. What Stornetta and Haber realized was that dishonesty by the system operator could be stopped if each certificate of notarization was linked to the previous and next certificates issued. The basic idea is that users submit hashed codes for the documents they wish to notarize, using a good one-way hash function, so that no one can create a document matching that hash code. The notarizer adds a date, rehashes, and sends back the hashed string. But the new hash is not just based on the date and on the hash code from the original document. Instead, it also includes the hash codes of the previous document sent in and the next one. In order to be deceptive, it would be necessary not only to create a fake hashed code for the original user but to create an entire chain of fake hashes involving everything submitted to the hashing authority. This is not possible. The practical implementation of this system, done by a firm named Surety, is to link each week's notarization requests not into a linear chain as described here, but into a tree. The root node of the tree is published as a classified advertisement in the *New York Times* each week. Any individual can verify their notarization certification against the number published in the *Times*, and nobody can create a fake certificate without the ability to change all the printed copies of the *Times* in all the libraries of the world.

6.5   *Summary*

This chapter has reviewed ways in which information is transmitted. Electronic information can be sent out as physical objects (CD-ROM) or through the computer networks that now pervade libraries. The Internet and the World Wide Web, in particular, provide a now widely accepted standard way for information to be accessed by users. The major problems are the lack of security and the lack of a way to pay for items on the Web. There exists underlying technology to handle many of the security issues; there does not yet exist a standard way of paying for electronic delivery. The problem is not assembling the technology that would provide payment mechanisms; the problem is deciding what they should be and how they will be administered. This will be discussed later in Chapter 9.

7

Usability and Retrieval Evaluation

MAKING COMPUTERS EASY to use is another Holy Grail of the software industry. Libraries accept a wide range of the public as their patrons and cannot force them to accept training. There has long been a mismatch between users of retrieval systems, who tend to think that the systems should require no training or experience at all, and the practicalities of actual systems; library schools, for example, often give a one-semester course in using online systems. Early experiments by Chris Borgman showed that a quarter of Stanford undergraduates had difficulty learning one of the commercial search systems (Borgman 1986). A practical digital library has to build systems everyone can use. This chapter will emphasize the user and the considerations in what needs to be done to make systems effective, not just available.

7.1 *General Human Factors Considerations*

The general science of human factors is called *ergonomics* and began with the study of physical tools and equipment, such as the shaping of handles and levers. Ergonomics is still referred to derisively as the "comfy chair" science. The basic principles of ergonomics come from cognitive psychology, and the research methods from that area are used in evaluating software. Two alternative technical solutions are implemented and tested on a group of subjects, traditionally under-graduates in elementary psychology courses.

Tests of this sort follow a traditional paradigm of scientific research. The subjects are divided into groups, each group using a different interface or trying a different task. For example, one group might be using an index language while another is using a free-text search system. Statistical measures are used to decide whether there is a significant difference between the conditions. The measures may be based on the accuracy, speed, or preferences of the users. Preferences may be based either on some choice (e.g., the amount of time the users choose to spend on some condition) or on questionnaires given to the users. Time taken should always be recorded, as a lot of good cognitive psychology data is based on human reaction times as a measure of how much processing is required in the brain.

Studies on human subjects need to done with care. For example, it is always desirable to run some preliminary tests before the main experiments. Subjects will think of things the experimenter did not anticipate, and it may be necessary to revise the experiment in consequence. Subjects have to be balanced in terms of their computer expertise, experience with the subject matter of the experiment, and so on. Normally this is done by randomization: the subjects are assigned at random to two different conditions. If two computer systems are being compared, they need to be balanced as well. If one has color screens and the other has black and white, unless that is the point of the experiment, the data are *confounded*, and it is likely to be difficult to learn anything from such an experiment. A critical point is response time of the systems, since people are relatively intolerant of slow response time, and again, unless this is the point of the comparison, response times should be balanced across experimental conditions. An even more serious issue is bugs in the software. All too often, an experiment produces confused results because the users hit new bugs in the process of testing that distort the results.

Often, an analysis of variance is done on the data to decide how much of the difference between the results can be assigned to different characteristics of the experiment. For example, an experiment might involve sixteen students, eight of whom had previous programming experience and eight of whom did not. Half might be given one text editor and half another. Thus four students of each degree of experience would see each experimental condition. At the end, analysis of variance would indicate the relative importance of the programming experience versus the particular text editor. Such experiments are often discouraging, since the variance among individuals in many computer tasks is very high. Thus, the result of many programming comparisons has been to discover that some people are better programmers than others. Compared with individual skills and with the difficulty level of the particular task to be done, the programming language used is almost unimportant.

In fact, the history of experiments of this sort is that they have been valuable in developing the details of interfaces but have not been as successful in generating new top-level paradigms. In the early days of computer time-sharing, attempts were made to systematically compare batch processing and time-sharing; the results were inconclusive until time-sharing completely overran batch processing in the marketplace (to be pushed out, in its turn, by individual workstations). Similarly the number of truly appalling human interfaces that have been successful in the marketplace is testimony more to the ability of determined users to overcome obstacles in their path than it is to the success of human factors research in program design. Getting to the marketplace first and establishing some kind of standard is more important than having good research support for your design.

Human factors research is going to become more important, however. The development of the computer interface is a major part of new software systems. More than half the code in many new software projects is running the interface, and the interface is often critical in someone's decision about which program to use (when there is a choice). However, the design of good interfaces is still as much an art as science, since there is still insufficient experimental data and good models of how to build an interface.

One principle from studies is the speed-accuracy trade-off that sometimes exists. If people can work more quickly, they may make more errors. Not always—more experienced people often work both more quickly and more accurately. We all know that someone competent in a language can speak it both more rapidly and more correctly than someone just beginning to learn it. For many tasks, however, there is some reasonable speed at which it can be done best. Asking people to read 2000 words per minute is not going to help them retain anything they are seeing.

A basic limitation in the design of many computer interfaces is the use of the display screen. Particularly for library information, there is often just not enough space to show everything that is wanted. This yields a set of trade-offs between packing the screen so tightly that the users are puzzled or frightened by the amount of information, or having too many choices hidden behind multiple levels of menus. Using an 80-character-by-24-line display is equivalent to looking at a newspaper through a 3×5-inch window and is likely to be frustrating for some users. A 640×480 pixel display is higher resolution than a TV screen, but it is not possible to read an ordinary printed page of text from a TV screen. Library projects using scanned images are particularly prone to need large bitmap windows, and they need to think carefully about how to use the amount of space available.

Another principal human factors issue is whether the users or the system designers are in charge of placement of windows and screen displays. The system designers often wish to take over the screen and position all the necessary windows and so on, avoiding problems with users covering up or deleting some key information. But that makes it impossible for users to adjust the display to their individual preferences and for the particular task they are doing. This is a special case of the general problem of how adaptable programs should be. Greater adaptability is sometimes good, but other times means that users cannot help each other (since the program is behaving differently for different people) and gives greater opportunity for people to become confused. In general, system design issues like this should be evaluated case by case.

Should computer programs be designed for expert users or novice users? This is another basic tension in system design. Often a system that has enough explanations and menu choices to help novices is annoying or slow for experts. There are two basic arguments:

1. Since most people who buy a program use it many times, they spend most of their time as expert users, and so the program should be designed for experts, perhaps with some aids for novices.

2. Since many buying decisions are made by people who look at a program in a store or a trade show for only a few minutes, programs should be designed for novices to increase sales.

Sometimes the decision is fairly obvious. Some programs by their nature are only run once in a while (e.g., the program that sets up vacation handling of electronic mail). Some programs by their nature are used mostly by people who use them a lot (e.g., programming language compilers). Other times it is clear that an organization has mostly permanent users, and other times the users are transitory. Libraries find themselves with many novice users. Relatively few people spend most of their working life in libraries. Many come in at the end of a semester or on rare occasions; the rule of thumb for university libraries is that you need one seat for every four students (to get through the exam-time crush).

How to train people to use programs that are only going to be used intermittently again varies with the task. In practice, people rely heavily on those with slightly more expertise. Libraries can run training sessions, but this is very expensive. Asked once whether it was true that the introduction of computers into dormitory rooms was going to develop college students who spent all their time alone, hunched over their machines, a Columbia librarian replied that since they had introduced the online catalog, they had seen many more students in groups. They rarely, she said, had seen people working together at the old card catalog; everyone used it by themselves. But at the computer terminals, groups of two or three students were frequently together, one showing the other how to use it. So had they improved student social skills by providing bad computer interfaces? Well, that was not the intent, but it was apparently what happened.

7.2   *Text Displays: Fonts and Highlighting*

Among the most important questions for digital libraries are those related to the willingness of people to read information from screens instead of from paper. Among the key studies done here were those by John Gould of IBM, who studied the reading speed of people from screens and from paper (Gould and Grischokowsky 1984). He found that although people read from conventional glass teletype screens 25% more slowly than they did from paper, improving the screens to 91 dots per inch and using grey-scale displays permitted people to read at about the same speed that they do from paper (Gould et al. 1987).

There are also principles derived from years of experience in the printing industry. People are used to reading, and prefer reading, lines not over 60 or 70 characters long. A 60-character line in 9-point type is about 4 inches long. This is why the lines in this book are five inches long; it makes for a comfortable single-column size. Material printed on 8.5 × 11-inch paper should be double-column to avoid excessively long lines. Although line lengths vary with type font design, the length of a line can usually be guessed by assuming that the average letter has a width one-half the type size, in points. Thus, in 9-point type the typical letter is 4.5 points wide, and at 72 points to the inch, 64 characters would require 4 inches. In designing computer displays, 80-character lines are a little too long to be comfortable.

At Bellcore, the SuperBook project (Egan et al. 1989) experimented with careful design of an interface for text display, with combinations of prototypes and testing on users. The result was a multiwindow interface organized so that users would retain an orientation of where they were in the book they were reading. One window displays a hierarchical table of contents, with fish-eye expansion and a mark for current position; another displays a portion of the text, and other smaller windows show any searching and general controls. An example is shown in Figure 7.1. In this example, a search has been performed on the word *zinc* (see bottom window), and 174 hits were found. The distribution of these hits across the sections of the document collection is given by the numbers to the left of the section headings in the table of contents, which is shown in the large left window. Note that 22 of these hits are in the "Enzymes" section. The actual article is shown in the window on the right, along with an arrow to move forward or backward. The icons in the right margin of the text window point to a footnote and a figure.

In 1990, during the CORE project, a comparison was done between people reading from paper and people reading from screens. Two kinds of screen interface were used: the SuperBook system for ASCII display and an image system for page images. The experiment, done by Dennis Egan, used five kinds of tasks involving searching and reading chemical information (Egan et al. 1991). Thirty-six Cornell students were divided into three groups: 12 got the journals on paper, 12 got an image display interface, and 12 the SuperBook interface. The

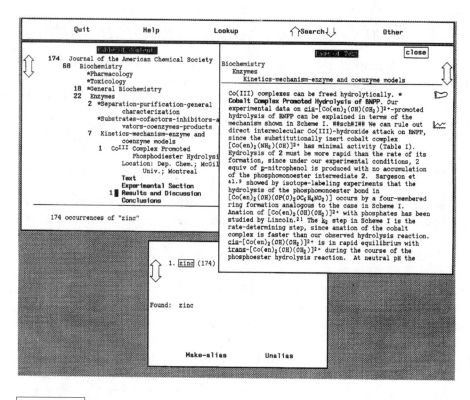

Figure 7.1   SuperBook

results, to oversimplify, showed that searching was much more effective with either computer system than with the paper journals and *Chemical Abstracts* on paper, while reading was the same speed on either system. Combining these into a realistic set of tasks suggests that the users would be much better off with electronic information.

For example, one of the tasks was to answer a simple question, something along the lines of "What is the P-O distance in hydroxyphosphine?" The answer was in one of 4000 pages of chemical journal text. Students had to locate the article with the answer and read enough of it to find the answer. Table 7.1 shows the results for the students using SuperBook, an image display system, and the traditional paper journals. Note that more than half the students with paper journals and paper *Chemical Abstracts* finally gave up after spending an average of almost 20 minutes looking for this. For tasks that just involved reading text, rather than searching, the time was comparable whether the students were reading articles on paper, on a screen displaying an image of the article, or through the SuperBook interface. Consistently, the computer interfaces were much faster for searching and competitive in time for simple reading; combining both kinds of tasks, they were both preferred and they

Table 7.1   Topic search results

Format	Time (min)	Score	Gave Up?
SuperBook	9.7	76%	8%
image	11.3	72%	1%
paper	19.5	23%	57%

let the students get more done. This data explains why electronic libraries are not only effective, but recognized as such by the users and generally welcomed. In fact, we had one student ask to stay after the experiment so he could keep using the system to find out something he needed for his course work.

7.3   *Image Displays and Compression Systems*

When designing screen images, there is a conflict between what the eye can see and what can fit on the screen, as described earlier. The most accurate experiment on this subject was done by Michael Ester at the Getty (Ester 1990). He found that people can see the differences in resolution quite clearly up to 1000 × 1000; above that resolution the gains in perceptual quality are lower.

To judge this yourself, here are some sample images. The base picture is Figure 7.2 (Color Plate), a book illustration by N. C. Wyeth, 1906. The resolution of that scan is 1075 × 1731 (300 dpi across the original book page). This has been reduced to half (537 × 865) and to quarter (268 × 432) resolution, and two excerpts from the picture shown at each resolution in Figure 7.3 (Color Plate). The set on the left show the man's face, and the set on the right show his foot with the saddle belts. Look at the saddle belts, for example. Notice that in the full-resolution image you can see the holes in the belts both in front of and behind the man's foot; in the half-resolution image, the holes in the belt in front can be counted, but not those behind; and in the quarter-resolution image neither set of holes is clear. Compare with the faces; note that the man's face survives the resolution loss better, since we have a much better a priori idea of what a face looks like than we do of how many holes there ought to be in those saddle belts. Also realize that even the worst of these resolutions is better than ordinary television.

We usually wish to reduce the space required by images, to save both disk space and transmission time. Many of the compression algorithms have been discussed already (see Section 4.2). In general, they operate by removing redundancy. If there is little redundancy in the original, compression will not save a lot of space. Images with large areas of a single color compress well, as do texts that contain many lines full of blanks. Conversely, if redundancy has been removed, there will be little compression possible. It never makes sense to encrypt first and then compress, for example; the encryption step should remove all the redundancy. If you ever find an encrypted file that gets noticeably smaller after compression, get a new encryption program. Conversely, compressing and then encrypting will produce a file that is extremely difficult for any cryptographer to decode, since there will be virtually no redundancy in the plaintext to use in breaking the cipher.

7.3.1   Text

The entropy of English, as shown by Shannon (1991), is about 1 bit per character. ASCII is normally stored at 8 bits per character. Often written text is so compact that there is little point in compressing it, but it is possible to compress it either by looking at pure statistics or at repeated strings. Letter frequency statistics, for example, are used in Huffman coding. Instead of the 7 bits that ASCII uses for each letter, a Huffman code assigns shorter codes to the frequent letters and longer codes to the rare ones (Sayood 1996). Morse code is an example of a code of this form, but it is not optimized for compression. A typical Huffman code reduces English to about 3 to 4 bits per letter. More powerful will be a code that works with repeated sequences such as the Lempel-Ziv algorithm. Such a code will also get to about 3 bits per letter on long enough texts.

7.3.2   Speech

The first step in compressing speech is to start with mu-law speech (8000 samples per second with 8 bits per sample) rather than CD-quality speech. Next, use the GSM algorithm from digital cellular phones. This algorithm is freely available and produces another factor of 5 compression, producing about 1600 bytes per second. Considerably better results can be achieved with a great deal more computing by using LPC (linear predictive coding). Fairly good intelligibility of speech at 300 or even 150 bytes per second is possible. Note that these algorithms will not handle sounds other than speech, whereas GSM can still compress music so that it is recognizable when decompressed. Of course, the best speech compression would be speech recognition followed by a program that resynthesized the original speech. A second of normal speech would have perhaps 2 words or 12 bytes. We do not know much about how to resynthesize the speech with the dialect, emphasis, and individual speech qualities of the speaker, however.

7.3.3   Images

Image compression was described in Section 4.2. In general, a book-type page will compress with Group IV fax compression to perhaps 30 KB; a very complex A4-sized journal page with small print, illustrations, and equations might take 100 KB.

Photographs can often be compressed to 10 KB with JPEG; although lossy, the loss is not perceived by users. We do not have good answers for very large detailed images such as maps; in particular, ways to search such images in the compressed format would be particularly useful.

7.4 Interface Controls: Menus and Keywords

When screen displays that were not limited to characters became feasible in the late 1970s, one of the most important steps forward was the invention of multiple-window interfaces. Window systems, once restricted to specialized machines and research systems, are now the standard on all workstations and PCs. Users are able to run different processes at once in the different windows and to look at one document while writing another.

Library systems today often still don't use window interfaces. Partly this reflects the fact that libraries were early adopters of networks for remote access; as users of the gopher protocols, they did not have the opportunities to use pictures. Partly it reflects cost pressures both to use cheap terminals within libraries and to allow users with lower-cost computers to access the systems without feeling second-class. And partly it reflects the industry that supplies online public access catalog (OPAC) systems and retained text display systems operating from mainframe or midicomputers through the early stages of the PC/workstation boom.

To many researchers in computer interfaces, the most important advance in interfaces was the desktop metaphor invented at Xerox PARC and popularized by the Apple Macintosh. With the conversion of most PC architecture machines from MS-DOS to Windows, this metaphor is now the most common way to control machines. It replaced such methods as IBM JCL (job control language, dating from the 1960s) and the command line interfaces that characterized most other systems.

The key ingredients of the desktop metaphor are iconic representation, click to activate, drag-and-drop, and pull-down menus:

1. Iconic representation means that each file or program is represented by an icon, which tries to show graphically what it is. On a Windows 95 machine, for example, Netscape Navigator is represented by a small ship's wheel, solitaire is a deck of cards, and the deletion routine is an image of a wastebasket (labeled "recycle bin").

2. Each file or program is selected by clicking on it once; to invoke it the user clicks twice. Normally a bar listing some choices is either at the top or bottom of the screen, and after the item is selected choices such as "rename" or "copy" can be invoked.

3. Drag-and-drop lets the user apply a program to a file by dragging the file icon to the program (holding down the mouse) and letting go over it. For example, files are deleted by dragging them to the recycle bin.

4. Pull-down menus appear when the mouse button is held over a command, and produce a list of choices that disappear when the mouse is released; if the mouse button is released while one of the choices is highlighted, that choice is invoked.

Other facilities are possible. For example, in many interfaces, moving a mouse around an image provides a panning capability for images too large to fit on the screen. Enlarging windows can be moved over images that are too small to view easily. Nevertheless, compared to command lines, this is an impoverished set of things the user can do. This makes life simpler; there are fewer choices. But it also means that complex arguments to commands must either be specified ahead of time or through pop-up forms.

There are strong advocates of interfaces based both on menus and upon command lines. The conventional wisdom is that keyword-type command line searches should be done by professional intermediaries (Krentz 1978), while novice users should only be asked to choose from menus (Shneiderman 1978). With time, however, more and more users are gaining interest in complex search systems; just as many people use word processing systems to achieve page layouts once requiring professional typesetting, computer users are beginning to do Boolean searches and other kinds of searching once done in library settings.

One comparison done in 1983 looked at two different interfaces to a library catalog (Geller and Lesk 1983). The research was done in 1981 when essentially no one had any familiarity with online catalogs. One interface was a search interface based on command lines, searching for keywords. The other was based on tracking menus through the Dewey decimal system.

In the keyword system the user could type any number of words; in these illustrations what the user types is shown in **bold**. Thus, in the first example below the user typed **chocolate** and responded to the prompt Which book? with **1**.

```
chocolate
1 items (1/1)
 1: Technology of chocolate.
Which book? 1
%T Technology of chocolate.
%A Kempf, N.W.
%I Oak Park, Ill., Mfg. Confectioner
%D 1964.
%P 118p.
%# 663.92/K32
```

```
%S Chocolate
%Z Copies at: PR
```

The system, to minimize training, did not care whether words were title, author, or subject headings. Thus:

butter pecan
```
2 items (1/2)
 1: Peanut butter and jelly guide to computers.
 2: Neuropsychology; the study of brain and behavior.
Which book? 2
%T Neuropsychology; the study of brain and behavior.
%A Butter, C.M.
%I Brooks-Cole.
%D 1968.
%P 211p.
%# 152/B98
%S Nervous system
%S Psychology, Physiological
%Z Copies at: HO MH
```

Note that failing to find **pecan**, the system ignored it and found the one word that did appear in the catalog. Coordinate index level searching was automatic. Thus:

salton kochen information retrieval
```
Postings:  salton: 4; kochen: 6; information: 2237-C;
           retrieval: 347
6 items (3/4)
 1: Theory of indexing
 2: Principles of information retrieval
 3: SMART retrieval system: experiments in automatic d
 4: Automatic information organization and retrieval.
 5: Growth of knowledge; readings on organization and
 6: Some problems in information science.
```

In this case six books have three of the four terms, as indicated by the numbers in parentheses.

The alternative menu system was based on the Dewey decimal classification hierarchy. The first display was always

```
0 000        Generalities, computing (280 groups)
1 100        Philosophy (87 groups)
2 200        Religion (5 groups)
3 300        Social sciences (306 groups)
```

```
4 400        Language and languages (71 groups)
5 500        Science (1063 groups)
6 600        Technology (applied science) (1175 groups)
7 700        Arts (64 groups)
8 800        Literature (8 groups)
9 900        History and geography (69 groups)
```

and the user chooses down which branch of the hierarchy to continue the search. The focus of the Bell Laboratories library is obvious from the number of groups in each main heading. Suppose the user now types **5**:

```
1 510 Mathematics (242 groups)
2 520 Astronomy (68 groups)
3 530 Physics (248 groups)
4 540 Chemistry (354 groups)
5 550 Geology (72 groups)
7 570 Nature (38 groups)
8 580 Botany (7 groups)
9 591.1 Sense organs (13 groups)
```

The average book was five levels down in the menus, but in the worst case it took ten decisions to get to

```
b 621.3815304 Transistor circuits (131 books)
1 621.381530401 Electronic circuits--Data processing (1 book)
2 621.381530402 Semiconductor circuits--Handbooks (2 books)
7 621.381530407 Transistor circuits--Programmed instruction (4 books)
```

Users had considerable trouble learning some aspects of Dewey; for example, psychology is neither science (500) nor social science (300), but is under philosophy (Dewey, of course, worked before William James, let alone Freud).

In seven weeks of trial, 900 people engaged in over 3000 sessions. Dropping all the sessions done by the library staff, people who did not identify themselves, and people who didn't do any searches at all, we had 1952 searches, of which keyword searches were 79% and menu searches 21%. After experience, even more were keyword searches: 71% of the first searches are keyword, and 84% of searches after the first. Of 208 people who did at least one keyword search and one menu search, they did 84% keyword searches in their next sessions. Even among those who were browsing (not looking for a particular book), they also decided keyword searching is better. Table 7.2 shows the data.

The keyword searches worked better as well as being preferred by the users: 65% of the known-item keyword searchers found their book, while only 30% of menu users found it (based on answers to questions they were asked at the end of each session). Confirming the subjective answers, 24% of keyword users failed to

Table 7.2   Percentage of keyword searches in sessions

Was User Looking for Some Particular Book?	First Search	Later Sessions	All Sessions
Yes	75.7	86.1	82.2
No	64.6	82.0	76.4
All	71.3	84.4	79.8

look at any full citations (implying that they didn't find any promising titles), while 55% of the menu users read no citations.

We found users typing about five commands per minute (we counted even a carriage return to see the next item in a list as a command). Despite the single-keystroke menu, it was no faster to use. The queries were extremely short: the keyword searches averaged a word and a half, with 55% of the searches being only one word. Retrospectively, this justifies ignoring sophisticated term combination commands. The most common search terms are title words (72%), followed by authors (40%) and then subject headings (36%). The users do not specify which field they wanted, and some words occur in all three kinds of fields, so the numbers do not add up to 100% (the catalog had items with authors with names like "Department of Defense Joint Aircraft Design Committee," which is how the subject words get into the author fields).

We also asked the users to compare the computer system with the old paper catalog. Keyword users reported the computer as easier to use, more complete, and less time-consuming. There may be some wishful thinking here; the average session time is 4 minutes. Perhaps they are getting more done than they used to, but few people spent 4 minutes at the old catalog. The menu users thought the computer was easier and faster but not as complete.

Most query languages are based on simple word matching. The standard technology in the library world for some decades was the Boolean query with truncation. Query processing proceeded by generating sets of documents and then combining them with Boolean operators: AND, OR, and NOT. The set retrieval is based on searches for words, possibly with truncation, and allowing searches for multiple words within some neighborhood. Searches can also involve *fielded* searching, in which the word must appear in a particular part of the document record, such as the author.

Thus, to use Dialog as a sample system, the search

```
S LESK
```

creates a set of all documents that contain the word or name *Lesk*. This will retrieve, for example, full text documents that mention *Lesk*. To retrieve only documents written by somebody named *Lesk* (i.e., with *Lesk* in the author field), the query might be

```
S au=lesk, ?
```

where the ? character indicates truncation. This retrieves all authors with last name Lesk and any first name or spelling; thus it would cover both initials and spelled out first names. In some Dialog databases it would have to be written without the comma.

To find documents containing the phrase "white whale," the user would type

```
s white(w)whale
```

where the (w) indicates *word adjacency*. Neighborhoods can also be specified, as in

```
s character(5w)recognition
```

where the (5w) string means "within 5 words." Any of these searches responds with a retrieved set of documents and its size. The user can then combine these sets with AND or OR or NOT, and type them out.

This kind of interface is believed too complex for naive users, and many of the Internet search engines use simpler searching procedures. On Alta Vista, for example, word adjacency is handled just with quotes, so one types "white whale" for a phrase search. And there is minimal fielded searching, since most of the Web pages indexed don't define fields. You can search for some fields (e.g., URLs) with prefixed strings; for example, url:lesk searches for *lesk* in an http string. The * character is used for truncation or internal variants (e.g., colo*r for *color* or *colour*). Neighborhood searches use the word NEAR, which means "within 10 words," trading simplicity for flexibility.

Search engines conforming to the Boolean search rules are often implemented using the standard protocol Z39.50, defined to permit clean separation of the client and server portions of a search system (ANSI 1992). In the Z39.50 protocol, a front-end system can send searches to a back-end retrieval engine, which would execute the searches, save up sets, and deliver values. Using this standard, it would be possible to buy a front end from one vendor and a back end from another. However, Z39.50 is definitely tied to the model of a Boolean search engine on a traditional document collection. It is not flexible enough to implement some other model of document retrieval.

The conventional wisdom on Boolean searches is that most users don't understand them. They confuse AND and OR, and they do not realize the effects of NOT. For example, suppose you live in New Jersey and are looking for plants that grow in the mid-Atlantic area and have red flowers. If you find that a search for red flowers AND mid-atlantic retrieves too many items that grow in Virginia but not further north, you should not just request red flowers AND mid-atlantic NOT Virginia since this will eliminate any plant that happens to grow in both Virginia and New

Jersey. In addition to the confusion created in users, some of Salton's experiments indicated rather little advantage to Boolean queries over coordinate-level matching (counting matching terms) (Salton and Voorhees 1985). As a result, although Boolean searches dominated early online systems, they are less common in the new Web search engines. Since the queries are extremely short (the average Alta Vista query is 1.2 words long), the lack of operators doesn't matter much.

Web search engines attempt to determine the relative importance of different words. A word used many times in a document is likely to be more reflective of the content than a word that is only used once. The exact details of assigning weights (importance) to terms by Web search engines is tricky to discuss. People sometimes attempt to fool the search engines so that their pages will come out at the top of search lists. Thus, they either put in words that they hope people will search for, or they add copies of the words hoping to make some term-weighting function decide their page should be listed first. As a result, the search engines do not publicize their techniques. For example, many have taken to ignoring the meta field in HTML, which is provided to let people insert keywords for searching. The reality was that people were found putting the entire dictionary into such fields, hoping to be retrieved by all searches. With that route blocked, there are now people concealing words in their pages either by writing them in the same color as the background or putting them in 2-point type so they appear to be part of a wallpaper pattern. It does appear that many of the search engines respond to the number of hits in the files, but they do not publish the exact algorithm.

Clearly, we are moving toward systems in which people do their own searching. OPACs are now routine, text searching on the Internet is common, and more complex search systems are being learned. New library users may need to learn how to use the library itself, as well as search systems. Even traditional bookstores, after all, have people who can answer questions. Can this be done online? Will a Web page substitute for a person to provide training?

In fact, some companies justify their Web site on the grounds that it answers questions that would otherwise require the time of their help desk. And certainly users get a lot of help from each other. But librarians still find that there is an enormous demand for courses in the use of the Internet and for help with computer problems. In fact, the very lead that libraries have taken in providing the public with search systems has meant that they get more than their share of questions, being the first search systems many people have come into contact with. Various tools have been developed to help with user training.

One extremely useful online tool has been the FAQ list. FAQ stands for "frequently asked questions," and FAQ lists are just that, lists of common questions with answers. There is a large archive of FAQs at MIT, and they have certainly been very useful for people with a reasonable amount of knowledge to find out more. There are rarely search systems for FAQ lists; they are each normally short enough to browse through.

One interesting experiment to try to improve help systems was the Answer Garden of Mark Ackerman (Ackerman and Malone 1990). This system tried to help with questions about X-windows. The idea was that a user would be presented with a series of choices about the user's question—for example, "Is this a client side or server side problem?" The user would then answer these questions, one after the other, moving down a discrimination tree through the system's information. Eventually, the user either finds the question or reaches the end of the tree. In the first case, the answer is with the question. If the user reaches the end of the tree without finding the question, then it is a new question, and it goes to an X-windows consultant who answers the question and posts the answer in the tree at that place. In this way, each question should only have to be answered once.

The Answer Garden has been implemented at MIT. The first screen, for example, displayed the choices:

```
Are you having a problem with:
  Finding information about X
  Using an X application
  Programming with X
  Administering X
  Using Answer Garden
```

It has been tested on a group of 59 users at Harvard and MIT (Ackerman 1994). It received consistent if not overwhelming use, and many of the people reported great value for it. Others, however, complained that the level of explanation was not right. It is difficult for an automated system to know whether the person confronting it is an expert or a novice and pitch its response appropriately; this is something people can do better. One advantage of the Answer Garden (and of any automated system) is that people perceive no loss of status in asking it questions, and so some people who might avoid asking for help from another person will feel free to consult the program. The reverse of this is that some contacts that might be made and might be useful are not made. It is likely that some training staff will be essential indefinitely.

7.5   Access Methods

Whether libraries in the future need to keep things, or will just buy access to them, is unclear. Many libraries may become "gateway libraries," which merely provide access to material stored elsewhere. This model has the great advantage that it postpones the work of dealing with any item until somebody wants it. Traditionally, libraries buy most of their content before anyone has actually seen it, and they commit to most of the cataloging and shelving cost before any user sees the book or journal. Thus, money may be spent on content that in the end no one uses. In a gateway library, until somebody tries to get at something, the library has minimal cost for it.

Conversely, however, users are not likely to be pleasantly surprised to find that the library has something but that it has to be obtained in a slow or inconvenient way. Nearly all items will come from a search, and we do not know well how to browse in a remote library. Users will need help doing their searches and adjusting them to retrieve a reasonable quantity of results. Also, it will be important for many users that response be fast and that the material be available at all times. We are all familiar with the undergraduate who sets out to write a paper the evening before it is due. If the contents of the library are only available by remote delivery during business hours, as with many of the fax-on-demand services, this major segment of the user base is not served.

The uncertainty that affects our use of digital information because of lack of cues as to the quality of the work is even larger when the work is coming from far away. Librarians or faculty will have to help users learn how to find out the background and context of works on the Web and help them judge what weight to place on different retrieved documents.

Many users of traditional libraries are not searching; they are browsing. They do not have a particular document, or even a well-formulated query, in their mind. For this purpose, the search engines provided on the Web, or in libraries, are often frustrating and inappropriate. Normal browsing is heavily dependent on visual scanning, going through fairly large numbers of items, looking at very little information on each, and picking out something to read. It is tolerable as a way of working only because it is usually done on some kind of classified collection, so that the general area is already selected.

Various innovative schemes have been tried to improve browsing, rather than searching. One plan that flourished in the 1980s was the idea of *spatial data management*, in which information is located by place rather than by keyword. It was invented as a model of the process by which people remember that they have put some document in this or that pile on a desk. Spatial data management was popularized by Tom Malone (then at Xerox) and others, and remains for a few items, for example in the way the Macintosh and Microsoft Windows interfaces allow the user to arrange the icons for files in any order. William Jones and Susan Dumais evaluated it and found that people are not very good at remembering where they have put anything (Jones and Dumais 1986). In fact, two or three characters of a name are worth more than spatial organization. They evaluated both real spatial organization (asking people to put documents into piles on a table) and the computer metaphor for the same thing.

Another metaphor that has been tried is the idea of retrieval by criticism, explored by Michael Williams in his Rabbit system (Tou et al. 1982). In the Rabbit interface, database query operates by having the computer retrieve random records subject to constraints. At the beginning, the machine simply returns a random record. Imagine, as in Williams's example, that the problem is to find a restaurant. The system picks a random one, and the user says something like "too expensive" or "too far north." The system now makes another random choice subject to the constraint. If the database can be described as a set of independent dimensions, each of which has a reasonable range, this process will quickly converge on acceptable answers.

Although the Rabbit model is attractive, few databases lend themselves to this kind of partitioning. One cannot see, for example, how to apply this to a conventional text-searching system; simply knowing a few words that you don't want does not restrict the search space much.

Although most library systems do not make much use of graphical screens, there are some interesting interfaces that do. For example, Ben Shneiderman has a "treemap" for hierarchical structures. In this model, moving down the tree one step changes the orientation of the diagram from horizontal to vertical and then back again (Johnson and Shneiderman 1991; Shneiderman 1992). For very complex structures, the treemap has the advantage of being able to show size relationships and categorization (through color). Figure 7.4 shows a simple treemap diagram.

A treemap can, for example, represent a file system. Each transition from vertical to horizontal packing is a step down in the directory hierarchy. Each set of items packed together is the contents of a directory. The relative size of the items in the

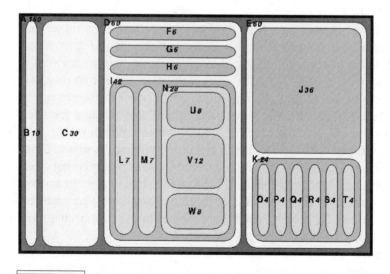

Figure 7.4   Treemap

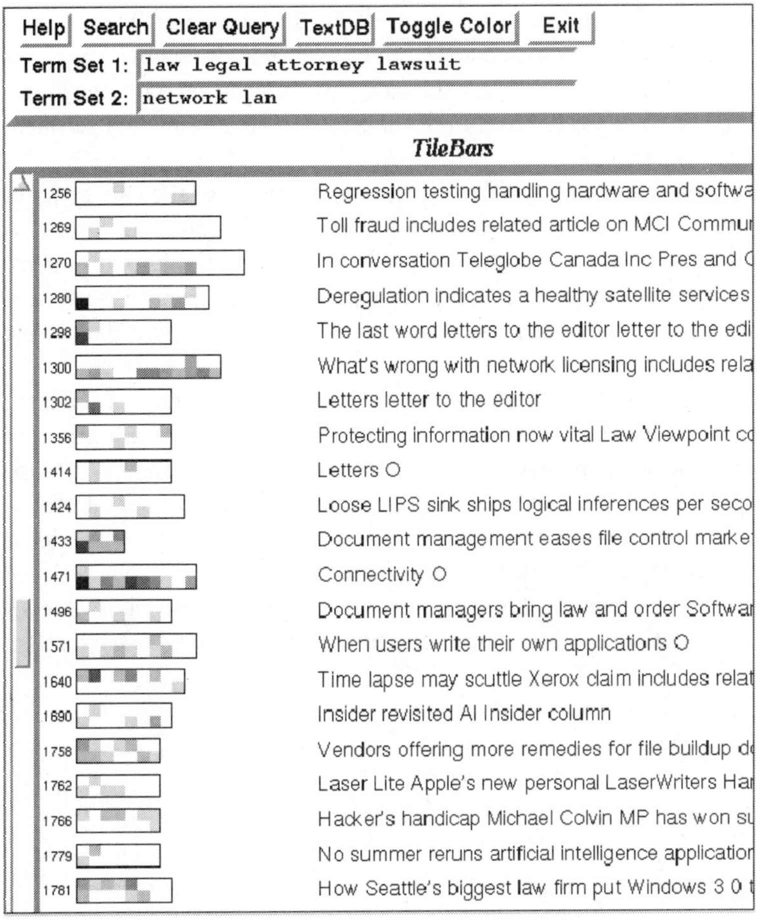

Figure 7.5   TileBars

diagram reflects their relative size in the file system. Color can indicate the kind of file (e.g., text, image, or program).

Some researchers are trying to indicate more than just a document ID in a retrieval presentation, instead of just a single list of documents. Marti Hearst (1995) has developed a display technique, called TileBars, that shows another approach to visualizing the results of a search. Each document has a row of squares; each row represents a set of terms, and each square is a portion of the document. The darkness of the square indicates the extent to which the terms are present. Thus, in Figure 7.5, document 1298 has matches at the beginning only, with a very dense match on *network* and/or *LAN*; document 1300 has a well-distributed use of *network* and a single portion relating to *law*.

Ed Fox, on the Envision project, has an interface that also combines a great many attributes to describe a retrieval list (Heath et al. 1995). In Figure 7.6 (Color Plate) documents are plotted using the x-axis to display publication date, the y-axis to show terms, and the color for degree of relevance. It is also possible to use shape to show yet another dimension.

These interfaces basically display lists of documents. Xia Lin of the University of Kentucky has represented a document collection using a self-organizing system. A rectangular space, intended to cover all semantic meanings, is divided into nodes. At first, nodes are assigned random positions in a term vector space (used to represent the coordinates of a position). Documents are then picked, and the closest node to each document adjusted so that the node will become even closer to the document. In this way, various nodes converge on the position values of different documents, and eventually each region of the space is associated with a group of related documents. The space is then tiled (divided into areas that do not overlap) and each area labeled with the corresponding documents (Lin and Soergel 1991). This process is known as the Kohonen map algorithm. Figure 7.7 shows 140 documents in artificial intelligence in this representation.

Note that the largest areas are for the most common topics (expert systems). This gives an overview of what topics matter and how they are related to each other.

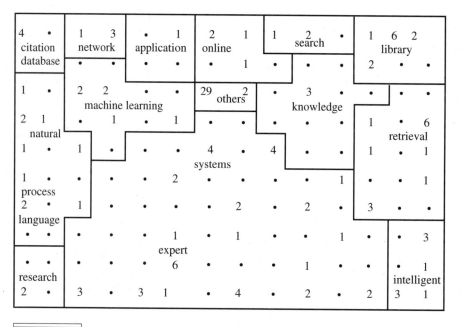

Figure 7.7   Kohonen maps

The difficulty with interfaces of this sort is likely to be difficulties when extended to very large collections, where it will be hard to find some way to indicate the location of every document.

The basic difficulty is the problem of summarizing the kinds of books in one area or another. We might like to have the result of a query not as "here are 200 books that matched the query," but "there were four basic topics, and 50 books in each, and here are what the basic topics are." How can this be done? One strategy is to use a library classification. Here is the result of a search for the word *screen* in a set of book titles with the number of hits in each part of the LC classification.

```
Type some kind of search query, one line:
Query: screen
Occ.      Subject                    Title (No. found 194)
143  P/Language and Literature  The face on the screen and other stor
 99  R/Medicine                 Toxicity screening procedures using b
 51  T/Technology               'Environmental stress screening, spen
 50  M/Music                    Broadway to Hollywood /Can't help sin
 30  L/Education                Finland /Screen design strategies for
 21  H/Social Sciences          National ethnic survey, 1980 /Mexican
 17  N/Arts                     The technique of screen & television
 12  --/--                      Alfalfa seed screenings as a feed for
 10  Z/Bibliography             Screen process printing photographic
  8  Q/Science                  NOS version 2 screen formatting refer
  5  --/--                      Screening inductees/An analysis of th
  5  S/Agriculture              Climbing and screening plants /The Co
                       .
                       .
                       .
Which category should be expanded? (n for none):
```

This shows the two main blocks of usage: words related to screenplays and the cinema, and words related to screening via tests for various conditions. At the bottom of the list is another meaning: hedge plants. If the S category is expanded, the result is

```
Type some kind of search query, one line:
Query: screen
Occ.      Subject                    Title
 2   SB427/Climbing plants.     Climbing and screening plants /The Co
 1   SB437/Hedges               Hedges, screens and espaliers
 1   SF961/Cattle -- diseases   Blood protein screening in healthy
 1   SH153/Fish-culture --      Efficiency tests of the primary
```

With these category labels a user interested in plants can now look through the categories SB427 and SB437, finding titles, such as "Shelter effect: investigations into aerodynamics of shelter and its effects on climate and crops," that do not use the word *screen* but are clearly relevant.

So far, most library catalogs only provide textual representations, despite the attractiveness of some of the graphical systems shown here. The rapid switch from the text-oriented gopher interfaces to the graphically oriented Web interfaces is likely to change this rapidly, and more work will be needed to decide which of these interfaces can cope with both the large quantities of information in libraries and the unskilled users who sometimes appear.

Whether any of these more detailed access methods can substitute for running your eyes over a set of shelves to find book titles that look interesting is not yet known. In principle, the cues used in shelf-hunting can be presented using one of the new graphics techniques, and the ability to organize books in response to each query should be helpful. Yet enough work has not been done to see that adequate cues are given to compensate for the lack of immediate observation of the size of the book or the recognition of a respectable publisher.

7.6   Retrieval Evaluation

User enthusiasm for a digital library depends on many things: the content of the collection, the cost of the system, the user interface, and so on. One aspect that can be systematically evaluated is the accuracy with which the system selects answers to questions. The standard methodology for this was defined by Cyril Cleverdon in the 1950s (Cleverdon, Mills, and Keen 1966). Cleverdon defined two measures, now known as recall and precision. The *recall* of a system is its ability to find as many relevant documents as possible. The *precision* of a system is its ability to select only relevant documents and reject the irrelevant ones. Thus, if we search for a query in a document collection, and there are 50 relevant documents in the collection, should the search return 40 documents, of which 20 are relevant and 20 are not relevant, it has a recall of 40% (20 out of 50) and a precision of 50% (20 out of 40).

There is a trade-off between recall and precision. Suppose we have some way of tightening or loosening the search strategy. For example, if the user gave the system three terms, and looked for any two of them, the strategy could be tightened by demanding that all three appear or loosened by accepting documents with only one term. If the strategy were loosened, more documents would be retrieved. It is likely that some of the new retrieved documents would be relevant, thus increasing the recall. But it is also likely that the new strategy would also increase the number of nonrelevant documents found, and in fact that it would decrease the precision (by introducing proportionally more nonrelevant documents than in the tighter search). In fact, you can always achieve 100% recall by retrieving every document in the collection, but the precision in this case will be close to zero. Conversely, if the system can retrieve a relevant document as its first response, by stopping there one can achieve 100% precision but probably with very low recall. Many systems operate at around 50% recall and 50% precision; half of what is found is relevant, and half of what is relevant is found.

It has become customary to plot recall against precision to show this trade-off. Figure 7.8 shows one of the very earliest such plots, made by Cleverdon as part of the Aslib/Cranfield study of index languages (Cleverdon, Mills, and Keen 1966). The care taken in this project to get good queries and relevance assessments was remarkable. The quality of the Cranfield work has not been equalled since, nor its economy (six staff years of effort for $28,000 on one project).

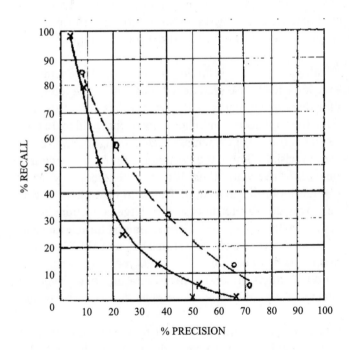

INDEX LANGUAGE III.5.a   SEARCH E
200 DOCUMENTS
(Index Language III.1.a   Broken line)

Figure 7.8   Recall-precision curves

In practice, the parameter changing along the curve is the number of retrieved documents. As more documents are retrieved, the performance moves to higher recall and lower precision; as fewer documents are retrieved, the performance moves to higher precision but lower recall. Ideal performance would be the top-right corner, where everything retrieved is relevant (100% precision) and everything relevant is retrieved (100% recall). Conversely the lower-left corner, where nothing useful has been retrieved, is the worst possible performance.

Retrieval algorithms are evaluated by running them against a set of test documents and queries. For each query, each algorithm being tested is executed, and for each result, the recall and precision are calculated. If the algorithm has variable parameters, it is often run with several values to produce different results (presumably moving along the recall-precision curves). All of the recall-precision results are then plotted and whichever algorithm has points closer to the top-right corner is better. In practice it is found that there is an enormous scatter among the results; some queries are much easier to answer than others, and the scatter across queries tends to be much larger than the differences between systems. The first lesson from these retrieval experiments is that the best thing to do for improved performance is to get the users to write better queries (or merely to get them to submit queries on easier topics).

The difficult part of a recall-precision test is finding the relevant documents for the queries. Originally, Cleverdon tried to use seed documents, or use the reference lists in documents as data for these experiments, but he was criticized for this, and it became standard to have the relevant documents chosen by people paid to do this. It is possible to examine only the retrieved documents, which is straightforward, but gives only a good estimate of precision. If only the documents found in the course of the experiment are evaluated for relevance, there is no way to guess how many other relevant documents might be in the collection. This kind of evaluation was started in the 1960s, when it was difficult to process very large collections. With small collections, it was feasible to have every document examined for relevance to each query. Gerard Salton prepared several such collections for the SMART project, and they remained the basis of such studies for the next 20 years. The largest of them was a collection of 1400 abstracts of aeronautical literature that Cleverdon had gathered, and this remained one of the standard retrieval test collections into the 1990s.

Many felt that these collections were inadequate, that they were too small. In 1990 Donna Harman of the National Institute of Standards and Technology (NIST), one of Salton's students, began the first of the TREC (Text Retrieval Evaluation Conference) experiments (see Harman 1995). Text retrieval researchers were presented with a gigabyte of text, half for training and half for experiments, and 100 queries. To estimate recall, the plan called for the first 200 documents retrieved by each system to be pooled and the entire set to be evaluated for relevance. The documents ranged from news wire stories to Department of Energy documents, and the queries were composed by professional analysts looking for information; as a result the queries are particularly long and detailed. Fifty of the queries were imagined to be standing profiles, so that it was acceptable to use the results on the first half of the collection to train or adapt the queries for the test on the second half. Fifty of the queries were imagined to be one-shot queries and no training could be done.

The TREC conference has been repeated each year, with new documents and queries. The document collection is now up to about 3 GB. Again, the scatter among systems exceeds the differences between them. Not only do the systems have widely different performance on different queries, but even two systems that may have about the same recall and precision on a query are likely to achieve it by retrieving entirely different documents. Some systems are also better able to deal with the entire set of queries. For example, some of the queries involve numerical comparisons ("companies with revenues above $100 million") but some of the purely text-oriented systems have no way of implementing this comparison.

There are two kinds of queries in the TREC experiment. Some queries are viewed as continuing ("routing"), and a set of documents is provided in advance that are known to be relevant; the queries are evaluated against a new set of documents. The other queries are new each time and called "ad hoc"; there are no relevant documents known in advance for such queries. Some systems do manual creation of queries for each ad hoc test; some do a fully automatic processing of whatever is presented to them. Many systems do the routing queries by ignoring the query and making a new query from the set of relevant documents (which, in aggregate size, are much larger than the query description).

As a result of the scatter in the results, it is not sensible to select a single "winner" of the TREC competition and suggest that it be used for all queries. One leading system from City University, London used term weighting, in which the weight placed on any term was roughly related to inverse document frequency (terms only appearing in a few documents are better content indicators). It also supplemented each query with a few dozen terms picked from the highest-rated documents, and it used passage retrieval (breaking long documents into shorter chunks for searching). Another high-performing system, the INQ101 system, from Bruce Croft's group at the University of Massachusetts, also uses term weighting, and query expansion using phrases detected in the collection. Salton's group did well using term weighting and massive feedback expansion (up to 500 terms added from the top 30 retrieved documents). West Publishing relied on a system similar to Croft's system but with expansion based on manually made synonym groups. Queens College, CUNY, sent in a system that uses spreading activation on passages (a technique that, to oversimplify, creates links between words as they co-occur). ETH in Zurich combined three methods, including vector spaces, Markov models, and links from phrases. Note the importance of expanding the queries; nearly everyone found this useful in getting better performance. This models the reality that librarians do better if they can get their users to talk more about what they want. Too much of a conventional question is implied rather than explicit, and making it explicit helps.

7.7   Summary

Again, this chapter describes a solved problem. We can build retrieval systems that work well and that work well enough that they are better than what people do now. We still have to think about accessibility for those with limited vision, inadequate computer displays, or no experience with keyboards and mice, but we have no basic difficulties building systems that work well enough to be effective.

Nevertheless, there are many difficulties with existing systems. Many tend to make inadequate use of graphical capabilities. Many offer inadequate guidance to users who have either retrieved nothing or have retrieved far too much. And many still suffer from the problems that users have negotiating their way through very large information collections. Research projects such as those described in this chapter address some of these problems, and solutions need to make their way into practice.

Perhaps most interesting will be the problems of representing item quality. In a conventional library, most material purchased is evaluated for quality at the time someone decides to buy it (usually by selecting reliable publishers or journals). In a gateway library that only fetches things on demand, how will there be an instant reflection to the user about possible bias or unreliability in the material listed? For example, would you wish to have the only information about disk drives be the press releases of some manufacturer, just because they were available free? Certainly this information might be useful, but with even less contact between the librarians and the users, how will novice users learn about the relative importance and reliability of certain kinds of information?

In one university conversation, a faculty member argued that this was not a library's business; he felt that faculty should assign undergraduate reading and that graduate students were sophisticated enough to appreciate degrees of bias or distortion. Many librarians would disagree and point out that their purchasing decisions today include quality and reliability considerations. In the future, how can we reflect these questions into an interface?

Collections and Preservation

IN A TRADITIONAL library, the collections are the most important part. Libraries all have rules and policies for what they collect, even if they are Richard Brautigan's Mayonnaise Library, which takes any book that publishers and other libraries have rejected. What should the collection rules be for digital libraries? What kinds of items should be acquired and retained? This chapter will focus on the split between those works that arrive in electronic form, compared with those that are converted from older forms, and on the division between those items a library holds itself and those it gets when needed from somebody else.

As mentioned earlier, actual possession of items is less important than it has been in the past. Since digital items may be transmitted almost instantaneously across even international distances, what matters in the digital age is not what the library has but what it can get quickly. A few national libraries with preservation as their goal may need to have physical possession of objects (since they cannot trust other organizations to keep them and continue to make them available), but for most libraries the right to get something for their patrons will be enough and may be cheaper than the actual possession.

8.1 Traditional Paper Collections

The traditional library acquires published material. Nonpublished materials went into archives, a related kind of institution. The fact that libraries acquired primarily published books and serials had several important consequences:

1. Some degree of quality control could be taken for granted. A book produced by a reputable publisher can be assumed to have some degree of integrity and accuracy. The library does not have to worry much about whether such books are plagiarized or fraudulent. As a consequence, most libraries do not have any procedure for examining the books they are buying to decide on their basic integrity. They may review their importance and significance for the library's users, but they rely on the publisher for some initial checking. In the digital world, where "publisher" may be some fifteen-year-old clicking away at his terminal, somebody else is going to have to verify the quality of the material.

2. All printed books bought recently have been produced in multiple copies. The specific copy the library had of any 20th-century book was rarely of great importance (again, with an exception for national deposit libraries). Press runs may have been small, but it was unlikely that the copy in any one library was unique. In modern publishing, printing fewer than a few hundred copies is completely uneconomic and is not done. In the digital world, this is no longer true. Unless there is coordination between libraries or between library and publisher, the library has no easy assurance that anyone else in the world has a copy of what it has. As a result, if it really cares about a particular item, it may have to think about how to keep it.

3. Published books are fairly static. Most books do not have a second edition, and if they do, it is clearly marked on the copy. Those few books that are regularly changed (e.g., almanacs that appear yearly) are well recognized. And the appearance of a book does not change as it is read, unless it is falling apart. Again, in the digital world, books may be much more dynamic. Each "reading" may be interactive and in some way change the book. The author or publisher may be revising constantly. The library has to think more carefully about what copy it has and what version it wants. Traditional rules such as "the best edition for scholarship is the last version published in the author's lifetime" make less sense in a digital world. The library is going to have to think about whether it wants to capture some version of a changing item. Will the readers prefer to know that they are always reading the latest version, or will they expect that if they take the same book off the shelf twice it will be the same? Can they duplicate work (a principle of scientific investigation) if the data sources used have changed between the original publication and the time the work is repeated?

For all of these reasons, it is important for libraries in the digital world to augment their collections policies with an understanding of the new problems of digital material.

In addition, of course, the old issues of collections policies continue. Few libraries can any longer afford what is called "comprehensive" collecting, meaning that every item of interest in a particular subject area is bought. Libraries must consider their audience. Are the patrons secondary school students needing introductory texts? Undergraduate students who need a variety of standard works? Or postgraduate students and scholars who want the most detailed material available? Vice President Gore is fond of suggesting that in the future a schoolgirl in Carthage, Tennessee, will connect to the Library of Congress. Any schoolchild might feel overwhelmed by the riches of that library; how will librarians provide some guidance, and will those librarians be in Tennessee or Washington?

Just collecting material that has been on paper is not enough. Digitally, we are now seeing online journals that are not now and never were printed. Some of these are published by professional societies with the same kind of refereeing and editing that apply to the printed journals of those societies. Among the best known are *Psycoloquy* (published by the American Psychological Association) and the *Online Journal of Current Clinical Trials* (published by AAAS and OCLC). These are expected to be the equivalent of print publications in quality and deserve equal consideration in libraries.

For many items, a digital version will be a substitute for the original and will be all the user needs. For other areas the digital version is only used to find items that the user will then look at in original form. Which items fall in which category? In general, the answer depends on whether the creator controlled the form of the work or not. For the typical printed book, in which the author wrote words but the page layout and book design were done by compositors and designers at the printer or publisher, it is not critical for the readers to see the original form. If digital versions can achieve the same readability and usability, the readers may switch. For works such as paintings, drawings, and some poetry, the original author did control the actual appearance that the viewer sees. Scholars often demand to see the original of these works, especially those who study brushwork or other details of creation. With books, a few users similarly study binding or papermaking and must see original copies, but this is a very small fraction of library users. With time, computer surrogates are becoming more and more acceptable even for some kinds of artwork or manuscript study, as displays improve and we learn about scanning. Even today, though, the overwhelming majority of library usage is from printed books for which digital substitutes can be used and for which digital display is preferable to the alternative of microfilm for decaying items.

In the digital world, there are even more kinds of material of unclear status. Although some online journals, as mentioned above, are edited to a standard equivalent to print publications, there are many mailing lists and other online files that have a variety of intermediate positions. They may be totally unrefereed, with content ranging down to the graffiti scratched into bathroom doors, or moderated with more or less effectiveness, or actually selected and edited into high-quality digests of information. Some of these may be of great value to the library's users, perhaps only for a short time but perhaps also for a long time. Libraries deciding what should be available to their patrons need to think about how to handle this material.

Today relatively few libraries collect this material. After all, the users can normally get it for themselves. However, the procedures by which online information may or may not be stored for the future are completely unsettled. Thus, the library community has to think in time about which of these online sources need to be saved, and if so, how to coordinate the saving of them. In some cases other organizations may handle this; for example a server at MIT attempts to store all the FAQ pages (frequently asked questions) from online newsgroups. Brewster Kahle, the inventor of WAIS (wide area information service) has established a new organization to archive electronic information. In the near future, libraries will have to decide if this kind of storage is their business or someone else's.

8.2 Traditional Preservation Problems: Acid Paper and Perfect Binding

What will survive of the contents of our libraries? We have only 7 of the more than 80 plays Aeschylus wrote. Of the books published by Cambridge University Press in the 18th century, for about 15% there are no surviving copies known. Libraries have users today, but will they also have users tomorrow? What of today will be here tomorrow? Digital technology has completely changed the meaning of this question. With paper, this is a question about survival of the physical object. With digital technology, which can be copied without error, a copy is just as good as the original. The question is not whether the original object will last; it is whether the process of copying can be continued and whether the original bits can still be interpreted. The major issue for preservation is regular refreshing. Even if some objects are physically durable, they become obsolete. Today you can hardly find a phonograph playing vinyl records or an 8-mm movie projector, and yet both technologies were once extremely common. Moving to new technologies is the only safe answer.

The technological inventions of 1800–1850 were not an unalloyed blessing for libraries. Books became much cheaper, but were made of paper that was less permanent. The use of chemical bleach, acid-process wood pulp, and alum-rosin sizes all produced paper with a life in decades instead of centuries. Acid paper is the major preservation issue facing libraries today. Most books printed between 1850 and 1950 were printed on this acid-process paper and have a much shorter expected life than earlier books. U.S. research libraries have about 300 million total books, representing about 30 million different titles. Of these, perhaps about 80 million are acid paper books covering perhaps 10 million titles. Considering books already reprinted, books already microfilmed, and some titles not to be preserved, there are probably about 3 million books that need some kind of treatment.

Other problems faced by libraries include the invention of perfect binding, the technique of gluing books together rather than sewing them. Early perfect-bound

Figure 8.1   Acid paper

books tended to fall apart after use, in a way familiar from used paperbacks. This has not been a major problem in U.S. libraries, which typically bought cloth-bound books; in France, where many books are only sold in less permanent bindings, it is more of a problem. Environmental problems also became more severe. Air pollution has become serious over the last century, and the advent of central heating in libraries without humidity control is not beneficial. Figure 8.1 is a sample document falling apart; it is not even very old—a 1958 railroad timetable, printed on newsprint.

Historically, the choices for a library with a deteriorating book were to simply put the loose, fragile pages in a box and ask the readers to be careful or to photograph all the pages and bind the reproduction. Neither is really satisfactory; boxing still leaves the individual pages deteriorating, and replacing the book with a copy destroys the individual copy. Some other alternatives, such as putting each page in a plastic sleeve, are practical only for items of great value. Each of these actions was a copy-by-copy solution. What became the traditional proposals for a large-scale solution were mass deacidification and microfilming.

Deacidification had been done, on a small scale. Books were disbound and the pages soaked in buffering solutions such as sodium bicarbonate or sodium diphosphate. After the chemistry in the page fibers was stabilized, the book was rebound. This is again too expensive except for rare books. Even sprays that can be applied without removing the pages from the book, but must be applied page by page, are too expensive for general use. The hope was for some gas that could be applied to many books at once in a chamber; the goal is to reduce the cost to about $5 per book. The Library of Congress pioneered a process using diethyl zinc, but this compound is very dangerous and a fire destroyed the pilot plant in 1985. Akzo Chemicals, Inc. eventually did try a pilot commercial service, but demand from libraries has been too low to support the work and it was abandoned in 1994. Other processes have been developed in Europe, but general interest has swung away from bulk deacidification as a solution. Even bulk deacidification still has the problem that it treats one book at a time; it is of little use to the New York Public Library that a copy of a deteriorating book at Harvard has been deacidified.

Microfilming is a more promising answer in many ways. Books are transferred to high-quality microfilm, a very durable medium. Typically reductions of 10X are used, with the book being photographed two pages per frame on 35-mm high-contrast black-and-white film. The original filming is always to roll film, although the copies made for distribution to libraries are often on fiche, with about 100 frames on a 4 × 6-inch (105 × 148-mm) microfiche. Microfilming costs about $30 per book, but it is easily copied once made. Thus, once a book is filmed in one library, the next library whose copy of the same title is falling apart can purchase a copy of the film fairly cheaply. In fact, large runs of books are sold on film or fiche by publishers such as Chadwyck-Healey, at costs down to $1 per book, permitting libraries that never had good collections in some areas to improve them quickly. It is also a cheap way for libraries that want to reach some target, such as one million volumes, to close the gap. Microfilming thus helps distribute works more widely, while deacidification does not increase the availability of copies.

Unfortunately, microfilm is not particularly liked by users. The advantages it provides, namely durability and compactness, are of value to the librarian not the reader. The reader sees that it is harder to get to a random page, you have to read from a screen, there is no ability to search, and in the early days of film you often had to read white on black. Microfilm also suffers from politics. It is much simpler to scan a large number of books at a few institutions than to scan a small number of books in each of many libraries; thus microfilming funds are more concentrated than, say, deacidification, leaving a lot of libraries who do not see enough local benefit to provide political support. Nonetheless, the United States has for some years had a major effort, funded by the National Endowment for the Humanities (NEH), to microfilm deteriorating books. About 600,000 books have been filmed under the NEH program; all are now more readily available and more likely to survive.

Libraries also have to worry about material that is not on paper. Images, for example, are today stored on photographic film. Black-and-white silver halide film is extremely durable, probably lasting for hundreds of years. Color films are more sensitive, and in fact some movie companies take their color negatives, make three black-and-white prints through different color filters, and store the result (interestingly, this is the original process for making color movies). Ektachrome is probably good for 25 years if stored properly and Kodachrome for 50. Although

Kodachrome is more durable than Ektachrome simply in terms of years, it does not stand up to repeated projection. If a slide is to be projected many times, Ektachrome will last longer. The failure, in either case, will be fading of colors. For movies, the film stock is more of a problem. Until the early 1950s, movies were made on nitrate-based stock, which is highly flammable. The newer "safety" film, which is acetate-based, is much better but does suffer from slow creation of vinegar in the film stock. With luck, it will suffice until digital takes over. Early movies, by the way, were deposited with the Library of Congress as paper prints, and many survive only in that form and are now being reconverted to acetate-based movie film.

A somewhat more complex situation is the problem of preserving sound recordings. Libraries have saved scores for centuries, of course. But saving actual performances only began at the end of the 19th century with piano rolls, thousands of which survive in the Library of Congress and represent the primary storage medium for about two decades of piano playing. Technology soon changed to wax cylinders; LC has some 25,000 of them. This exemplifies the problems with new technology. Both the piano rolls and the wax recordings are reasonably durable if not played, but there is almost no equipment left in the world that can play them. The Library of Congress is forced to preserve not just the recordings, but the machinery as well.

Sound recording then moved on to vinyl and tape. These pose widely different kinds of preservation issues. Vinyl recordings, if not played, are quite durable, but they are very vulnerable to damage (scratching) when played. Magnetic tape, by contrast, is sensitive to temperature and humidity and is not very durable under the best circumstances. Yet it is very widely used for sound recording, not just by commercial cassette producers but by libraries collecting oral histories and such material. The problems in the United States are aggravated by the lack of a legal deposit requirement for sound until the 1970s. As a result, many early recordings are not in the Library of Congress and need to be sought in other collections.

More recently, of course, vinyl records have also become obsolete. The new technology is the audio CD. Audio CDs are durable and digital—almost an ideal solution from the standpoint of a library. However, given the history, libraries must also worry about the future obsolescence of CDs. Also, as with the readers who wish to hang on to the smell and feel of paper, there are audiophiles who claim that analog sound has some quality that makes it better than digital.

CDs, like every other kind of storage that requires a playback machine, could in principle become unreadable while still looking in good shape. The problem of knowing the state of a collection, previously only requiring visual inspection, for many kinds of material now requires some kind of sampling and playback. CDs, fortunately, are very durable. Short of idiots scratching labels into them with diamond markers, they are not likely to become unreadable.

They might, of course, be supplanted by some other kind of storage. Libraries somewhere have 8-track tape, wire recordings, and the visual format used on sound movies. The most serious threat today is the digital versatile disk (DVD), which will have 10 times the capacity of a CD and about the same production cost. Does this mean that the Library of Congress will need to have engineers repairing CD players in a hundred years?

It should not need to. CDs, unlike all the previous formats except player piano rolls, are digital. So a copy should sound exactly the same, and it should not matter whether a library keeps the original or migrates to a new format. And yet, you might think that vinyl records could be discarded when the same performance is available on CD, but there are people still attached to the vinyl. Will there be people in the future who develop an emotional attachment to the physical form of CDs?

8.3 *Digitizing Special Collections and Archives*

Libraries also house much material that is not in the form of traditional printed books and serials. Among the most common special collections in libraries are music (printed and recorded), maps, manuscripts, rare books, drawings, advertisements, photographs, and slides. Newer kinds of special collections may include videotapes or oral histories; older kinds might be papyri, Inca quipu, and any other kind of material written on something other than paper. Figure 8.2 shows examples of different scanned items.

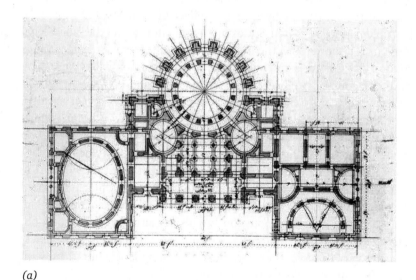

(a)

Figure 8.2   *(a) architectural drawing, (b) old letter, (c) notebook of C. S. Peirce, philosopher, (d) photo of Robert E. Lee*

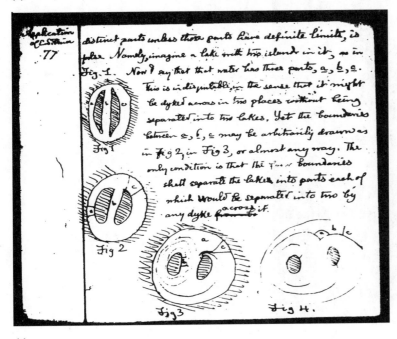

(b)

(c)

(d)

Figure 8.2   *(Continued)*

An important issue with special collections is that they may not be cataloged down to the individual item level. Collections of photographs, for example, may simply be placed in folders at the level of perhaps 100 photos per folder and the entire folder given a catalog record. For example, the National Air and Space Museum (Smithsonian) videodisk on the history of aviation has a few hundred pictures under the label *Amelia Earhart*. Some of these are photographs of her plane, her cockpit, her navigator, and so on. As a result you cannot pick a photograph at random from this file and assume that it is a picture of Earhart herself. Collection-level cataloging makes it difficult for the user to decide whether there is an answer to a question in the particular folder. In traditional libraries this was dealt with by delivering the entire folder to the user and having the user flip through it. Digitally, browsing may be more tedious and complex and not serve the purpose.

To address this kind of material in the digital context raises two questions: first, can we digitize what we have now? And second, what new kinds of special collections will there be in a digital world?

In terms of digitization, each kind of material must be discussed separately:

1. *Maps.* Although maps can be scanned, they pose a severe problem in terms of size and accuracy. Maps are printed on very large sheets and yet contain small items that must be visible. A sample 1:25,000 Ordnance Survey sheet measures 15 by 31 inches and yet contains letters (in a blackletter font, no less) that measure 0.75 mm high. Even assuming that the Ordnance Survey would grant permission to scan this map, the scan resolution would have to be over 300 dpi, and given the sheet size it means that the full map would be 4500 by 9300, or 125 MB of uncompressed data. The Library of Congress has a flatbed map scanner that scans 24×36 inches at 600 dpi, 24 bits per pixel; multiplying out, a single scan is nearly 900 MB. Some current maps can be obtained in digital form, but conversion of old maps will be expensive for some time to come.

2. *Music.* Recorded music has been discussed earlier. Sheet music can be scanned, but OCR for sheet music is not well developed, making it difficult to search the scanned music or arrange for a program to play it. There is an interesting possibility with recorded music: it is possible to produce a score from the sound, which may be more useful for searching.

3. *Photographs, drawings, advertisements, slides, and other graphical items.* These again must be scanned. They pose severe cataloging problems, and it is hard to make flat recommendations for the kind of digitization that will be needed. Photographs of natural scenes, for example, will have wide color spaces to represent, while an artist's pencil drawing may have only grey values.

4. *Museum-type objects:* papyri, scrolls, pot inscriptions, bone carvings, and so on. We really do not know much about what kinds of digital images of these items can serve what functions. In practice we can imagine photographing them and then scanning them, but individual evaluation is necessary to decide when (as with papyri) the digital image may be more useful than the original, and when (as with three-dimensional objects) the digital image is likely to be only a finding device.

Although this sounds pessimistic, there are successful examples of digitizing special collections. Harvard, for example, has scanned and converted to PhotoCD some 80,000 posters from their Judaica collection. This was a quite cheap operation ($2 per poster) done by a commercial firm. Again, however, note the particular circumstances. Posters are not made to be studied with a magnifying glass; they are expected to be read at a distance and are printed with large type. Nor do they usually contain subtle colorings. Thus, the resolution of PhotoCD is adequate for them. Posters are also flat and on paper and, although large, can be handled easily enough if adequate space is available.

Special collections also pose the problem that sometimes they have artifactual value. Unlike books, they often contain unique items, and the items are sometimes museum quality. As a result, the digitization must not destroy the original, and users are more likely to insist that a digitized version is merely a finding aid rather than a substitute for the original.

In the digital world, there will be new kinds of special collections entering libraries. Libraries do not really know what to do with videotape, let alone interactive computer programs. As scholars want to have access to these items, what will be required? The computer science department at Berkeley set out some years ago to recover all the early versions of the UNIX system, since the first one widely distributed was version 6. This required rebuilding some old drives to read such media as Dectape, which became obsolete a decade earlier. Libraries cannot do this in general, but they are going to have to think about what new kinds of digital materials should be considered under the heading of special collections.

8.4   *Sharing of Collections among Libraries*

Libraries, for years, have been vexed by the lack of space for books. In 1902 the president of Harvard wrote an article recommending moving little-used books to an off-campus site (Eliot 1978). Another option has been division of the burden of book purchasing. Libraries in the same geographic area have often shared collecting responsibilities. Harvard and MIT, CMU and the University of Pittsburgh, and other groups of universities have divided up the responsibility for subject areas. There are now nationwide cooperative agreements for collecting various kinds of foreign publications.

Collection sharing has been backed up historically by the interlibrary loan process. Almost any library is eligible to borrow books from this system. OCLC operates a service using its union catalog to allow libraries to find a nearby holder of any particular book. The delays involved in mailing books from one place to another, however, have made this less than satisfactory for scholars. Furthermore, the book leaves the loaning library for a fairly long time, which may inconvenience them. As a result, in more recent years there has been a tendency to order photocopies or faxes of the particular pages needed.

Faxing copies of articles has been limited by the provisions of "fair use" in the copyright law. Fair use is an exception to copyright that was intended to support the relatively minor copying needed for scholarship and in some sense derives from the desire to let people make notes with pen and ink in libraries. For copying to qualify as fair use (and thus not require permission or payment), the law sets down four tests:

1. What is the purpose of the use? Educational uses are viewed more favorably than commercial ones.
2. What is the nature of the copyrighted work? Photographs and music (including song lyrics) are more protected than text.
3. What is the amount of the copying, both absolute and relative to the size of the original work? The more copied, the harder it is to argue fair use.
4. What is the effect of the copying on the market for the work? For example, copying out-of-print books is easier to justify than copying in-print books.

There are various guidelines circulated by libraries, although many users don't seem to adhere to them. Typical copying guidelines limit users to the following:

1. Prose: 1000 words or 10% of a work, whichever is less (except that a whole article may be copied if less than 2500 words)
2. Poetry: up to 250 words
3. Illustrations, cartoons, and so on: one per book or journal issue

For libraries requesting photocopies from other libraries, the guidelines limit copying to five articles from the most recent five years of a journal. A library needing more articles than that from the particular journal should buy its own copies (or pay copying royalties).

Dissatisfaction with the amount of photocopying led publishers to create the Copyright Clearance Center (CCC) to handle payments for photocopy royalties. Instead of trying to describe "fair use," the publishers simply said that people could make copies if they paid a particular royalty, which is printed at the bottom of each article. Royalty payments (minus about one-third administrative fee) are forwarded from the CCC to the publishers. For large companies that do a great deal of photocopying, the CCC negotiates bulk arrangements and distributes the payments based on a sampling process.

Supplementing library photocopies are the commercial document delivery services. Several companies, such as the Information Store, will find and fax or mail a copy of any article on request. They pay the fees imposed by the CCC and as a result charge perhaps $10 per article copied. Some libraries also operate extensive document delivery services; perhaps the best known is the Document Supply Centre of the British Library, located at Boston Spa, Yorkshire. However, libraries such as the John Crerar Library in Chicago also do considerable on-demand photocopying. Photocopying is not an answer to the budget problems of libraries, however (Hawkins

1994); the United Engineering Library in New York was unable to support itself that way despite a large journal collection.

In the digital world, shared collecting, like everything else, is going to become more complex. Since libraries will often be purchasing not just—or not even—a copy, but access rights to something that may or may not be on their premises, what rights will they have to redistribute it to other libraries? In CD-ROM sales, the library typically has no right to network for off-site use. Publishers will prefer to have no off-site use, of course. Under these circumstances, can libraries share collecting at all? Remember that shared collecting is not just a way of saving money on purchasing books; it is also a way of saving money on deciding what to purchase and on cataloging. Even if publishers say to libraries, "We have pay-by-the-use arrangements; it will not cost much to buy access to a rarely used publication," this will not reduce the library's cost in deciding whether it needs this publication or whether it is worth cataloging.

8.5 *New Kinds of Material and Their Durability*

Libraries can expect to receive much digital material that is new in both format and content. There will be Web pages, created by individuals and corresponding neither to journal articles (Web pages are not refereed) nor book manuscripts (Web pages are much shorter) nor most letters (Web pages are addressed to the world at large, not a single individual). There will be interactive software, including multimedia CD-ROMs, which is generally akin to published material but is very hard to evaluate for content. All of these objects will have the property that they cannot be evaluated without some kind of machine, and the interactive software may require particular kinds of equipment. Will every library have to collect all kinds of hardware so that they can check whether the material on their shelves is still in working order?

A library that feels that it has some patrons who wish to learn a foreign language already has the choice of buying books, CD-ROMs, videotapes, and audiotapes. Shortly it will have more ambitious multimedia programs on offer, Web pages, and downloadable shareware and priced software. Which are most important? What are the rules for using it? Which of these materials correspond to textbooks and which to advanced study materials? All of that may depend on the kind of interaction: we can easily imagine programs that watch the responses of their users and adjust from secondary school to postgraduate courses in some subject. Admittedly each of these materials could be studied to decide whether a library should buy it, but no library has the time to do so. A CD-ROM is already much harder to inspect than a book; a Web page will be even worse.

Again, each of these kinds of material may have different legal restrictions on what can be done with it. The library may be faced with material that cannot be lent out, but only used on the premises. Some material will become worthless quickly once the technology to run it becomes obsolete. This will pose a hard purchase decision, no matter how valuable the material is right now.

And, of course, the ability to combine new and old material will be vitally important. Just as an example, Figure 8.3 (Color Plate) is an overlay of a map of New England from 1771 with a modern view of where the boundaries really are. The old map was scanned; the newer map is a vector representation, provided by the U.S. government.

Libraries will have to come to some agreement on the appropriate acquisition policies for digital material. There is already shared cataloging; there may have to be shared evaluation of some of the more ephemeral material. Key questions will include the following:

1. Is anyone else proposing to maintain copies of this? If the material is coming from a commercial publisher, is it likely that the libraries (again excepting national libraries with a preservation mission) can normally expect the publisher to do what is necessary to keep it into the future? Do libraries have a legal right to try to maintain a copy?

2. Has this been peer-reviewed or in any other way checked and reviewed? If not, the default action may be not to spend effort trying to save it.

3. Are there scholarly references to this material? If so, how are those going to be fulfilled in the future?

4. Can a library obtain legal permission to do what needs to be done to make this available to library patrons? Can it share the material with other libraries?

Many have suggested that libraries should be "gateways" more than repositories for digital material. But what they do not recognize is that in the future, it may be just as expensive to be a gateway as to be a repository, given the conflicting needs of users, the publishers, and the copyright law.

One saving feature of digital information is that much of it can be saved with very little difficulty. Pure ASCII text can be stored very compactly and indexed automatically. Thus, a library could decide (aside from some copyright issues) to preserve the entire contents of netnews and incur relatively little cost. In fact such services are given away on the Internet today (see for example DejaNews) with merely the hope of advertising revenue to maintain them. So we might find that the modern version of an archive (stored, not evaluated, not cataloged in detail) was an electronic pile of free-text indexed messages or Web pages with only an overall disclaimer, while elsewhere in the digital library there would still be serious publications maintained to traditional standards. Gaining prestige would involve moving your writings from the archive pile to the library pile. The

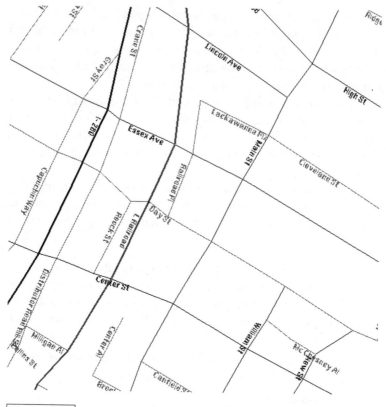

Figure 8.5   Vector map file

Cambridge University Library, for example, has two catalogs, one for material they select and one for material they receive via legal deposit and consider of less value.

Libraries in the future are likely to have both material that has been converted from older formats and material that is new, just as they do today. Depending on the need, either may be better. For example, Figure 8.4 (Color Plate) is part of a fire insurance map of Orange, New Jersey, dating from early this century, and Figure 8.5 is from the TIGER map file of Orange. There is a great deal of information in the old map that simply is not in the modern database, and just knowing that I-280 has been built across the map is not compensation. But remember that the TIGER file is automatically searchable, whereas there is no way to find a street in the old map except to look for it by eye. And the scanned old map is more than 100 times as large as the TIGER map. The last century devoted effort to both beauty and detail that we have traded for functionality and efficiency. Libraries are going to have to keep both kinds of data: the new and the old.

Figure 8.6   Diskettes (8-inch, 5.25-inch, and 3.5-inch) and CD-ROM

Table 8.1   1996 costs of nearline and online storage

	WORM Jukebox	Magneto-Optical Jukebox	Winchester Disks	CD-ROM
Capacity (GB)	300	40	9	.55
Cost	$150K	$30K	$2K	$.2K
Size (cu ft)	20	4	.1	.3
GB/cu ft	15	10	20	2
MB/$	2	1.3	4.5	1

Magnetic disks are the standard online storage medium. They are very sensitive to dust, but the most common current form, the Winchester technology, comes completely sealed. The usual warranty on a disk now runs five years. Again, however, regular copying is likely to be worthwhile. Each generation of computer disks is sufficiently smaller in size and larger in capacity that conversion often makes sense for economic reasons. Figure 8.6 shows different generations of diskettes.

Table 8.1 shows the 1996 costs of online and near-line storage technology. *Online* means immediately accessible; *near-line* is used to describe jukeboxes that are accessible without operator intervention, although it may take 15 seconds to a minute to load a platter into a reading device.

As mentioned before, a book such as *Pride and Prejudice* is about 0.5 MB. If we had most of our literature available in ASCII, we could store it more cheaply online than on paper. WORM (write once, read many) is a kind of optical storage in which the changes made are irreversible; this kind of storage system is attractive

Figure 8.7   Tape formats (clockwise from top left): steel, DECtape, $1/4$-inch, 8-mm, DAT, and $1/2$-inch

to libraries and others since it cannot be overwritten either intentionally or by accident. It can still be lost or destroyed in a fire, however, so some kind of second copy is always needed.

Magnetic tape is the oldest important digital storage medium that still matters to libraries and archives. Magnetic tape is a film of iron oxide on a substrate, originally steel but now mylar; samples are shown in Figure 8.7. Tape is an extremely economical way to store information, as shown in Table 8.2. It is commonly used for emergency backup and for offline storage of large amounts of material.

How long will it last? Digitally, this is the wrong question. Even tape, which is relatively fragile by the standards of many other computer media, is more vulnerable to technological obsolescence than to physical deterioration. I no longer know where I could find a 7-track drive or an 800-bpi tape drive. Even the newer 6250-bpi drives are disappearing as the world switches to 8-mm or 4-mm cartridges.

As another example of obsolescence, punched cards (see Figure 8.8) were made from quite strong paper. Waste paper dealers would pay two to three times the price of newsprint for it. Stored under reasonable humidity, it would certainly last for decades. But today you would only find a card reader in the Smithsonian or companies specializing in rescuing old data. Linear recording half-inch magnetic

Table 8.2   Properties of some digital media (1992)

	WORM	8-mm Exabyte	DAT
Capacity (GB)	6	5	1.3
Cost	$340	$5	$9
Wt (oz)	40	3	1.5
Dimensions (in.)	12.75 × 13.5 × .6	4.0 × 2.6 × .75	3 × 2.6 × .6
Volume (cu in.)	103	5.5	2.4
GB/cu ft	100	1100	480
GB/lb	2.4	27	14
MB/$	17	1000	140

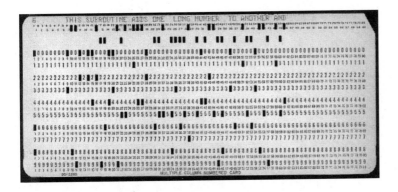

Figure 8.8   Punched card (used 1880–1970). At 80 bytes per card, it stored 160 KB/10 lbs or 16 KB/lb. Digital 8-mm cartridges store about 27 GB/lb

tape, since 1964, has been through 7-track and 9-track widths and at least the following densities: 200, 556, 800, 1600, 6250, and 31,250 bpi. Readers for any of the early densities would be very hard to find.

The lifetime of magnetic tape depends enormously on storage conditions. It also depends on the quality and type of the original tape. Helical-scan tape, for example, is less durable than linear recording tape. And tape intended for the consumer video market is thinner and likely to be less durable than tape intended for data applications. In fact, consumer videotape is probably the worst problem for libraries. It will neither last for many years nor will it stand many playings, and as video material it is hard to digitize. A frequently advertised service is to take people's 35-mm slides and convert them to videotape. We hope that the people using such a service know that while the slides are good for decades, the videotape will probably be gone in 5–10 years.

In general, few people rely on magnetic tape for decades. However, if stored properly, Table 8.3 shows some lifetime estimates posted on the Net by Ken Bates of DEC's Subsystems Performance Engineering Group. The key to long life is storage at low humidity and low temperature. Ideally, you would keep your tapes in a dry freezer (but be sure to defrost before use under circumstances that would prevent condensation!). Figures 8.9 and 8.10 show expected tape life and advice for the best storage conditions (Van Bogart 1995).

Table 8.3   Expected media lifetime

Media	Life (Years)
9-track tape	1–2
8-mm tape	5–10
4-mm tape	10
3480 cartridges (an IBM tape format)	15
DLT (digital linear tape) cartridges	20
magneto-optical	30
WORM	100

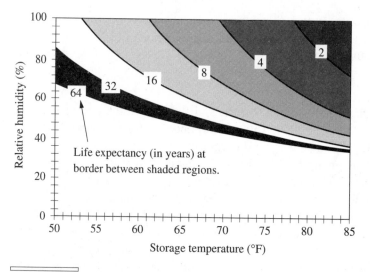

Figure 8.9   Tape life

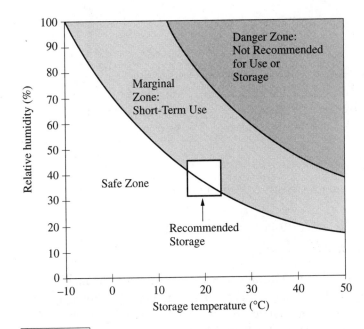

Figure 8.10   Tape storage recommendations

   Perhaps the most important thing to remember about durability of digital information is that permanence depends on copying. The devices used to store digital
information become obsolete quickly. Where today is a paper tape reader, a punched
card reader, a reader for 8-inch floppies, or a DECtape drive? Libraries must expect to have to copy material in a few years whether or not the physical media are
durable.

   Here are some of the hardware formats that have existed over the life of
computers:

- floppy disks in 8-inch, 5.25-inch, and 3.5-inch size
- digital linear-recording mylar-based magnetic tape, 1/2 inch, densities of 200,
  556, 800, 1600, and 6250 bpi
- punched paper cards (rectangular hole and round hole) and punched paper tape
- digital helical-scan mylar-based magnetic tape in 4 mm and 8 mm
- various linear tape cartridges such as 3480, QIC (quarter-inch cartridge), and
  DLT
- magnetic tape and disk jukeboxes (IBM datacell, digital video jukeboxes)
- removable cartridges for various kinds of large magnetic disks (IBM 2314, DEC
  RK05, RP05)

Table 8.4

For Sale in 1985		For Sale in 1995	
Wordstar	PFS:write	Microsoft Word	Clearlook
Leading Edge	Samna	Lotus Word Pro	WordPerfect
Multimate	WordPerfect	DeScribe	Accent Professional
Microsoft Word	Xywrite	Nota Bene	Xywrite

- magneto-optical cartridges (mostly 5.25-inch but some 8.5-inch and 3.5-inch), in several styles
- WORM optical storage, some 12-inch, some 5.25-inch
- CD-ROM and CD-R media

Hardware lifetimes seem to be typically 5 to 10 years. Even if the medium you have is not completely obsolete, it may still pay to abandon it. Why should a library store 1600-bpi ½-inch reels, which hold 46 MB in 140 cubic inches, when it can store 8-mm cartridges, which hold 5 GB in 5.5 cubic inches? Instead of .5 GB per cubic foot, the library can hold 1000 GB per cubic foot. It is not the shelf-space saving that matters so much, but the handling costs are lower. The new cartridges are also easier and faster to load, as well as taking less time to get off the shelf. Maintenance costs are also higher for old rather than new equipment, and may rise as the old stuff goes off the market. And even if a library wished to try to keep old equipment running, eventually the lack of spare parts will do it in.

What is even worse than the variety of hardware formats is the plethora of software formats. There are many more software formats than there are hardware manufacturers, and they have flourished for even shorter times. Table 8.4 shows the word processing programs advertised in a 1985 issue of *Byte* compared with those advertised in 1995. Dealing with old software is even worse than dealing with old hardware. There are many more software formats, and they come and go much more rapidly than do hardware formats. Software formats may be extremely complex, even deliberately so (to keep people from switching to competitors' products). They might be kept running by simulation on modern machines, and some work of this sort has been done. A full emulation for the PDP-10 exists, for example, to rescue the old software for it (including nearly everything done in AI research in the 1970s, for example). But, in general, we will need to convert old formats to new formats, preferably standard ones (Born 1995). This may not be easy. For example, Microsoft Word 6.0 will not read a Microsoft Word 1.0 document. Word 3.0 will, however, and Word 6.0 will read Word 3.0, so if you have saved the intermediate program, the conversion can be done.

The image world is actually in better shape than the ASCII world, however, since there are more accepted standards for images. In text representation, not only are the older formats obsolete, but they may have different capabilities than newer software. For example, the EBCDIC and ASCII character sets have different characters in them: EBCDIC has no curly braces {}, and ASCII does not have the hook character for "logical not" ¬. The collating sequences changed, so that putting a file in order means something slightly different. More recent word processor languages have introduced still more capabilities. Suppose a library has a catalog prepared in the 1960s. It is unlikely to have accent marks indicated for foreign titles. Should those now be inserted? The amount of work required to do that will far exceed any other costs in preserving the old title list and may in fact be more work than redoing the entire job.

The worst situation of all is in databases. Commercial database systems change even more than image or text languages, and there is less context from which to decide what something means without the program or the database schema. A document with the formatting commands garbled may still be worth something. A table of numbers without the labels is essentially worthless. And the job of editing a database to move it to standard relational format can be immense; again, depending on what was in the original database, there may be undecidable issues requiring reference to some other source of information.

The message, of course, is to use standard formats. Refreshing SGML is likely to be straightforward by comparison with WordPerfect. Similarly, JPEG will be readable in the future. At a minimum, since these formats are described in public sources, you could always write your own program to read them, which may not be true of proprietary formats. We may find ourselves with a new kind of professional, a "digital paleographer," who specializes in understanding the formats used by bankrupt software vendors.

Fortunately, the costs of copying are decreasing rapidly. If we assume a 50% decrease in cost every five years, then any long-term cost for data migration is small compared with the cost of the first copy. The key to survival of digital information is systematic and regular copying, not air conditioning.

8.6   *Summary and Responsibilities to the Future*

We do not yet have collection principles for a digital library. There are no published lists of recommended holdings or details of what a library has to have for university accreditation. Furthermore, a digital library is more dynamic than a paper library; items will come and go more rapidly. This gives digital librarians an opportunity to look more carefully at what is used and what is useful and to design collections that follow the needs of users more quickly than was possible in the past. The switch to access instead of purchase should leave us with better future collections, not just larger ones.

The problems of editing older formats to create current documents is harder. If the old format has some property that it is hard to convert to the newer format, how much effort should be spent trying to imitate or emulate it? Is it better to preserve the actual appearance of the older format, or its spirit? These issues resemble some of the problems we have always faced in other areas. What should be saved under the heading "Beethoven's Ninth symphony"? The score? A studio recording? Or a live performance with audience reaction? We can go to a church that existed in Bach's day and perform one of his keyboard works on the organ using 17th-century performance techniques. The result will be sound waves almost the same as those Bach's listeners would have heard. But the impression will be different. To our ears, the organ is not the standard keyboard instrument, and it will always sound old compared to the piano and the keyboard synthesizer. And Bach is no longer the most recent composer; we have heard Beethoven, Brahms, and the Beatles. Many of the same issues will arise in digital preservation. Are we trying to produce the best possible copy of the old object or something that will serve the same function to a modern reader or audience? Homer is certainly valuable in ancient Greek, but may be more useful in a translation. At times we may not be able to do anything satisfactory. We do not know what a David Garrick stage performance was really like, nor an oration by Cicero. And what should we do to preserve the work of Julia Child or Jacques Pepin? Print their recipes? Videotape their cooking? Freeze-dry the food? Or take a gas chromatograph trace of the smell?

Economics

ECONOMIC JUSTIFICATION FOR libraries has been hard to achieve. The economies of scale in publishing and in libraries make it hard to come up with suitable prices; in addition, the wide disparities in the use of material in libraries make cost recovery pricing additionally unsatisfactory as a base for funding libraries. The economics of libraries is tied to that of the publishing industry and depends critically on the economies of scale in publishing. Over the years, publishing has increased its economies of scale significantly, and digital publishing is making those economies even larger. This chapter discusses how digital libraries can be paid for, beyond the simple issue of whether they can simply be cheaper than the paper libraries we have had until now. This chapter is not really about libraries; it is about the sale of digital information in general, not just to and by libraries.

To confuse matters, the job of libraries is expanding. Once upon a time, library patrons were always physically present in the building where the books were held. Now libraries provide remote access across the campus and across the world. They do fax delivery, electronic displays, and other methods of information access. They provide sound recordings, videos, multimedia, and computer files. They have a tradition of providing access to books for no charge. Should that tradition also apply to these new services and these new users? Some of the new services appear to be filling needs previously filled by bookstores, journal subscriptions, and other paid-for activities. Some might be quite expensive to continue operating (e.g., levels of computer support counseling adequate to deal with much modern software). Does that mean that libraries should charge for these services, and if so, on what basis?

Digital libraries are going to need a new model for funding. Among the possibilities are

- institutional support, as most of them now have
- charging users for unusual services, perhaps including assistance
- charging users for everything
- finding support from advertisers
- finding some other mechanism for support—for example, pledge breaks on the Internet (public appeals for donations)

Libraries will also have to realize that there are many other organizations hoping to be the supplier of digital information for a fee, including publishers, bookstores, computer centers, and other libraries. Can libraries extend their reach into areas these organizations now serve? Or will the other organizations extend theirs, cutting back the use made of libraries? The model of a library is that it provides information free, reducing costs by sharing those costs among a community of users. Will that model survive in the digital world?

Libraries suffer to some extent because few of their transactions are monetized. Thus, people have little feeling for what the library costs and also have great trouble assigning a value to it. José-Marie Griffiths and Don King (now at the University of Michigan) have done many studies on the perceived value of libraries (King, Castro, and Jones 1994). For example, they surveyed libraries in corporate organizations (Griffiths and King 1993). The typical corporate research organization spends a range of $400–1000 per year per professional employee. If this is compared with what it would cost to replace the library with other sources of information, they report numbers showing a 3:1 return on investment. Table 9.1 compares the cost of documents from inside and outside a company (per professional staff member per year). So, they argue, the cost per professional per year would be $3290 to obtain

Table 9.1

	Now
$515	library subscription cost
$95	library
$840	professionals finding cost
$4100	professionals reading cost
	No library
$3290	getting document
$840	professionals finding cost
$4100	professionals reading cost

the same documents outside, compared to $610 in a library, or a savings of $2680 per employee per year, greatly outweighing the $800 or so that might be spent on the library. And the information found in libraries does generally benefit the people that use it. Table 9.2, again from King and Griffiths, compares the cost to find different items against the savings claimed from having found it. King's data (see Figure 9.1) also show that those who read more are the more productive employees;

Table 9.2

Item	Cost to Acquire	Savings Reported
Journal article	$37	$310
Book	$83	$650
Tech. report	$77	$1090

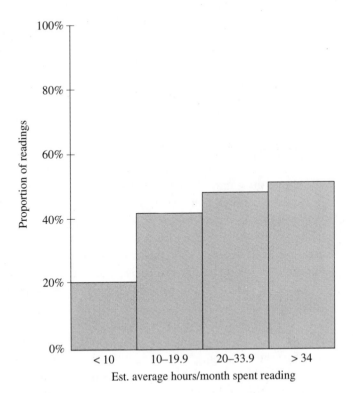

Figure 9.1   Proportion of readings that achieve savings vs. time spent reading

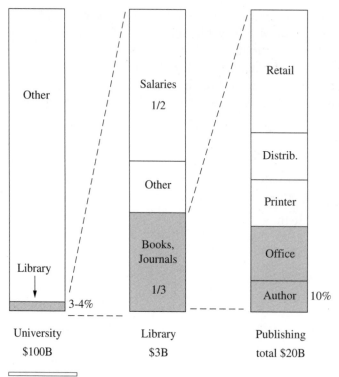

Figure 9.2   Library economics

and the more people use the library, the more likely they are to make savings by doing so.

It is commonplace to talk about information exchange as a circle in which scholars write articles that are published, stored in libraries, and then read by scholars. Figure 9.2 summarizes very roughly a financial view of libraries. The average U.S. university spends about 3% of its budget on its library; with the university establishment as a whole spending $100 billion per year, this means that about $3 billion per year goes to libraries. Of what the library receives, about one-third goes to buy books, with half going on staff and the rest on computers and supplies (the typical U.S. university does not monetize building costs, which would probably be about one-third of the current budget if they were calculated). Finally, of the money spent buying books from publishers, only about 10% goes back to the authors. Thus, viewing the university as a system designed to move information from inside one head to inside another head, there are many inefficiencies in the system. This has been viewed by digital futurists as a great opportunity, but so far neither librarians nor anyone else have been able to improve the system.

9.1   *Traditional Economics and Economies of Scale*

The mantra of the traditional economist is "price equals incremental cost," based on supply and demand curves. These curves show the changes in price as more or less of some commodity is needed in the marketplace. As drawn by economists, these curves look something like Figure 9.3. The demand line says that as the price of something goes up, the quantity that people are asking for at that price goes down. The supply curve here suggests that as the quantity needed of something goes up, the cost to provide it also goes up. Where the curves cross, transactions take place. As an example of a real demand curve, Figure 9.4 is a plot of Don King's showing the number of times a week that a corporate researcher will visit a library, plotted against the time it takes to get there (time is money) (Griffiths and King 1993).

In a supply and demand plot, the price at the crossing point is the cost at which one more unit can be produced, that is, the *incremental cost*. Thus, the economic rule is that price will equal incremental cost. The shaded area is the *surplus value*, the amount of money the producer left on the table: people would have paid more than the price at the crossing point for goods. If the seller is able to charge a different price for each purchaser, and can know which purchasers will pay how much, the seller can capture this money. The most familiar example of this is in the sale of airline tickets; airlines use nontransferability of tickets to keep people from buying tickets from each other, and they use rules like advance purchase or

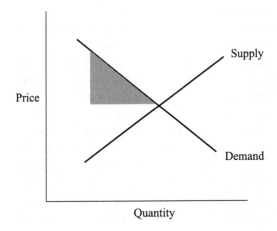

Figure 9.3   Supply and demand curves

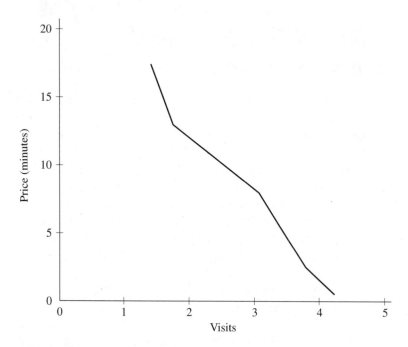

Surveys of professionals in 21 organizations (N = 73,303; n = 7,366)

Figure 9.4   Visits to library

Saturday night stay requirements to separate the business travelers, willing to pay more, from the leisure travelers.

All this assumes, of course, that as more and more of some product is demanded, the cost of producing it goes up. This assumption is reasonable for the 18th-century Cornish tin mines that Adam Smith was thinking about; as you need more tin, the miners must either dig deeper or dig up less rich ores, and in either case their cost per pound of tin increases. However, this has nothing to do with modern publishing and even less with digital technology. In these new technologies today, we have economies of scale; it costs *less per item* to produce many items than to produce fewer.

With digital technology, the problem is even worse. Digitally, the incremental cost to view something is very close to zero. Even the few staffing expenses that might increase with the number of users in a paper library are hardly there digitally. Worse yet, the ease with which electronic information can be copied and transmitted raises expectations in the minds of users that copies will be free or cheap. This then frightens the publishers, who still need a way to cover their average costs if they are to be able to produce material.

In printing journals or books, the costs of typesetting, editorial, and press make-ready dominate. The American Chemical Society estimates 75% of its costs are startup, and other journal publishers agree. HMSO (Her Majesty's Stationery Office, the official British government publisher) prices *Hansard* (the Parliamentary proceedings) at £12 per day, expecting to break even on sales of 5600 copies. The incremental cost of a copy is £1.07, so that 91% of the cost is startup. If startup costs are divided among more and more copies, the cost per copy decreases. Conversely, if press runs start to get shorter, the price per copy will have to go up if the publisher is to break even on the book. In electronic information there is the further difficulty of a low barrier to entry. People can go into the business easily; it doesn't cost a lot to set up a Web site (compared with buying a newspaper printing plant, for example). The combination of low entry barrier and low incremental costs often leads to price wars alternating with monopolies; the airline industry is the most familiar example, and U.S. railroads behaved similarly in the late 19th century.

9.2   *Scholarly Publications Today*

Libraries are finding it increasingly difficult to buy books and journals. The steady increase in the cost of publications as well as the steady increase in the number of publications is outrunning the financial resources of libraries. Since libraries respond by cutting the number of books they buy, publishers print fewer copies of books intended mostly for sale to libraries. And that means that the prices have to go up again, putting even more financial pressure on the libraries. Figure 9.5 shows the number of books purchased by U.S. research libraries, compared with the number of books published (Cummings et al. 1992).

Consider, as an example of the problems caused by current printing economics, the cost of *Chemical Abstracts* (*CA*). In the 1950s, the preprocess costs of *CA* were

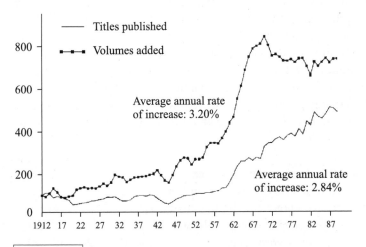

Figure 9.5   Book purchases vs. published titles (1912=100)

paid by a group of chemical companies, *CA* cost dozens of dollars per year, and individual chemists subscribed to it. Today it costs $17,400 per year, and even large libraries have trouble finding the money to subscribe. The number of subscriptions drops regularly, as library after library cuts back, and despite the best efforts *CA* can make to mechanize and become more efficient, the cost of the publication goes up (of course, its size also increases, as the amount of published chemistry continues to increase). Fortunately, many *CA* users are now online, providing access for people at institutions that no longer subscribe on paper.

The number of scholarly periodicals continues to increase as do their subscription prices. And libraries, faced with increasing expenditures for new equipment, have ever greater difficulties keeping up with the costs of publications. Libraries spend about one-third of their budgets on materials purchases and few get budget increases comparable to the journal price inflation. As a result libraries increasingly have less material directly available and get more of it from remote sources. About the only option for a paper-based library faced with price increases that it cannot pay is to stop buying material and obtain it on demand instead.

9.3 *Models for Library Funding*

Why should there be libraries at all? Harold Varian (Dean of the School of Information and Management Systems at Berkeley) has described libraries as "buying clubs" in which different individuals who would like to have some resource, but who cannot each afford to buy it, pool their money to buy one copy that is shared (Varian and Roehl 1997). Computers used to be bought like that. Is this an adequate model in the digital world?

Consider one of Varian's examples that tries to take into account both economies of scale and different users placing different values on the same item. Traditional economic pricing may not work out in such a case. Suppose it costs $7 to make the first copy of some object and the second copy is then free. Suppose there are two customers, Smith and Jones. If Smith will pay $6 and Jones will pay $3: (1) at a price of $3, the manufacturer gets only $6 and cannot stay in business; (2) at a price of $6, the manufacturer gets only $6 and cannot stay in business. There is a total of $9 available, more than the cost of production of two items, but no single price that is acceptable.

Some other assumptions seem equally frustrating. If Smith will pay $8 and Jones will pay $3, then the item can be produced, but Jones will not get one. Perhaps the most counterintuitive is the case when Smith will pay $20 and Jones will pay $8. The most lucrative choice for the manufacturer is to charge a price of $20. Smith pays it, and Jones, even though willing to pay more than the entire cost of production, doesn't get a copy. But no lower price than $20 will bring the publisher more money. Varian discusses two solutions to this paradox: price discrimination and bundling.

Some industries with this kind of problem move to different prices for different users. This may take the form of defining different services in a way that leaves the public with a perception that different value is being delivered, but still let the manufacturer gain economies of scale. For example, airlines put people paying widely different fares on the same airplane, and the same postal service letter carriers deliver different kinds of mail. In the publishing business, a traditional separation was hardcover against paperback editions. In the context of digital libraries, many ftp sites differentiate between local users and remote users, or between authorized and anonymous users, and then limit either the number of connections or the number of requests that can be made by the less preferred users. Other possibilities include restrictions on bandwidth, on time of day, on currency of information, or on amount of information.

Another answer, and one historically relevant to libraries, is bundling. In the first case, when Smith will pay $6 and Jones will pay $3 but the production cost is $7 for both of them, suppose there are two such publications. Suppose that for the second publication Smith will pay $3 and Jones will pay $6. Then they can each pay $8 for both publications together and the publisher can recover the $14 cost. This is what libraries do: they let people who place different values on different items get together to buy them. And, in this set of assumptions, the publishers are better off because the buying club is there.

Unfortunately, buying clubs do not always help the publisher. In this example, for example, since the price was set at $8 for both or $4 for each publication, there is an item for which Smith had been willing to pay $6, but gets it for $4. Could the publisher get that extra $2 from Smith? Perhaps the price for the publications could be raised to $9 for both. But what if there is also a Robinson, and Robinson will only pay $4 for each publication? Then $4 is still the best bundled price; it is not worth forfeiting the $8 from Robinson to get $2 more from Smith and Jones. The publisher can wistfully think that if it were possible to sell specific copies to specific purchasers at known prices, then each of Smith, Jones, and Robinson could be charged the maximum they are willing to pay. In terms of the supply and demand diagram, the entire surplus value could be captured by the manufacturer.

In the above discussion, it has been assumed that each of the buyers is going to get a copy of the publication. Of course, in general with libraries the number of copies bought is less than the number of patrons interested, since they are sharing the copies by borrowing them. Public libraries started as a commercial business in the United Kingdom in the second quarter of the 18th century, as a way of loaning copies of the book *Pamela* and other novels. Eighty percent of the rentals then were fiction, and 76% are fiction today. Partly this reflects the public desire for entertainment (how often do movie theatres show documentaries?); partly it reflects the unlikelihood that mystery novels will be reread. The smaller the chance that a reader will want to go through the book more than once, the less the advantage of owning rather than renting or borrowing a copy. Even if the library is providing copies at no incremental charge, the cost of traveling to it will still discourage its use for books that will be needed frequently.

The idea that public libraries should be paid for by taxes rather than their users is a U.S. invention transferred back to Europe. Private lending libraries survived on a fairly large scale in the United Kingdom until a few decades ago (Boots, the chemists, were well known for their lending services). A few examples of subscription libraries still survive (the London Library in the United Kingdom and the New York Society Library in the United States). These, however, charge by the year rather than by the book borrowed, so they are a different economic model. Many university libraries charge nonaffiliated users, although the charge is often more to limit the demand on the library than it is a way of raising revenue.

The private rental library familiar to most of us is the video store. Prerecorded videotapes started out around 1979 at prices of $90, and some stores started renting them for $5. By 1988 the purchase price was down to $50 and the rental price down to $2. From the standpoint of the movie studios, this was a lot of money slipping through their fingers: people who might have bought a movie were choosing to rent instead. Although the studios tried to discriminate, with different prices for tapes to be rented rather than tapes to be retained by a consumer, they ran afoul of the "right of first sale" doctrine. This rule basically says that when you buy something you can then do what you want with the physical object. It prevented the movie companies from selling a videotape and then claiming to control whether or not it could be rented. So, in 1988 Disney decided to start selling some of its tapes cheaply ($15–25) to see if they could get more money than they were getting in rentals, and changed the market completely.

Again, items that will be viewed more than once are a better candidate for purchase than rental. It is not an accident that Disney is the studio that started selling tapes; they make children's movies, and children are the most likely customers to watch the same video over and over again. Among movies intended for grown-ups, people are more likely to watch a comedy than a drama twice. Thus, as Varian points out, Hollywood took *Fatal Attraction* and produced 500,000 copies to sell at $89.95 each, while the "press run" for *Good Morning Vietnam* was 2,000,000 copies to sell at $29.95 each. Clearly the first was expected to be a rental title, while the second was a sale title. Documentaries, even more likely to be watched more than once, are typically sold; when was the last time you saw an ad to *rent* the Time-Life history of anything?

The movie studios also try price discrimination, in those areas where they can. Although once tapes are publicly sold people can do what they want with them (except copy them), there is a carefully staged delivery of the movie. First it is placed in theatres at $7.50 per viewing; then it goes on pay-per-view at $5 per viewing;

then to video rentals at $2 per rental; and finally to cable TV and then broadcast TV. Intermixed in all of this are hotel and airline viewings, plus sequential delivery around the world. The goal is to find the people who are desperately anxious to see this particular movie and get them to pay the higher price, while still getting some money from those who don't care much which movie they see.

Which model is likely to appeal to the operator of a digital library? Private rental libraries for books are no longer viable, but video stores certainly are. Why? The answer is the incredible concentration of video rentals: 80% of the rentals each week are the top 20 films. Thus, there is a predictable demand for a few films and the sharing of costs works well. By contrast, book sales are distributed over an enormously larger number of titles. In typical years the United States produced 462 movies (1994) and published 49,276 new books (1992). The large number of new books makes it difficult to concentrate demand.

Despite all of these comments, electronics is spreading very rapidly, particularly through CD-ROM. Simon & Schuster expects to get a quarter of its $2 billion revenues from electronic products. But they are not yet ready to publish on the Net itself: "We don't think there is safe commerce on the information superhighway . . . Until we can be assured of copyright protection and until we can be assured authors and Simon & Schuster will be paid for our work, we are reluctant to post copy on the Internet," according to Simon & Schuster's Andrew Giangola (senior VP of communications).

9.4 *Paying for Electronic Information*

There are a great many ways in which publishers might choose to charge for digital material. Donald Hawkins published a review of information pricing in 1989 that listed, among other charging mechanisms, connect time, CPU usage, fee per search, fee per hit, and download fees (Hawkins 1989). All of these have one or another kind of problem: the users may not understand them, the charges may be unpredictable, or they may encourage unreasonable behavior. Vendors normally wish to charge for smaller and smaller units of activity, following traditional economic advice to allocate costs as well as can be done. This minimizes the risk that somehow the publisher will suffer from some kind of gaming behavior in which someone finds a hole in the charging method that allows them to get a great deal of service for less money than had been anticipated. But charging many small amounts for small transactions imposes high administrative costs.

In fact, some publishers do prefer simpler systems. Journal publishers, for example, are accustomed to subscriptions. Subscriptions give them many advantages, such as predictability of revenue, a six-month advance on the average payment (for yearly subscriptions), and no problem with bad checks and debt collection. Thus, they would often like to keep the prepaid subscription model in the digital world. The certainty and simplicity are worth something to them, too.

The other side is represented by some computer scientists proposing models involving micropayments in which each tiny use of anything would be paid for separately. Ted Nelson, who coined the word *hypertext*, has now proposed the name *transclusion* to describe the process by which people include quotations from other documents. In the future, instead of quoting an author's words, other authors would provide a pointer to them. The act of following this pointer would incur a charge, paid by the reader. As Nelson wrote, "Every document will contain a built-in 'cash register' . . . but the system only works if the price is low. If the price is high then different users will [use and] hand each other dated [paper] copies" (Nelson 1996). In the future, in his view, this sentence would not be copied out in my writing; a reference to the file would be included, and as someone read this page they would pay a small amount to him for that sentence. He believes this would change the way we transmit information, or, to quote his words, "Open transmedia—unique in power to aid understanding and to solve the copyright issue—represents a vital singularity in the great family of media cosmologies."

Ted Nelson has been followed in his desire for micropayments by CNRI (Vint Cerf and Bob Kahn) and also by such groups as Marvin Sirbu's NetBill project at CMU (Sirbu and Tygar 1995) and Tenenbaum's CommerceNet (Tenenbaum et al. 1995). All believe that a detailed, byte-by-byte charging algorithm is both fair and implementable. However, many librarians feel that per-use charging is basically a bad idea, since it will discourage use of the library. There is an old saying, "A month in the lab can save you an hour in the library," but if people are charged for setting foot in the library and not for the time they spend in their own lab, scientists and engineers are likely to hesitate to use the library.

Among the models followed by commercial publishers are the following (Krasilovsky 1995):

1. *Monthly subscription fees.* Times Mirror, for example, charges $6.95 per month. The Electric Library at http://www.elibrary.com charges $9.95 per month for 150 newspapers, 800 magazines, and thousands of books (a total of one billion words, or the equivalent of about a 20,000-book library).

2. *Per-minute fees.* Services such as America Online (AOL) will remit 10–20% of the money they collect per-minute from their subscribers (typically they charge a few dollars per hour) to the online information provider whose information is being browsed. This only yields a few cents per minute, or perhaps $1 per hour, however. By comparison, the traditional online industry got $1.145 billion from about seven million hours of connect time in 1993, or an average of $146 per hour (Williams 1995). Figure 9.6 shows, for example, the revenues and profits of Mead Data Central (Lexis/Nexis). They have shown steady growth

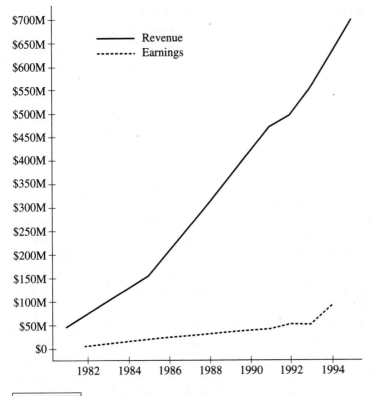

Figure 9.6 Revenues and profits of Mead Data Central

in revenues, but profits have lagged behind as competition from Westlaw cut into what was once a Lexis monopoly.

3. *Bounties for signing up new users.* Again, the online services, trying hard to grow, will pay publishers whose content attracts new customers. In fact, during 1994 Time, Inc. received $448,000 from AOL as bounties and only $118,000 for per-minute reading fees.

4. *Transaction fees for downloading.* Publishers selling magazine articles, for example, can charge each time an article is downloaded. Mead Data Central, for example, using Open Market Systems software, sells articles to small businesses for prices ranging from $1 to $5 per article.

5. *Advertising.* This is the most common use of online presence: to notify prospective readers of new books or to provide tie-ins of online material to existing printed matter. For example, the Electronic Newsstand offers tables of contents and some articles from a variety of magazines as a way of attracting traditional subscribers.

6. *Cost avoidance.* Online information can replace some calls that used to be made to customer service; although this is perhaps less important in publishing, in the computer industry help-line costs are very important and reductions can easily justify a Web site (one manufacturer informally claims savings of $4 million per year).

On balance, a great many articles are available online today for free, particularly scientific papers, and a great many more available for a price. Full-text books are still rarely available online except for out-of-copyright works, although there is considerable access to reference works through the paid services.

There have been some suggestions that online availability of information, even free, would stimulate the sale of paper books. John Ousterhout's Tcl/Tk book was available online, and it appears that online readers then often went out and bought the paper copy (Ousterhout 1994). On the other hand, the *New Republic* used to put its entire text online free via the Electronic Newsstand and gave up doing that, feeling that it was cutting into sales. It seems unlikely that giving away text online is really a good way to boost sales of the equivalent paper book, but it is probably not a one-for-one substitution either.

All of the simple payment schemes run into difficulties providing off-site access to the library material. Obviously, the library would like to provide off-site access. In fact, on many campuses that have been wired, the library was often the first general information source for the students and faculty, with the online catalog for the library preceding the online phone book and course directory. But use from student rooms poses increased possibilities for abuse and increased difficulties charging for some users and not for others. Some libraries must, in addition, deal with either traditional or legal rights of alumni or the general public to use their collections; typically publishers insist that these rights only apply to those who physically appear at the library building.

A possible model as a solution to this problem is the simultaneous-use site license concept in software. Many software programs are now sold to large organizations on the basis of "n people at once may use this program," and the purchasing organization pays proportional to the number of simultaneous users. This arrangement allows them to let everyone use a program without perceiving an enormous cost for a program that people only use once in a while; yet for those programs that are so important that a hundred people at once may be using them, the vendor gets a fair payment. Since use within the organization is fairly open (usually enough licenses are bought to cover even busy times), there is little incentive for anyone to cheat (Blyskal 1983).

The serious question is whether there is enough financial support for the information on the Web. Traditional scholarly magazines are not advertiser-supported; who will pay for the material libraries want? Will there develop any tradition of editorial independence on the Internet, or will ads only appear on Web pages that plug those products? At present, the economic balance is as follows:

1. AT&T, by offering Internet connectivity free for a year, has cast gloom on anyone's ability to make money by selling connectivity.
2. Content sales are still few and far between.
3. Sales of goods are growing rapidly, but no one knows what level they will reach.
4. Advertising may not be lucrative enough, especially for the more scholarly uses.

9.5 *Access versus Ownership*

The speed with which digital information can be transmitted makes it relatively unimportant whether the information is stored in a particular library, so long as that library has the ability to get it when someone needs it. The earlier discussion of library cooperation discussed shared collecting (see Section 8.4). In principle, a library in a digital world hardly needs any collections of its own at all; it only needs the data communications resources and legal permissions to access the material its patrons need.

This model also fits well with the desires of the publishers to retain control of the material they provide. If libraries do not own material outright, but have only bought the right to access it as needed, then the rules under which they can deliver it to their patrons are specified by the contract between the library and the publisher. For example, the publisher can try to limit the ability of the library to loan or deliver the items off its premises or to allow use by people unconnected with the school. Just as the libraries see opportunities to expand their "markets" by delivering information directly that had previously been obtained from bookstores, the publishers see ways to bypass the libraries and sell information directly to students and faculty.

The likelihood that libraries will not own information outright raises future dangers. At present, when a library cancels its subscription to a journal, it at least retains ownership of the issues it has already bought. In the future, if all the library had was a license to access the material, when the subscription is canceled, the library will lose the rights to the material it had previously provided to users. This may not matter much, since the subscriptions that are canceled are likely to represent material that was not much used. The reverse problem may also arise. When something goes "out of print," will this mean that the publisher no longer supports access to it? If the library does not own a copy, does this mean that there is no longer *any* way for the users to read it?

Even the temporary contract raises issues libraries will have to face. Most libraries have not historically charged their users, nor kept track of what they did with the books they borrowed. Publishers may also wish to approve of users (for example, an educational discount for student use of a law resource may only apply to students enrolled in the law school, not to other students). And the collection sharing that libraries have begun to rely upon to control costs may be forbidden by the license agreement.

Licensed access may require per-minute or per-byte charging and may require a degree of record-keeping that is against traditional library ethics and may offend some readers. The publishers are likely to want to have the most detailed possible record-keeping and pricing, since it will be part of their marketing methods. They will argue, with some justice, that per-unit pricing will make it possible for libraries to acquire rights to access material that they could not afford if they needed unlimited-use rights. But the libraries are not anxious to get into the charge-back problems and would rather have the security of budgeting provided by unlimited-use licenses.

9.6   *Importance of Administrative Costs*

Economic studies, to be valid, must consider administrative costs. The fear of piracy has introduced enormous problems into the operation of network publishing. John Garrett, VP of Business Development for Planet Direct, reports that when IBM produced a CD-ROM to commemorate the 500th anniversary of the Columbus voyage, they spent over $1 million clearing rights, of which only about $10,000 was paid to the rights holders; all the rest went into administrative costs.

Many holders of intellectual property insist on maintaining very close control over their work. Irving Berlin was known for choosing which theatrical company would be allowed to perform which of his works. The copyright holder may wish to get as much money as possible, or may want artistic control, or may wish to prevent further reproduction of something now believed to be erroneous or embarrassing (Stowe 1995). Or, even more frustrating, the copyright holder may be hard to find, too busy to answer mail, or refuse to sell any kind of license out of fear of making some kind of mistake with new technology. A class of my students assigned to write letters to intellectual property owners asking for permission to digitize something and put it on a Web page, and offering to pay, only got six answers from eighteen letters after two months. And only two of the six actually offered a license.

As guidance toward what is actually being charged, in their replies to these letters, the *New York Times* asked for $100 per month to put an article on a Web site, and *Sports Illustrated* wanted $250 for a picture. Picture Network International advertises rates of $30 for an image to be used on a Web page.

Unfortunately, the laws are being changed to make the administrative costs ever higher, partly at the request of copyright holders wishing to have even more power relative to users, and partly as a result of the United States' bringing its laws into agreement with the Berne Convention. Until 1976 published materials in the United States had to carry a copyright notice that included a date and the name of the copyright holder, and the material had to be registered with the Copyright Office. When the United States ratified the Berne Convention, it became unnecessary to place a notice on works, and with the next revision of the law it is probable that there will be virtually no advantage to registering a work with the Copyright Office. As a result a future reader may be faced with documents that show no date and no author and are not registered in any central office. How is the user expected to determine whether the work is still in copyright or to find the appropriate rights owner from whom to buy permission?

In other intellectual property areas, clearinghouses have been used to reduce administrative costs. The best-known examples are probably those in the recorded music area. ASCAP (American Society of Composers, Authors, and Publishers), BMI (Broadcast Music, Inc.), and SESAC (Society of European Stage Authors and Composers) license large numbers of works for a blanket fee. For example, radio stations pay about 2.5% of their gross income for a blanket license to play all the music they want. Few musical works are licensed on a one-time basis. ASCAP overhead is about 20%.

Similarly, for traditional photocopying of journals, the blanket license organization is the Copyright Clearance Center of Salem, Massachusetts. Although its procedures provide for very detailed per-copy pricing, in practice it is moving to blanket licenses as well, with sampling techniques to decide on the fee. There is now an additional Author's Registry trying to provide low-overhead licensing payments to authors.

In photography, there are large photo agencies that can provide millions of photographs upon request. Among the best known are Picture Network International (owned by the *Chicago Tribune*), Hulton-Deutsch (which owns or has rights to the BBC, Fox, and Reuters archives), the Bettmann Archive, the Bridgeman Art Library, SIGMA, the Image Bank, and Black Star. A new company, CORBIS, which is owned by Bill Gates, has been buying digital rights to many pictures (including the Bettmann Archive and the works of Ansel Adams).

Historically, individual photographers tended to sell one-time rights to their pictures. Thus, magazines sometimes cannot put their full content online because they do not have the right to do anything with the illustrations other than print them once. This has already made difficulties in building online systems for some current popular magazines.

All of these organizations have problems with intellectual property protection that predate computers. For example, the musical organizations regularly inspect bars and restaurants to see if they are playing recorded music without a license.

Nevertheless, they seem in better shape than those areas where no standard contracts exist. Furthermore, those areas that have compulsory licensing do not seem to be particularly troubled. Playwrights in the United States, for example, can and do decide which theatre companies they wish to let perform their works. Songwriters must allow any singer to record a copy of any song (that has been recorded once); a standard royalty is paid via the Harry Fox Agency. The compulsory license does not seem to be a disaster for songwriters.

In some countries, government-imposed charges attempt to compensate authors for the use of intellectual property in or from libraries. In the United Kingdom, for example, there is a "public lending right," which provides payments to authors when their books are borrowed from libraries. A similar scheme operates in Australia and paid $4.8 million (Australian) to 8800 authors and publishers in 1995–96. More interesting is the tax on blank audiotape that is imposed in Germany, with the proceeds paid to composers.

Electronic distribution has moved from ftp sites through newsgroups (and mailing lists) to the Web. Most of these systems allow anyone to send out anything, leading to names like "netnoise" (for netnews) and to Purdue University's Eugene Spafford's likening of Usenet to a herd of elephants with diarrhea. Online distribution provides for the availability of machine-readable data tables. In some areas, such as biotechnology, this is essential, and so that field now depends upon electronic information distribution. The appeal of electronically distributed preprints is also obvious: speed, total author control of format, and no hassle sending out paper. Preprint distribution has no refereeing. However, since in general refereeing serves not to reject papers altogether but to route them to a more suitable place (most rejected papers appear eventually, just in another journal), some see this as a minor problem.

And certainly preprint distribution is popular. High-energy physics now depends entirely on a bulletin board at Los Alamos National Laboratory run by Paul Ginsparg. It has 20,000 users and gets 35,000 hits per day. There are 50 hits on each paper, on average (this does not mean that each paper is read 50 times; some other servers routinely connect and download each paper meeting some criteria). When, a few years ago, Ginsparg felt overwhelmed by the clerical work involved in maintaining the physics preprint service and proposed giving it up, the outcry from physicists around the world was sufficient to persuade his management to give him an assistant (Taubes 1993).

A problem with such an unrefereed and unevaluated bulletin board is that people do not know what to read. In the old days physicists could rely on *Physical Review Letters* to select important papers for consideration. Now, without refereeing, people tend to read only papers written by someone whose name they recognize. Thus, the use of electronic distribution has had the side effect of making it harder for a new physics researcher to gain public attention.

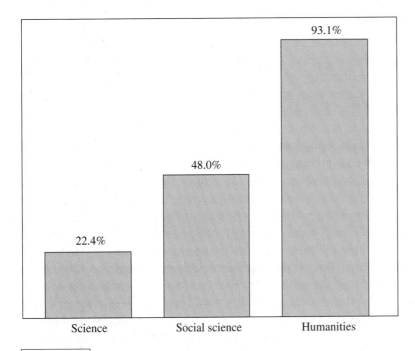

Figure 9.7 Fraction of published papers not cited in 10 years (original published in 1984)

For academics and university libraries, scholarly journals and monographs are an important part of publishing. These publications usually do not pay significant royalties to their authors; in fact, they may charge them. The authors publish to get tenure or reputation. And the publications are much more driven by authors than by readers; in fact many are hardly read at all. So many are trying to publish that the number of papers is enormous, most of them inaccessible except to specialists. Figure 9.7 shows the fractions of papers published in 1984 that were not cited in the next 10 years; clearly much publication is going only into a wastebasket.

Harvard subscribes to 96,000 journals and has 2000 faculty members. Does anyone believe that the average faculty member is reading 50 journals? Françoise Boursin reports a 1993 study claiming that 90% of primary journal articles are read by nobody at all (Boursin 1995).

Andrew Odlyzko of Bell Laboratories has written eloquently on the problems facing mathematics publishing, as an example (Odlyzko 1995). Although there were only 840 research papers in mathematics published in 1870, Odlyzko estimates there are now 50,000 papers each year. A good mathematics library now spends $100,000 per year on journal subscriptions, plus twice as much more on staff and equipment. The cost of all the journals, added up, is $200 million per year, 35% of which is spent in the United States. This means that the United States spends as much money buying mathematics journals as the National Science Foundation spends on doing mathematics research. It means that the average university mathematics department, if it gave up its library, could have another faculty member. If, as Odlyzko estimates, fewer than 20 people read the average published paper, the cost per reader is about $200. Thus, any kind of pay-per-view is out of the question; nobody expects that a mathematician would pay $200 to read a typical paper.

In an effort to deal with increasing costs, some journals began to institute page charges in the 1960s. This practice places some costs on the authors, and furthermore helps the journals to balance their costs. Suppose that a journal were able to raise enough money from page charges to cover the initial costs of composition and make-ready, and only charged the subscribers the printing, binding, and mailing cost (the incremental costs). This would leave the journal in an admirable situation: it would not matter if either the number of articles submitted or the number of readers changed. Since the authors were paying the costs proportional to the number of pages, and the readers the costs proportional to the number of copies printed, either could fluctuate with no effect on the other. In reality, no journal can raise that much money from page charges, and so the number of pages must always be limited by the amount of money raised from the readers.

Page charges would have another enormous advantage, namely, that they would decrease the incentive for theft. If we imagine a publication system in which the readers paid only the real incremental cost of copying the pages they received, they would be unable to gain anything by cheating (if they can really copy them for a lower cost than the publisher can reproduce them, they shouldn't be wasting their time reading journals, they should be competing in the printing business). Any significant contribution by page charges to the journal cost brings the subscription price closer to incremental cost and decreases the cheating incentive.

Finally, page charges would reflect the realities of the situation. Few scholars are going around complaining that there is not enough to read. But they are trying to publish ever more papers, as tenure becomes ever harder to get. Page charges would reflect the true vanity press situation and put some degree of pressure on people to publish less.

Despite these arguments, page charges are dying out. The problem is that the subscription costs are paid by libraries and the page charges are paid by the authors or their departments. Thus, by publishing in a journal with no page charges, the author can shift costs away from a personal research grant (or department funds) and over to the library. And there is little the library can do about it.

What is not clear is why much of the scholarly publication needs to be on paper at all. This system is entirely under the control of the university; if people could get tenure for online files, they would not need to get their university to pay Reed Elsevier to chop down forests to distribute their words. Steven Harnad has led the charge for replacing the entire scholarly journal system with an all-electronic system (Okerson and O'Donnell 1994). He is the editor of an online journal, *Psycoloquy*. Harnad estimates that the cost to the American Psychological Association of providing journals like his is perhaps 25 cents per member per year, that is, too cheap to bill. Online journals are appearing everywhere, but as yet do not have the prestige of the good paper journals. And, as a result, they do not attract the best papers. In 1993 the Royal Society took a survey and found that authors would not put their best papers in online journals, for fear that they would not get proper credit for them. Similarly, when OCLC and AAAS began printing the *Online Journal of Current Clinical Trials*, in the first year they got relatively few submissions, and little of what they did get was about clinical trials (most of the submissions were self-congratulatory letters about electronic publishing). This lack of prestige is frustrating since the system is entirely under the control of the universities; it is not the publishers forcing people to print things that few want to read.

However, more and more electronic journals are appearing, and the prestige of the journals is also growing. In the United Kingdom the official research assessment process values online publication as equal to paper publication. When Harvard or Stanford gives someone tenure for an online publication, the balance will tip. Harnad guesses that around 2010 about 80% of the journals in the world will have stopped paper publication.

9.7 *Electronic Commerce*

What will pay for the Internet in general, even if not library publications? The Internet in 1995 saw major businesses start to use the Web. For many years the Internet had been a research tool; in fact there was an "acceptable use policy," which prohibited commercial use of the Internet. Now the Internet is full of commercial companies trying to get rich. There is still no accepted model of how to get rich; some want to sell access to the Net, some wish to live off advertising, some plan to sell content (books, pictures), and others to sell goods that will be delivered in the mail.

There are some conflicts between these different goals, since each would like the other services to be free. Those who sell access, for example, would be best off if the content was provided free after users had connected. Those who sell content would obviously prefer access to be cheap. And those who sell ads need the content available in such a way that the ads can be tied to it; the Dilbert comic strip, for example, introduced random names for its files to keep people from accessing the comics without getting the ads along with them.

Just running a Web site does not guarantee riches; Time Warner is said to have lost $8 million in 1995 running its Web site (Hill and Baker 1996). Perhaps selling goods online will replace direct-mail catalogs. The *Economist* pointed to arguments about whether sales tax should be charged on goods sold on the Web, and said that it knew the Internet had arrived when it was used for tax avoidance ("Taxed in Cyberspace" 1996). In 1995 about $300 million was sold on the Web, and in 1996 it was about $500 million (Knecht 1996). The largest category of goods sold is airline tickets, but commerce is spreading rapidly through computer parts, audio CDs, and books. Projections for 1998 range from $3 billion to $46 billion for the value of goods sold on the Web. To put these numbers in perspective, catalog shopping is about $53 billion per year in the United States.

The rise of online shopping has, predictably, produced the shopping robot (although some of you may think you already know someone who deserves this label). Andersen Consulting has prepared a program, BargainFinder, that checks around the CD stores on the Net looking for the lowest price on the items you want. Not surprisingly, many of the stores block the robot; they want a chance to impress the buyers with their service or stock and not be rejected by a price-shopping program.

Selling connections to the Web is presently more lucrative. The number of subscribers to online services is shown in Table 9.3. Internet access is estimated at between 30 million and 50 million, since many users have access through a school or business (see Figure 9.8). *USA Today* on July 25, 1996 reported that 35 million people over 16 years old used the Internet in the first quarter of 1996 just in the United States, although 40% of those use it less than 2 hours a week. Table 9.4 shows some estimates of the future growth in Internet connectivity. Nicholas Negroponte has predicted a billion users by the year 2000 (Negroponte 1996).

Vast amounts of information are available on and distributed from the Web. The Web, as of March 1997, contained about 2 terabytes of text content, comparable to a library of 2,000,000 volumes. The site at Walnut Creek (a distributor for free software and shareware) sends out 1 terabyte a month; this is comparable to a major monthly magazine. Almost all of this material is still available free. Much of it is posted to raise the reputation of either individuals or corporations. Some of it is provided as an alternative to help lines or customer service.

Table 9.3

1994	6 million
1995	9 million
1996	15 million
1997	22 million

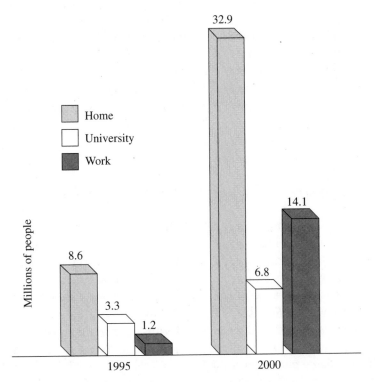

- Home, university, and school usage overlap significantly
- Work includes only companies with more than 20 employees

Figure 9.8 Internet users

Table 9.4 PC and Net access growth (numbers in millions)

Year	PCs with Internet Access	PCs
1994	13.6	153
1995	28.3	184.6
1996	52	233.7
1997	91.6	266.4
1998	133.2	303
1999	184.3	326.8

Some of the more popular content is advertiser supported. Rates for Internet advertising have dropped throughout 1996 and are now under 2 cents per exposure. Nevertheless, some $10 million per month is being spent on Web advertising, mostly at a few very popular sites. Most library publications, of course, have never been advertiser supported in the past, and it seems unlikely that they will be soon. Advertising is also not likely to distinguish material on the basis of quality rather than readership.

9.8   *The Future of Quality Information*

When I was learning elementary probability, I was told that if a million monkeys sat at a million typewriters, they would eventually write all the works of Shakespeare. The Internet has shown that this is not true (a remark adapted from an earlier line by Blair Houghton of Intel, quoted by others).

More fundamentally, does the switch from paper to electronics mean a loss of quality? In an interview with *Publisher's Weekly* (Milliot 1996), Ian Irvine, the chairman of Reed Elsevier, said that Elsevier was seeing no drop in submissions to its journals, that it rejected 80% of those submissions, and that the rejected manuscripts are "what's being put out over the Internet," also adding, "Information you get for nothing (over the Net) is worth nothing." The low quality of the typical netnews group is certainly familiar.

The physical quality of electronic materials is no longer at issue. Some years ago, online distribution was associated with ASCII-only formats that could not support equations, images, or even reasonable type fonts. In those days paper journals had a clear advantage in display quality. That has now reversed. Online material can include not only all the usual typography and illustrations, but also color pictures, sound excerpts, and animation. All of these are hard for any paper journal to include at reasonable cost. In addition, online material can be searched and reformatted by the user. The gap in physical quality is now in favor of the online material.

Steven Harnad and Andrew Odlyzko argue that the intellectual quality of printed journals is maintained by the refereeing process, not by the fact that subscription prices are so high (Okerson and O'Donnell 1994; Odlyzko 1995). They believe that electronic journals could have equal or better quality than paper by maintaining refereeing standards and procedures, and in fact Harnad does this with the electronic journal that he edits, *Psycoloquy*.

What must be recognized is that the refereeing process introduces some delay. Those who like the immediacy of writing a paper this afternoon and having it read in India an hour later cannot have this along with refereeing. Thus, the fast-reaction bulletin boards are likely to be low quality. At least in this context we cannot have both fast and good information. The difficulty this introduces on the bulletin boards is that people read only those papers written by somebody whose name they recognize, making it harder for new scientists to break into the circle of those who get attention.

Other changes are likely to result from the fact that online journals do not have page limits. This lack of page limits may mean that editors may become less careful about asking authors to limit what they write. More importantly, it is likely to mean that prestigious journals, which get far more submissions today than they can print, will expand at the expense of marginal journals. If this shrinks the total number of journals, it might become easier to deal with the literature, although the prestige value of the best journals will shrink somewhat. Again, we will be relying more on searching and less on editors to find what we want. This is not, however, inherent in electronics; there is no reason why an electronic journal editor could not impose size and quality limits, accepting the resulting need to hassle the authors. It just can't be blamed on the printer, the way it is today.

The reverse problem may also appear. There is no reason why electronic journals with low overhead might not accept shorter articles. There are undoubtedly those who imagine that if there had been electronic journals 90 years ago, Einstein could just have sent in the five-character message $E = mc^2$. Some of them will then think that their most recent one-liner is worth sending to a journal. Few of them will be right. Fortunately, the editorial overhead in handling very short submissions is likely to discourage this.

As an alternative to refereeing, we might decide to try and rely on the behavior of individuals reading papers, as in the community-rated movie experiment described earlier. If a system permitted it, for example, a reasonable way to select references on electronic libraries might be to read anything Ed Fox (of Virginia Tech) or Bruce Croft (of the University of Massachusetts) had spent at least an hour with. Whether anyone would like having people know that much about what they were doing is less likely; in corporate research it would clearly be viewed as a danger. Whether a technique could be found for anonymously recommending articles that could not be manipulated by people looking for attention is not clear.

What this means is that we can have high quality in electronic journals, but we are going to have to fight for it. So far there is no automatic refereeing program. In fact, the advent of spell checkers has probably made the serious job of editors a little bit harder, since there is less correlation than there used to be between those authors who have bothered to correct their errors in spelling and grammar and those who have bothered to get their equations right. Decent quality online is going to require the same refereeing and high-level editorial work that is required for paper. Since most of that work is unpaid, it does not follow that online journals have to be expensive. But if the work is not done, we will be back to the "great graffiti board in the sky."

9.9 *Summary*

Economics is emphatically not a solved problem. Many earlier chapters ended with my facile assurance that we could build workable systems. And certainly the Web has been a very successful way of distributing free information—library catalogs, computer parts lists, or CD titles for sale. But we do not have a way to support the creators of information who need a way to be paid. This chapter has reviewed the economic methods used by online publishers today and the hopes for funding the Web in the future. It has not, however, found a clean, acceptable answer.

Economic problems interact with many issues of library collections and quality. Will we find students using cheaper but less accurate information? The cost of printing books placed some kind of floor under the quality of what was printed; a Penguin paperback might not have the durability of a hardbound book, but it would still provide a reliable text. Online, there is nothing to stop random people from presenting totally corrupted texts as accurate, whether through incompetence or maliciousness. And if there is no economic incentive to provide quality material, we may find bad material driving out good.

Similarly, the ability of libraries to gather material from remote sites encourages cutbacks in actual holdings. Will libraries coordinate what is saved and what is abandoned? How do we see to it that the present structure by which libraries share collecting responsibilities and preserve at least one U.S. copy of important works remains? The incentives for university administrations, and thus for libraries, may be to cut back to frequently used material only and hope that someone else will keep the rare material. I am told that when the Ayatollah Khomeini came to power in Iran, there was not a single copy in the United States of any of his writings, all of which had been published overseas (Bielawski 1996). How can we avoid this in the future, if economic pressures encourage libraries not to acquire books until needed? What kind of pricing will see that both common and rare materials can be created and purchased by libraries?

Finally, economic problems also interact greatly with intellectual property rights issues. What can be charged for is strongly related to the legal rights of the owners of the works. And whether the legal framework is well matched to the economic framework is a major question, to be discussed in the next chapter.

Intellectual Property Rights

ISSUES RELATED TO intellectual property law are the most serious problems facing digital libraries. As the early chapters have discussed, we have a wide choice of technological solutions. But we cannot solve the economic problems that arise from intellectual property law. Publishers are too familiar with the destruction of the software game industry in the early 1980s by illegal copying and by the amount of piracy facing the software industry today in some foreign countries. They see statements on the Net such as the following (from *netnews*, April 1996):

```
RHONDA announces its existence in CyberSpace promising to rob
books from the rich and give them to the poor.

RHONDA stands for Robin Hood -- Online Network Distribution
Anarchy. Like Robin Hood in Sherwood Forest RHONDA robs from
the rich and gives to the poor. Specifically RHONDA intends to
provide the poor with electronic books including classic
literature and textbooks and revolutionary manuscripts and all
manner of text that will help educate the poor and lift us
from our poverty. We will make these works available via
the Internet.

. . . We refuse to recognize any copyright claimed on any
text. "PropertyIsTheft!" We claim the right of eminent domain
on text on behalf of society. Books come from the minds and
mouths of the People so books rightfully belong to the People.
```

Publishers do not yet see adequate technology to protect their information, nor do they have policies for dealing with it if they did have the technology.

It is normally accepted that protection of intellectual property is necessary to encourage people to create it. How much protection is required, however, is not clear. The market does not always work smoothly. For example, early in the history of aviation the Wright brothers had many of the most important patents and Glenn Curtiss had others. Neither would license the other, so no one in the United States could build a state-of-the-art airplane. This lasted until World War I, at which point the military services realized that American pilots would be shot down and killed if the best planes couldn't be built, and forced cross-licensing on the patent holders. Another interesting contrast is type font design. The shapes of letters can be protected in Europe but not in the United States (although U.S. companies can trademark the font name and copyright a particular digital representation of the shapes). You would think, if the lawyers and economists were right, that all type font advances would take place in Europe. In fact they currently happen in the United States (since they are largely tied to laser printer details).

However, most digital library proponents completely agree that creators of intellectual property should be paid for it. The problem, as discussed above under administrative costs (see Section 9.6), is that we need practical ways of doing this. History does not show that relying on the owners of intellectual property will produce fair and smoothly operating schemes; they may not even act in their own self-interest. For example, some years ago in a famous case named *Sony v. Universal*, two major movie studios sued to block the sale of video cassette recorders in the United States. They lost. As a result of losing, the movie industry now makes more money selling videotapes than it does selling theatre admissions. How can we arrange the rules and procedures for selling information in digital form to be fair to creators, users, and the intermediaries?

10.1 *History of Copyright Law*

There are three basic forms of intellectual property protection: copyright, patent, and trade secrecy. Trade secrecy (restricting access to your company's information and making anyone who gets the information sign agreements to keep it private) is not of great relevance to libraries. Copyright laws, on the other hand, are a primary concern for digital libraries.

The first copyright law dates from 1709 and was designed to offer authors and publishers protection against pirated editions of books. Traditionally, developed countries have always wanted protection for their work, and undeveloped countries have argued lack of foreign currency, general poverty, and other reasons why they should be permitted to avoid paying for it. In the 18th century, Ireland was known for pirated editions of English books. In the 19th century, the United States was a major pirating country. And now Asian and eastern European countries are perceived as the main villains.

The United States did not pay royalties to foreign authors until 1891. It started paying them not because Congress responded to the pleas of foreign authors, but because U.S. authors complained that American publishers were ignoring them in favor of foreign writers to save on royalties. This exact scenario has recently been replayed in Europe, where the software companies in eastern Europe argue for enforcement of copyright and antidumping laws because they have enough trouble competing with Microsoft at its prices in hard currency, let alone having to compete with pirates. What has changed from the last century is that it is much easier to export intellectual property. When, in the 1950s, the Soviet Union reprinted *Chemical Abstracts* without permission, they cost *CA* its sales in the Communist bloc, but not its sales in other countries. Now, China appears not only to produce pirate copies for internal consumption but is exporting to other Asian countries, including places (such as Hong Kong) where substantial progress had been made reducing local piracy. Figure 10.1 shows the *Economist*'s estimates of software piracy. Similarly, piracy of music is widespread in many countries.

Copyright is a technique to protect a form of expression. Its goal is to encourage authors, and in the United States it is based in the Constitution: Art. I, sect. 8 lets Congress "Promote the Progress of Science and useful Arts, by securing for limited Times to Authors and Inventors the exclusive Right to their respective Writings and Discoveries." Copyright does not protect useful objects. In fact, if something is useful, that will be a legal argument that it should not be protected by copyright.

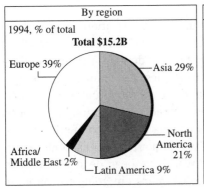 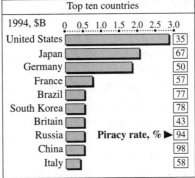

Figure 10.1 Software piracy losses

Nor does it protect ideas, as opposed to the way they are expressed. Copyright prevents other people from making copies of your work, or providing a public performance of it, or creating derivative works (translations, movie versions, and so on).

The length of time that a copyright is valid has been getting longer. Under the original 1709 British law, it lasted 14 years. The U.S. law until 1976 provided for a 28-year term with an extension valid for another 28 years, or 56 years total. In 1976 the United States changed its law to provide for a 75-year term on an interim basis; in the future copyright terms here will match the Berne Convention, life of author plus 50 years. Some details in the process for extending the copyright law meant that any work that was up for renewal in 1964 or later is treated as if the copyright had been renewed. In summary, in the United States any work published before or during 1920 is out of copyright. Those that were published between 1920 and 1936 and not renewed have lapsed and are also in the public domain, as are works published since 1920 that were not copyrighted for some reason. The reason for a lack of copyright may be deliberate; for example, all U.S. government works are in the public domain. You may freely photocopy (or scan) a U.S. Geological Survey map. Or it may be an accident; in the past books published without proper notice, or which were not registered in the Copyright Office, became public domain.

The flat 75-year term in the United States means that a very few creators, for instance Irving Berlin, lived to see some of their compositions ("Alexander's Ragtime Band" comes to mind) pass into the public domain. This was not true in Berne countries that already had a "life plus 50" rule. So, for example, the stories of Sir Arthur Conan Doyle were under that law public domain in the United Kingdom (since Doyle died in 1930) but only those published before 1920 were public domain in the United States. Conversely, *Caesar and Cleopatra* is public domain in the United States (written in 1899) but is still under copyright in the United Kingdom, since Shaw died in 1950.

A revision to the U.S. copyright law is now under consideration. In it the term will be extended by 20 years. Instead of the situation of the last few years in which each year, another year's worth of books became public domain, the threshold for possible copyright will stay in 1920 for two more decades. The temporary copyright rule will be 95 years from date of publication, and the eventual rule, aligning with Berne, will be life of author plus 70 years. The retroactive extension is obviously aimed at international trade considerations, as Pamela Samuelson (Berkeley) has pointed out (Samuelson 1993). Even Congress would not believe that a more generous copyright law would encourage authors who have been dead for 50 years to produce more works. The logic is that if the Germans are going to charge us royalties on books published in 1921, we might as well charge them royalties similarly. At least in the United States, books already in the public domain stay there. In the United Kingdom the corresponding law has been applied even to works already public, so that Sir Arthur Conan Doyle's writings are *again* copyrighted in the United Kingdom.

The U.S. proposed law revision also contains several other minor changes to the advantage of the copyright holders. The need to provide notice on a publication is gone, and virtually all incentives to register the copyright will disappear. The publishers are trying to arrange digital distribution so that it is not called "publication," since that will incur the obligation to deposit in the Library of Congress and the right to allow "fair use." If digital distribution is either called "performance" or something new, neither of these burdens will be placed on the publishers.

More important to digital libraries is the relation of the new law to digital transmission. The proposed law defines any digital transmission as copying, so that, for example, a purchaser of an electronic copy of a text would not be allowed to pass it on to somebody else (unless this is done by handing them a physical object). Compared to the current rights available under the "first sale" doctrine, this will be very restrictive. There will also be no digital fair use. Thus, viewing a Web page will be the same as making a copy, and the copyright holder will have the right to refuse to let you do that (Samuelson 1995). The proposed law revision does give libraries the right to do digital copying for preservation purposes. Under the current 1986 law, libraries may only make analog copies (photocopies, microfilm, fax) to replace deteriorating books; they may not make digital copies.

A major change that did go in the direction of loosening copyright control came from the Supreme Court in 1991. Historically, copyright was viewed as a way of protecting creative work. In addition, however, a tradition had arisen of protecting intellectual work in general, even if it was not creative. This was called the "sweat of the brow" standard; if somebody did enough work, they were entitled to protection for it. However, nothing in the laws as passed by Congress enabled protection for noncreative effort, and in 1991 the Supreme Court (*Feist Publications, Inc. v. Rural Telephone Service Co.,* 111 S. Ct. 1282) held that sympathetic as they were to somebody who spent a lot of effort piling up some data, if there was no creativity involved, it was not protectable. The *Feist* case involved white pages telephone directories, and the Supreme Court felt that alphabetizing names was not creative enough. As a result, telephone books in the United States became fair game, and there are now many CD-ROMs selling copies of the U.S. phone books.

The courts seem to have felt that they were being unfair in letting people copy significant amounts of work, and so the threshold for calling something creative has been set fairly low. In two 1991 cases (*Bellsouth Advertising and Publishing Corp. v. Donnelley Information Publishing, Inc.,* 933 F. 2d 952; 11th Cir. and *Key Publications v. Chinatown Today,* 945 F. 2d 509, 514; 2d Cir.), the courts have held that yellow pages phone directories are creative and may be protected. Baseball box scores are now officially creative (*Kregos v. Associated Press,* 937 F. 2d 700, 705; 2d Cir. 1991), but horse racing charts (*Victor Lalli Enterprises v. Big Red Apple,* 936 F. 2d 671, 673–74; 2d Cir. 1991) and radiator parts catalogs (*Cooling Sys. & Flexibles, Inc.*

v. Stuart Radiator, 777 F. 2d 485, 491; 9th Cir. 1985) are not. In other countries this kind of problem is compromised. The United Kingdom has a special 25-year protection for "typographic arrangement," which will protect merely the particular typeset version of a book that is out of copyright, so that in the United Kingdom you cannot just photograph an Oxford version of Dickens, say, and reprint it. The phone book issue is dealt with in the EC with a special "data compilation copyright" that lasts for 10 years. A late 1996 World Intellectual Property Organization proposal for database protection would address this problem by creating a new right in data compilations. This proposal has already attracted much debate for its lack of a fair use exemption.

The proposed new law would also introduce the concept of "moral rights" to the United States. Moral rights are separate from copyright and derive from a French tradition. They give the creator of a work the right to be identified as the creator and the right to prohibit destruction or degradation of the work. For example, moral rights would have allowed Noguchi to object when a sculpture of his was cut into pieces in 1980 by a landlord trying to get it out of a building that did not have large enough doors (and in fact, the Visual Artists Rights Act of 1990 now provides such protection for public art). Moral rights cannot be sold. For example, I can transfer the copyright in this book (and typically would have to do so to get it published), but I cannot sell somebody else the right to be named as the author. Moral rights can be waived, however, and in moral rights countries, contracts will frequently have to provide for such waivers. The introduction of this right into the United States, with no history of getting such waivers, is likely to create chaos, especially as the courts start to interpret it. For example, in Canada, the Eaton's department store in Toronto has a sculpture depicting some flying geese. For Christmas one year they tied red ribbons around the necks of the geese. The sculptor protested and won; he felt the ribbons diminished his work.

Finally, a small note for those of us who treasure one small exemption in the copyright law. Recognizing that if you needed the permission of a copyright holder to parody his work, few parodies would ever get written, the courts have allowed an exception for satire. Berkeley Software is well known for selling a screen saver named *After Dark*, which shows toasters flying across the screen. Delrina attempted to market a screen saver that showed Opus the Penguin (licensed from Berke Breathed) shooting down toasters. Berkeley sued for copyright enforcement. Delrina defended claiming protection as a satire. The list of participants in the case was remarkable; Mark Russell showed up on the side of Delrina and the Irving Berlin estate on the side of Berkeley. In *Delrina v. Berkeley Software*, Judge Eugene Lynch shot down Delrina, saying (1) that this was commerce and not literature, and (2) that the toasters were too similar in design. Although Opus eventually resumed shooting down toasters, but with propellers instead of wings, the precedent is set that you cannot legally parody a computer program. All of this ignores the fact that toasters with wings were originally drawn for a Jefferson Airplane album by artist

Bruce Steinberg in 1973. The Jefferson Airplane sued too, but lost for failure to copyright the album cover under the law at time of publication.

10.2 *History of Patent Law*

The other most relevant intellectual property protection is the patent law. Patents are to protect devices or processes. Patents must cover something useful, new, and not obvious. Since copyrights cover things that must not be useful, while patents must be useful, it would seem that nothing could be both copyrighted and patented, but that's not true. A computer program can be covered both ways: the idea or algorithm underneath can be patented, while the text of the program, the form of expression, can be copyrighted.

For software, copyrights protect against someone who simply copies the code and attempts to resell it. Patents stop someone who would rewrite the code, so long as the underlying algorithm is reused. However, software is not what the original patent law had in mind, and sometimes it is a pretty rough fit from software to patents.

Patents are much shorter term than copyrights. Traditionally, in the United States, they lasted 17 years from date of issue. A recent change in the law made them 20 years from date of application; since most patents issue in under 18 months, this is usually a slightly longer term. From the standpoint of computer software, either number is still so long as to be comparable with the life of the field. There is also a special kind of patent called a design patent, which can be used to protect industrial designs such as bottle shapes; they have a different life but have not been used much for software.

For many years, the question was whether software should be patentable at all. Traditionally, methods of business are not patentable. In a famous 1876 case, *Baker v. Selden*, a set of accounting forms was held not patentable. The best precedent for computer programs seemed to be player piano rolls, which were copyrighted, not patented. This did not satisfy some software companies or authors, who did not like the fact that copyrighting a program only keeps someone from using your text; they can legally reimplement the same solution in their own code. Patents give an absolute monopoly on the method; even someone who independently reinvents the idea cannot use it.

Early in the days of software, in fact, the solution to software patenting was to convert the program into a circuit diagram and patent the circuit. This approach could be used to stop somebody from using the same process in a different program. But it was clear that this was unsatisfactory, and the patent lawyers kept trying to patent the actual software algorithm directly. The Patent Office tried to fend them off.

The first step in the legal process was *Gottschalk v. Benson* (1972), in which Bell Laboratories tried to patent a binary-to-decimal conversion algorithm. The algorithm was very simple—in fact it might have been known to Euclid—but both sides agreed not to raise the novelty issue. They thought that this was a good test case as the algorithm was so simple that the judges could understand it, often not the case with computer programs. Unfortunately for the patent applicants, the Supreme Court justices not only understood the algorithm but realized they could do it in their head. As a result it looked to them like a constraint on how you could think, and they rejected the patent saying that any process that consisted entirely of "mental steps" was not patentable.

So the next case was *Diamond v. Diehr* (1981), about a patent application for a rubber curing plant control system that was certainly so complicated that nobody was going to do it in their head, and in fact was inherently linked to a nonmental process (the rubber plant). The Supreme Court now agreed that software patents were legal, and the Patent Office began to issue them. Today there are over 1000 software patents per year. Since software is a relatively new field, it is often hard to establish what should be considered obvious in terms of "prior art," and many patents issue that some consider obvious. The League of Programming Freedom attacks software patents regularly. And Bernard Galler (University of Michigan) has founded the Software Patent Institute in an effort to assist the patent office by creating a database of prior art and helping train patent examiners.

It also does not appear that major software companies rely on patents the way hardware companies do. Figure 10.2 shows that the leading hardware manufacturers get about 1000 U.S. patents per year, while the leading software companies get very few. It does not look as if the patent system has been closely tied to in-

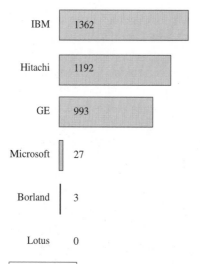

Figure 10.2   U.S. patents issued (1994)

dustrial success in software. There are some famous hardware patents that led to large industries: Alexander Graham Bell and the telephone, Chester Carlson and the photocopier (Xerox), or Edwin Land and instant photography (Polaroid). There are no such stories for software.

The difficulty that the patent office has evaluating software patents also means that some of them have taken a very long time to issue. This has raised the issue of "submarine patents," patents that no one knows about but suddenly appear to disrupt an industry. It is perfectly possible for someone to invent something, develop a program, start selling it, and only later discover that a previously written patent has just issued and controls the process (a time bomb patent). The best-known example is probably the Pardo patent (U.S. 4,398,249), which looks like an invention of the spreadsheet. The application was received in 1970, but the patent did not issue until 1983; under the law at that time, it does not expire until 2000. The Pardo patent had no effect on the early development of the spreadsheet industry (which was carried on by Visicalc and Lotus). Nevertheless, litigation about it affects the current industry. There are even patents that have taken more than 20 years to issue; at least one has taken 40. Under the new law, patents of this sort will be much less important since the term of 20 years from filing would mean, for example, that the Pardo patent would have expired in 1990. Patent applications would also become public after 18 months.

The designer of a digital library, for better or worse, is going to have to be sensitive to what algorithms are already patented and consider what to do about them. For example, the JPEG compression method is not subject to the LZW patent and may be preferable to GIF.

10.3 *Other Legal Risks*

Other legal risks that may affect digital libraries are appearing as well. Libel and trademark infringement are perhaps the best known, but the biggest threat on the horizon is strict liability.

Some problems arise from the use of old materials in new ways. For example, in the early 1950s Disney hired Peggy Lee to sing in *The Lady and the Tramp*, for which she was paid $3200. Some 40 years later Disney released the video version and Peggy Lee sued, claiming Disney did not own the video rights to her voice and song. She was awarded more than $3.2 million in damages for copyright infringement. Similarly, libraries may have to worry about whether, when something is converted, all the necessary rights were obtained originally from the creators or performers.

Traditionally, in the case of libel, the law distinguished between authors and publishers, who were responsible for what they wrote and distributed, and organizations like the post office or printing plants, who were viewed as providing general services and were not responsible for knowing the detailed content of what they transmitted or produced. Libraries, bookstores, and magazine stands, as well, were historically immune from libel suits; no one really believes that a bookstore owner reads all the books in the store and is ready to stand behind their content. There is, however, a recent case in the United Kingdom in which the then prime minister, John Major, sued and won a libel action against not only *Scallywag* and the *New Statesman*, the magazines that had published the libel, but against the printers and distributors (W. H. Smith and John Menzies). So far this is not the law in the United States.

Where does an online service provider or a Web site manager stand in this rule? Are they responsible for what they transmit, or not? Stratton Oakmont, a suburban New York brokerage company, objected to something said about them on a Prodigy bulletin board. Although they had paid a $2.5 million penalty for securities law violation, they objected to a description of their behavior as "fraud" and "criminal." They sued Prodigy and won. Prodigy had been advertising itself as the "family friendly" online service and employed people to read and approve messages for its chat groups, with the intent of keeping out obscenity. The court held that this turned Prodigy into a publisher and found it responsible for libelous statements posted by their users. Congress was so distressed by this result that it reversed it in the Telecommunications Reform Act of 1996. Actions taken to limit obscenity can no longer incur legal liability. However, the more general question is still open: are the Internet service providers, or the other online services, responsible for what is sent out through their systems?

Would a library be responsible? Not, one expects, if all it does is put books on a shelf in the traditional way. But the many suggestions that libraries should provide more services, including recommending specific items, selecting particular bits of Web pages, and so on, all move closer to what has traditionally been publishing. And to the extent that libraries try to gain the advantages of publishing (e.g., being able to claim that information they are passing along has a better-than-usual chance of being valid), the more they incur the risks of a publisher as well.

Trademark law has also started to appear on the Internet. The problem here has been that traditionally two different companies may use the same trademark as long as they are in well-separated businesses. HP hot sauce and HP electronics (Hewlett-Packard) coexist, as do Sun Oil (Sunoco) and Sun Microsystems. On the Web, however, there can only be one www.sun.com and it belongs today to Sun Microsystems. As between legitimate trademark holders, the rule is first come, first serve. The domain name authority today belongs with Network Solutions, Inc., of Herndon, Virginia, which has an NSF contract to operate the InterNIC registration service. They charge $50 per year for a domain name, with an initial signup of two years.

The worst problems are going to arise as international business on the Web grows. TBS, for example, may well be Turner Broadcasting to an American, but it is Tokyo Broadcasting to a Japanese. Right now the Web encourages foreign companies to use national domains (e.g., `tbs.co.jp` for Tokyo Broadcasting). Not surprisingly, other countries do not think the United States should have special rights for `.com`, and it is not clear how this situation will be handled. Similar problems arose with toll-free 800 numbers, which have been partially alleviated by deciding that the international toll-free 0800 code will be followed by eight digits rather than seven, meaning that few national freecall numbers can move without change to the new space, and providing a sufficiently larger number space that congestion may be less important.

Perhaps the most serious legal problem eventually will be strict liability, raised by Pamela Samuelson (1993). Traditionally, in the United States, the warranty on a book merely said that the paper and binding would hold together. The content was not warrantied. If you read a book on investment strategy and go broke trying to follow its advice, the publisher is not responsible. The rules are different for stockbrokers; if they give sufficiently bad financial advice, they are liable for discipline and damages. What about an electronic program that gives financial advice? As yet we do not know.

It seems likely that in the not-too-distant future somebody will sue an online provider for sending out bad information and win. The questions, as with libel, will be whether liability only attaches to the Web page owner or to other people in the transmission chain. Given the number of Web page owners who are young and without financial resources, the tort lawyers will be very anxious to be able to sue somebody large, like a phone company. Will libraries also be held liable? Again, the more they position themselves as "information providers" and claim to be reviewing, editing, or improving the Web pages or whatever else they take in, the more chance that they too may have to take responsibility for the consequences.

Realistically, we can expect an insurance industry to arise to deal with the potential liability issues, and libraries may have to buy insurance against these problems.

10.4 *National Information Infrastructure Dangers*

The national information infrastructure (NII), as well as being useful to educators and businesses, carries with it risks when used by bad guys. At the moment the "four horsemen of the NII" are drug dealers, foreign espionage agents, terrorists, and child pornographers. And of those, at least to Congress, the greatest danger is child pornographers.

The result was the Communications Decency Act, joining existing state laws that prohibited certain kinds of pornography on the Net. The act has already run into legal trouble, since it was insufficiently precise about defining the prohibited material. The question of what kind of indecency restrictions should exist on the Net is turning into a major public policy issue. Reconciling the right of free speech with the desire to keep people from pushing pornography at children is going to be difficult. The use of programs that attempt to scan the Net for dirty words is being circumvented by porno vendors who instead of giving their sites names like "XXX Super Hot" call them "Barney" and "Sesame Street." Educators report that over the last two years this has become a serious problem.

There is also danger from traditional distribution methods, of course. The DVD worries some of the movie studios, for example. They typically release movies six months earlier in the United States than in Europe; what will happen if Europeans buy DVD disks in the United States and carry them across the Atlantic? As a result it is likely that there will be DVD-NTSC and DVD-PAL, so that U.S. disks will not work in European players. The concept of deliberately introducing incompatibility may strike others as crazy, but it appeals to the studios, at least until digital transmission to theatres, by removing the need to make multiple prints of movies, eliminates the reason for not distributing movies simultaneously around the world. And the studios are anxious for DVD *writing* devices not to be marketed until some kind of copy protection hardware is included in them, just as with DAT drives.

Perhaps the most important issue in the copyright law revision is the question of responsibility for enforcing copyright law violations. Suppose a Web site contains an illegally copied work. Whose problem is it? The Internet community would like it to be only the problem of the site creator; the publisher should attack the site owner directly. Publishers would like to be able to place the responsibility for enforcement on the company that is hosting the site (and on anyone else as well). Their position is that suing the site owner, who may well be a 14-year-old with no financial resources, is unproductive. If the responsibility is placed on the Internet service providers, they hope, they can both collect damages and have a workable enforcement mechanism.

At the time of writing, it appears there will be a compromise, with a requirement that on detecting an infringement, the publisher will notify the Internet service provider, and the provider will then have to block access to the site. There will be fixed penalties for a provider that does not do so. The major question left is whether the provider is liable for damages that are incurred before notification.

As mentioned in Section 6.4, U.S. cryptographic technology export laws are also a major NII issue. The U.S. government is trying to retain the ability to wiretap with court order for law enforcement purposes and has proposed that encryption devices contain hidden keys kept by the government and available with a warrant. This proposal, the so-called Clipper chip, has not met with much welcome from other countries or many private organizations. A replacement proposal for commercial key escrow organizations does not seem to be catching on either. Private corporations will have to think about alternate administrative processes; with modern cryptography, if all my files are encrypted with a password that nobody else knows and I am suddenly taken ill, no one else will be able to salvage them for my employer.

Anonymity on the Internet is also a major issue. At present, people visiting Net sites have their originating computer net address, but not their individual user name, reported to the site. Electronic mail is normally delivered with an electronic user identification. However, people often use pseudonyms for their email, so this user identification is less useful than it might be. Nevertheless, on request, systems administrators can be asked which actual user has any particular name. Those requiring still more security have sometimes gone through an anonymous remailer. Anonymous remailers are machines that take any message and pass it on with a new, anonymous address. The remailer keeps enough records to permit replies to the message, however. The best known such server was in Finland, but it has been closed down as a result of legal actions preventing the operator from preserving the anonymity of his users.

Somehow, the Internet community has to decide whether anonymity is a good thing or not. Each side can point to its favorite cases: the democratic political dissident in a dictatorship or the terrorist planning a bombing. The practical politics of the situation, however, is that a continued defense of anonymous email leads to an increased prospect of government regulation on a stricter scale.

10.5 *Intellectual Property Protection*

The hope of the publishers is that some technology will arise that protects their intellectual property effectively. At the moment, there is a substantial fear of theft. The U.S. balance of payments in intellectual property is positive by $46 billion, but it is believed that another $15–17 billion is being lost to piracy.

What are the techniques used today to keep people from stealing online intellectual property? Here is a list of current and proposed technologies for this purpose:

1. Fractional access
2. Control of interface
3. Hardware locks ("dongles")
4. Repositories
5. Steganography
6. Cryptolopes, or secret envelopes
7. Special hardware
8. Economic approaches
9. Flickering

10.5.1 *Fractional Access*

Mead Data Central has 2.4 TB online. You can steal a few hundred bytes, but not find somebody else who wants those bytes enough to pay for them. For a large enough database that is doled out in small units, it is not practical to do small-scale cheating. Large-scale copying, with advertising of the result, will come to the attention of the copyright holder and can be shut down legally.

This is not, however, an answer for textbooks; the entire book is often of use to the reader, and the typical user knows who else is in the class and would want a copy of the book. In general, sales of individual, self-contained items can't just rely on providing access to only small parts of the material.

10.5.2 *Control of Interface*

If people can only access material through a proprietary interface, they may have trouble back-translating it to something easily redistributed. Imagine, for example, reverse engineering one of the complex screen displays of a modern browser. This approach is relied on by many CD-ROM vendors; the format on the CD-ROM is private and the software to access it is on the CD-ROM. It is hard to try to arrange any other access to the material. Again, if someone does this and tries to market the result, they will come to public attention, and it is too hard to do on a small scale.

10.5.3 *Hardware Locks ("Dongles")*

If some part of information access can be made to depend on a piece of hardware, then nobody without that hardware can use a copy. In a typical case, part of the access program (e.g., the decryption key) is kept out in the hardware, which must be on the machine. In the extreme case, an entire special-purpose machine is designed only to run the vendor's programs; video games are the practical example.

More usually the special-purpose hardware looks like a parallel or serial port (a plug on the back of the computer used to connect printers or other devices), which normally acts like a cable and just transmits through whatever it gets, but which traps and responds to a few special commands. An example is shown in Figure 10.3. These devices, however, meet considerable consumer resistance and also cost enough that they can only be used to protect fairly expensive products (they cost perhaps $20 apiece).

10.5.4 *Repositories*

The idea behind repositories is that if there was a copy of everything copyrighted in one place, unauthorized copies could be found mechanically. Stanford, for example, explored a case of Net plagiarism by comparing papers from a specific source with the online database of technical reports. Such a repository could either rely on

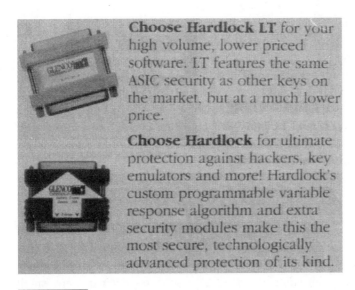

Choose Hardlock LT for your high volume, lower priced software. LT features the same ASIC security as other keys on the market, but at a much lower price.

Choose Hardlock for ultimate protection against hackers, key emulators and more! Hardlock's custom programmable variable response algorithm and extra security modules make this the most secure, technologically advanced protection of its kind.

Figure 10.3   Hardware lock

copyright signature codes included in a document, or it could generate its own signatures and do searching.

Among groups trying to build a repository are InterTrust (previously known as Electronic Publishing Resources [EPR]) and CNRI (Corporation for National Research Initiatives), which is working with the Copyright Office. The European Union has Imprimatur (Intellectual Multimedia Property Rights Model and Terminology for Universal Reference). There is a consortium called the Electronic Rights Management Group and also the Electronic Licensing and Security Initiative.

10.5.5   *Steganography*

The word *steganography* describes hidden messages. Originally it meant the kind of cipher in which the first letter of each word spelled out a secret message. Sherlock Holmes solved such a cipher in "The Adventure of the Gloria Scott." Steganography has been extended into the idea of "digital watermarks" that are hidden in digital materials. The idea is that each copy sold would be labeled with a different identification number, and illegal copies could thus be tracked back to the original purchaser so that legal remedies could be pursued (Komatsu and Tominaga 1990). These codes have the difficulty that they may be easily removed, and they may be hard to insert. It is easier, for example, to find spare places to put extra bits in a picture (where low-order detail can be adjusted with little notice) than in text (Matsui and Tanaka 1994).

There are many research efforts on digital watermarking now, including projects at MIT, NEC, AT&T, and smaller companies such as ARIS Technologies. Normally, the goal is to have a mark that is not noticeable to the user and yet is hard to remove. Many of the most trivial suggestions, which would involve manipulating the low-order bits of an image, would be removed by any kind of lossy compression and decompression, or even just by low-pass spatial Fourier transforms. More complex and robust processes might involve, as at MIT, adjusting overall grey densities in different parts of the picture. The eye is not very sensitive to absolute levels, so this kind of coding passes unnoticed. Because it is not in low-level bits, it survives JPEG or other compressions.

Placing digital watermarks in text, as opposed to pictures, is harder. There is no spare space in ASCII text to hide anything. Lawrence O'Gorman and others at Bell Laboratories came up with a scheme that manipulates the spaces between letters or words, or the exact shapes of letters, as shown in Figure 10.4 (Berghel and O'Gorman 1996; Brassil et al. 1994). Again, as with any scheme that depends on detecting pirates and then suing them, legal procedures against many small infringers with limited financial resources are not effective.

10.5.6 *Cryptolopes, or Secret Envelopes*

This heading covers the general technology of supplying information in encrypted form, with software that decrypts it under rules provided by the copyright holder. *Cryptolope* is a word referring to a particular system of this sort at IBM. Information is distributed only in encrypted form, and the access software controls the ability to print or download. The idea is that the user can do what they want with the encrypted version; in fact redistributing it might even help the copyright holder. But when the user asks to view the material or print the report, some kind of financial transaction may be started.

For IBM, cryptolopes are part of their Infomarket. IBM is providing a large set of software designed to facilitate information sales on the Web. The cryptolopes can implement a wide variety of policies for selling information. The information owner can choose to allow or forbid viewing, downloading, copying, printing, or whatever. So long as the user stays within the limits of the program, the policies are secure. As with other techniques, the user, having obtained a screenful of information, may be able to capture it with screen dumps or some such system, and then abuse it.

Similar technology is sold by InterTrust, which has Digiboxes and NetTrust, or by Release Software Corp with its AutoPay. Some users might not appreciate one of the statements about AutoPay, that it can scan the user's hard drive looking for competing products and adjust the price accordingly.

A long-term worry that has been raised by Clifford Lynch of the University of California is what happens to encrypted material in the long run. If libraries only buy access to material, and at any given instant it is only encrypted, how does it

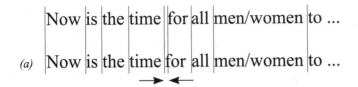

(a)

(b)

(c)

(d)

(e)

Figure 10.4   Bell Labs document marking. Examples *(a)* and *(b)* show word-shift coding. In *(a)*, the top text line has added spacing before the "for"; the bottom text line has the same spacing after the "for." In *(b)*, these same text lines are shown again without the vertical lines to demonstrate that either spacing appears natural. Examples *(c)*–*(e)* show feature coding performed on a portion of text from a journal table of contents. In *(c)*, no coding has been applied. In *(d)*, feature coding has been applied to select characters. In *(e)*, the feature coding has been exaggerated to show feature alterations

become generally accessible 50 (or 70) years after the author has died? Publishers are under no affirmative obligation to assist books into the public domain, and perhaps when the current sales are no longer lucrative, they will simply forget about the book. With no library having an unencrypted copy, it will be gone. It may be essential to require that at least one clean, unencrypted copy be deposited with the Library of Congress.

10.5.7   *Special Hardware*

Another possibility for protection with encryption is not to rely on software, but to put decryption hardware directly into an output device. For example, an audio card could include a digital-to-analog converter with a decryption chip, possibly with a unique key for this particular chip. To download music, the user would provide the ID of that particular audio board decryption chip; it could be used to make a special password that would be used to encrypt the music so that it could only be decrypted by that particular chip. Copies would be useless to anyone else. Similar technology could be in video cards, laser printers, and other devices.

10.5.8 *Economic Approaches*

It would be ideal, of course, if some pricing strategy could remove or alleviate the piracy problem. The existing pricing strategies are often very frustrating. For example, CD-ROMs use a technology designed to stamp out millions of pop records. Yet the price of some library CD-ROMs is so high as to encourage the library to do networked delivery as a way of sharing the resource, prompting fears that the networked access would in some way produce abuse. Few publishers, however, have arranged for libraries to get multiple copies of CD-ROMs on the same site, with the extra copies at the site being very cheap.

Among possible economic solutions, for scholarly journals page charges might make it possible to reduce the per-issue price to the point where copying just did not have enough economic incentive, as discussed previously. More generally, site licenses at least remove the issue of cheating within an organization. Many university libraries are likely to pursue this route for acquiring material so that they have no policing requirement within their university. Institutional sponsorship of publications, although going out of favor, would also mean that piracy was less relevant. And, of course, advertiser-supported publications do not care if people copy them. Aside from site licenses, it seems unlikely that any of these suggestions would cover most library material. Perhaps someday we will have pledge breaks on the Internet.

10.5.9 *Flickering*

Is there a way to let people see something and read it, but not capture it by screen dumping? This would seem contradictory, but a proposed solution relies on retinal persistence, the ability of the human eye to average rapidly changing images. Movies and television work because a human eye presented with images changing 24 or 30 times per second tries to average the result, rather than perceive the separately changing images (as it would if the images changed every second or every two seconds). Computer screen dumps, on the other hand, capture an instantaneous appearance. They don't do any time-averaging over the screen appearance.

Thus, imagine taking a text to be displayed and adding random bits to the background. Do this twice, producing two bitmaps that contain all the bits in the letters plus perhaps 50% of the remaining bits turned on at random. Then rapidly

```
Piece out our imperfections
with your thoughts;
Into a thousand parts
divide one man,
And make imaginary puissance.
Think, when we talk of
horses, that you see them,
Printing their proud hoofs
in the receiving earth;
For 'tis your thoughts
that now must deck our kings.
```

Figure 10.5   Flickering for protection

alternate between these bitmaps. The human eye will perceive the steady letters as letters; it will take the irregular flickering bits in the background as equivalent to a 50% grey background. After all, this kind of display is how to use dithering to represent a 50% grey rectangle. So the eye will perceive steady letters on a grey background. Any screen dump, however, will capture the background bits and the resulting screen image is almost useless.

Figure 10.5 shows this process. The top two bitmaps, if merged together, produce the appearance of the lower image (the text is from the prolog to *Henry V*). In a static paper, it is not possible to show the flickering, so the lower image is 100% black letters on a flat 50% grey background. However, if read on a screen with about 30 repeats per second, this is roughly the appearance that results. An even higher flicker rate would be desirable; rates as low as 15 repeats per second cause the changing background to appear as an annoying Moire-like pattern, rather than as a steady grey level. The separated bitmaps, although barely readable by the human eye, have been tried on OCR programs, with no useful output. The eye is, of course, much better than an OCR program at deciding what represents a possible letter and what is random noise.

The density of the background can be adjusted. Clearly, moving to a lighter background (fewer dark bits) produces a more readable image, at the expense of making it easier to imagine an OCR program that can deal with the separated bitmaps. Tests suggest, however, that even 10–20% of random bits added to a bitmap will make OCR ineffective. Note, however, that this figure assumes a normal letter size; if the letters are greatly enlarged relative to the dots, the noise is easier to remove.

Figure 10.6   Flickering, lower density

Figure 10.7   Flickering letters

The flickering is annoying, but the text is readable. A screen dump of the window gives one of the two bitmaps with the cluttered data. Even with only a 25% dark-bit density level these can only be read with considerable annoyance by the human eye, and certainly not by an OCR program, as shown in Figure 10.6.

There are various choices in this system. The random bitmaps can have any grey level. In particular, if the background grey level is about 10%, you get a very easy-to-read onscreen display, but a reader can make out the cluttered images when isolated easily as well (although OCR programs still fail). If the background level is 50%, the display is now a fairly dark background but still quite readable when flickered. The individual cluttered images are then not even easily recognizable as text by eye, let alone readable.

Another choice is to have the background flat white, and flicker between two images of the text, each of which has half the bits from the letters. This produces a different impression: instead of seeing good letters against a flickering grey background, flickering letters appear against a clean background. The half-images are recognizable as text but not easy to read (and again won't make it through OCR). This form, shown in Figure 10.7, seems a little harder to read than the steady-letter, flickering-background form (and it is easier to imagine how it might be attacked with bit-cleanup techniques).

Note that it may not be desirable to have too many background bitmaps. If a method of attack is to capture both images and try to logically AND them to uncover the letters, the more random backgrounds that are used, the more likely it is that the letters will be apparent. It is also possible to combine the idea of flickering backgrounds and flickering letters, with perhaps a 25% background and a 75% letter density.

Another feature in this program is to "wobble" the text up and down the screen slowly. This wobble doesn't bother the reader as much as the flickering, and it defeats a pirate who might try taking 100 screen dumps in succession and averaging the result. With the text wandering up and down the screen, the averaging will be destroyed.

This idea does not work as well with displays of pictures rather than text. Without the familiar letter shapes to guide the eye, the addition of noise to a photograph of a real scene makes it considerably noisier, rather than being an apparent "background." However, the digital watermarking techniques are applicable to pictorial images. Thus, the flickering technique is applicable exactly when the watermarking techniques are not and fills a slot in copyright defense technology.

Intellectual property protection is a practical application of the Turing test. Turing had proposed that machines would be "intelligent" when a person exchanging teletype messages with both a machine and a human could not tell which was which (Turing 1950). The desire to allow a person to read information, but not to have a machine copy it, is effectively a need for a way to be sure what is at the other end of your communication line. The same problem has come up with the desire of some online stores to block price-comparing robots; they only want people, not programs, to connect to their site.

10.6 *Summary: Future Research and Law*

Again, this chapter has described an unsolved problem. Many of the most important future issues of digital libraries involve legal questions. Should the United States extend or limit protection in these new digital areas? Will greater protection encourage the creation of digital information, or will it bog us down in rights negotiations? Perhaps the most important problem will be to reduce administrative costs, perhaps with some kind of compulsory licensing scheme. Although print publishers have argued against compulsory licensing, it seems to work in the songwriting business. Perhaps a voluntary clearinghouse will be acceptable; the Copyright Clearance Center, for example, has most important publishers as members.

We also need ways of authenticating publishers and users. There is nothing in an electronic message that can be inspected to convey age or authorship. Cryptography does provide solutions to this problem, but the complexities of U.S. export regulations and the lack of agreement on implementation means that we do not have routine, commonly agreed authentication procedures, and we will need them to build economically reliable systems.

There are many details of legal procedures that will make great differences to libraries. Should collected facts be eligible for protection, and if so, should the protection be as long-lived as creative works? Should a document converted from one form to another acquire some kind of protection, and if so, what? How much responsibility do libraries, communications carriers, and others have for stamping out undesirable uses of their services? How much privacy are readers entitled to?

Perhaps the hardest choice to make is when laws should be used and when contracts. If there are no laws protecting some kind of information, we are likely to see elaborate contracts, raising administrative costs. A legal framework for information economics, however, is likely to be slow to enact and change, and this is a rapidly changing area. And finally, the international nature of the Web makes it harder for either U.S. law or U.S. contracts to operate in isolation from the rest of the world.

11

International Activities

THE PREVIOUS CHAPTERS have described potentials: how to store information, how to pay for it, how to protect it. There is a great deal of activity, in which things are really being done. This chapter looks at many of the existing digital library projects and what kinds of work are going on. In some ways, the Web itself is the largest digital library project, but there are many specific contributions to it, in a wide variety of places and organizations.

11.1 *Information Policy, Not Industrial Policy*

The Web is worldwide, and digital library research exists in many countries. Many countries have identified information technology as some kind of national goal, as in Singapore, which has declared its intent to become the "intelligent island." After memory chips, and after software, content in digital form may be another industry that countries are targeting as a way of gaining international advantage. As noted before, it has enormous economies of scale and sufficiently low entry costs that even small countries can try it.

Several nations have major digital library initiatives underway. One contrast is whether these programs are focused around libraries or around computer science research departments. The United States is at one extreme: the digital library effort is run by NSF, and it focuses on computer science research, building new tools and new methods of access. The collections involved are of less importance. Japan is at the other extreme: the major digital library effort is run by the National Diet Library and focuses on collections. European countries are directing their efforts in a mixed mode, less toward either end of the balance.

Another contrast is the difference between some projects that are very international and some that are trying to exploit particular resources that they have. In some nations, the culture supports working on the nation's own history and library collections; in other nations, the culture supports access to international information. Countries also may have specific skills that they can exploit: Singapore has many people who are expert in both English and Chinese; Switzerland, people skilled in several European languages; and Japan has expertise in devices, displays, and the like.

The degree to which the publishing community is involved and is working with the digital library effort differs from country to country. In the United States, publishers are involved in all the digital library projects and work frequently with universities. This is less common in some other countries, particularly if the digital library project is defined merely as "save the national heritage" and doesn't work on anything modern.

Information delivery, viewed in retrospect, is a U.S. success story of government stimulation of a new industry. Beginning in the 1950s, NSF and other government agencies funded research in information retrieval. Today, information retrieval is an enormous industry and is dominated by the United States. U.S. Department of Commerce estimates for 1993 for "databases and information services" show exports of $735 million against imports of $88 million. Even with Japan, the U.S. balance is $94 million of exported services against $10 million of imports. In the larger general area of "information services" (including large amounts of the software industry), in 1994 U.S. exports were $3.2 billion against imports of $0.4 billion. The industry is large, with information retrieval in general (including financial services) selling $13.5 billion in 1993 in the United States and a 25% growth rate in online service subscribers (while consumer subscribers grew even faster, 44%). About 30% of sales of U.S. online services are to foreign customers.

Everyone recognizes that this industry began with federal funding. The *Encyclopedia of American Industries* (Hillstrom 1994) says, "Government investment in the 1960s initiated many of the private information retrieval services that dominated the market in the 1980s and early 1990s. For instance, DIALOG sprung from a venture between the National Aeronautics and Space Administration (NASA) and Lockheed Corporation called Project RECON. ORBIT Online, which was recently acquired by Questel, was developed as a result of System Development Corporation's work with the National Library of Medicine. As another example, industry giant Mead Data Central got its start from seed money provided by U.S. Air Force projects." In addition, BRS began with a project from the National Library of Medicine as well.

NSF, in particular, started the text search industry, which relies heavily on techniques developed in programs funded originally by the Office of Science Information Services more than 30 years ago and which NSF has continued funding. Text search today is a $500 million per year business. Among the largest companies are Dataware (selling the BRS software that can be traced back to original government funding) and Personal Librarian (traceable to work funded by NSF at Syracuse University). However, this is a very competitive marketplace—the eight largest companies taken together have only perhaps one-third of the market.

Retrieval systems hold out promise in entirely new areas. For example, clothing manufacturers report that 27% of clothing costs are avoidable with better information (e.g., excessive inventory or lack of product), while only 10% of the costs are wages. Thus, clothing manufacturers can gain more by introducing better information systems than by paying their workers zero (Charles 1994).

U.S. government funding is still stimulating new efforts in retrieval. The National Science Foundation funded Bruce Croft at the University of Massachusetts, and his software is the base of the Thomas system at the Library of Congress, which has put congressional information online for everyone. Mosaic began at the National Center for Supercomputing Applications at the University of Illinois, funded under the High Performance Computing and Communications (HPCC) program, and its derivative Netscape went public in 1996 with an implied market value of over $2 billion. World estimates of network users are shown in Figure 11.1.

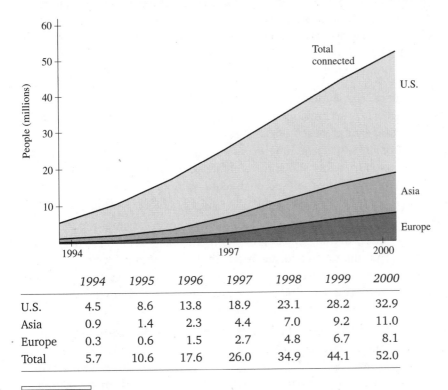

	1994	1995	1996	1997	1998	1999	2000
U.S.	4.5	8.6	13.8	18.9	23.1	28.2	32.9
Asia	0.9	1.4	2.3	4.4	7.0	9.2	11.0
Europe	0.3	0.6	1.5	2.7	4.8	6.7	8.1
Total	5.7	10.6	17.6	26.0	34.9	44.1	52.0

Figure 11.1 People on the Internet in the U.S., Asia, and Europe

11.2 *United States*

In the United States, NSF, NASA, and ARPA have funded six important digital library efforts, called the Digital Library Initiative (DLI). These programs each involve a large consortium of cooperating institutions, but the principal sites are at six universities: the University of California at Berkeley, the University of Michigan, the University of Illinois, Stanford University, the University of California at Santa Barbara, and Carnegie Mellon University. Each is doing both digitization and research in the use of electronic materials; each university and its partners are exploring a different area. This program was specifically designed to advance technology rather than just convert material, however, and includes many areas of research in access and cataloging of online materials.

11.2.1 *University of California at Berkeley*

To go briefly through these projects, Berkeley's collection is based on environmental information (papers, state documents, environmental impact statements, photographs, maps, and so on). The Berkeley collection now has 50,000 pages of reports and expects to grow to 300,000 pages. It has 30,000 photographs and plans for 560,000. They have 50 MB of data from dams, water flows, and so on; they expect 1 GB. Including various other kinds of data, they expect 3.5 terabytes in the final collection. Led by Robert Wilensky, Berkeley researchers are also developing several kinds of new technology for digital libraries (Berkeley 1995):

1. *Image content queries.* Berkeley, with the help of Xerox PARC, is running a system that classifies colors and regions in pictures. Users can then search for pictures with large orange areas, or red dots, for example. This system is integrated with the conventional textual searching, so that a query could look for photographs of dams in Sonoma County showing green areas. Even higher level is the use of color and shape matching to detect such features as people, animals, trees, and so on, which is still under development but shows some promising results.

2. *Database extraction from documents.* Many of the environmental reports in the collection are tables of numbers. Berkeley is writing parsers for these documents to extract the information in a formal representation so that it can be transferred to a database or spreadsheet. Thus both numerical and textual queries can be addressed to documents that report measurements such as the yearly fish population or water flow, along with discussion.

3. *Multivalent documents.* Given the availability of some documents in multiple forms (text, image, database, and so on) Wilensky has devised a representation that he calls "multivalent documents" to describe the multiple forms. Users can search or view any representation. For example, if some documents were translated into Spanish, users could choose to view that form, even if

they had searched in English. Processing of the multiple representations is also supported; for example, cut and paste works with images as well as with text.

4. *Natural language processing*. Berkeley is working on lexical disambiguation (see Section 5.2) and quotes an accuracy of 81% for assigning words to senses.

Much of the success is possible because Berkeley not only does OCR, but also is able to tag the position of specific words on the recognized page. Berkeley is also beginning to merge in other digital library resources, such as maps.

11.2.2 *University of Michigan*

The University of Michigan has one of the broadest and highest-level digital library projects, led by Dan Atkins (Birmingham 1995). Michigan is using earth and space sciences as its subject domain, and includes journal articles, books, and video and audio recordings of scientists discussing research questions in the collection. Two key aspects of the project are scalability and education:

1. *Scalability*. Michigan uses agents to help unify the different collections; in their model, digital libraries can be added to forever, and with entirely new organizations, since as a new collection arrives, the central agents route appropriate queries to the new server. They call this process the *conspectus search*: finding which collection is appropriate for which query.

2. *Education*. Michigan has deployed both an "Internet Public Library" and a system that reaches into public schools. Researchers at Michigan such as Elliot Soloway believe in "inquiry-based education" as a major improvement in teaching styles in the public schools and are trying to develop this potential using the Internet and the digital library resources.

Michigan again is trying to merge the DLI project with its other digital library efforts such as JSTOR (Journal Storage; see Section 3.7), TULIP (The University Licensing Program; see Section 11.2.7), and "The Making of America" (see Section 11.2.7).

11.2.3 *University of Illinois*

The University of Illinois is using scientific journals as its base collection, with a goal of 100,000 documents from many scientific publishers (largely professional societies) and 100,000 users across the Big Ten universities in the midwestern United States. Bruce Schatz is the project leader (Schatz 1996, 1997). At this point Illinois has five journals from three publishers and is making the SGML to HTML process smoother. Their major effort has been on defining semantic spaces. They use automatic term expansion computed on a parallel machine and term-term correlation methods. Preliminary evaluations of this method look promising.

11.2.4   *Stanford University*

The digital library effort at Stanford, led by Hector Garcia-Molina and others, is mainly an infrastructure project (Stanford 1996). Although there is a collection of computer science literature, the main effort at Stanford is basic networking and database infrastructure to support digital libraries. The Stanford goal is to allow many different projects to interwork at a low level, in terms of exchanging search services, billing, and so forth. Instead of the Web, where all documents are in the same format, HTML, Stanford envisages systems that describe themselves in a formal model and then are linked by their database software.

11.2.5   *University of California at Santa Barbara*

Unlike the previous projects, the main content of this digital library work is not text. Santa Barbara (UCSB), headed by Terry Smith, is working on maps, aerial photographs, and other "spatially indexed" information in their Alexandria library (Alexandria 1996). They cooperate not only with the other Digital Library Initiative projects, but also with a group of NASA-funded efforts to make earth observation data more readily accessible.

1. *Spatial indexing and retrieval.* UCSB tries to determine, for each query and library item, the "footprint" on the earth, which may be a precise point or area, or may be fuzzy. Geographic names or coordinates are mapped to the footprint, which can then be used for spatial retrieval. Given the size of the images, UCSB is also researching technologies for rapid response to image data, including multiresolution image storage and display.

2. *Image processing.* Like Berkeley, UCSB is also interested in analyzing images. In their case, a key question is partitioning: dividing the image into areas, which can then be characterized by texture, color, and location. This process can be used to find particular kinds of land use in aerial photographs. Their edge location algorithms are doing very well, holding out hope for queries such as "Find a photograph of Ventura County in the 1950s showing orchards." Figure 11.2 shows a sample of the partitioning algorithm from their Web site.

11.2.6   *Carnegie Mellon University*

Finally, Carnegie Mellon University (CMU) is working on digital video; their collection will eventually contain 1000 hours of videotape from WQED (the public television station in Pittsburgh). The CMU project is named Informedia, led by Michael Mauldin, Marvin Sirbu, and others; it now includes about 200 hours, composed of about 50 hours of science documentaries from the Open University and 150 hours of broadcast news shows (Mauldin 1996). Several different technologies

Figure 11.2   Image partitioning

are brought together to try to provide access to this material, including image and voice recognition. Video is partitioned into scenes, as in Section 4.5, and different techniques are applied to the scene and the accompanying soundtrack.

1. *Image analysis.* Images from the video are partitioned, and then image features are found and categorized for search. Users can pick particular frames and then look for others that are similar. Research is under way on classifying frames (meetings, real events, speeches, and so on).

2. *Speech recognition.* Although some of the video is closed captioned and thus comes with a reasonably accurate transcript, CMU is using automatic speech recognition to handle uncaptioned material, to align the captioning with the spoken words, and to allow spoken questions. This work builds on a long history of speech recognition research at CMU (the Sphinx system).

3. *Face recognition.* CMU software looks for faces in the video and attempts to match them with names in the voice transcript. Again, this work is preliminary, but there is moderate success. Color values and shapes are used to find faces, and then a face similarity algorithm attempts to match them up.

4. *Natural language understanding.* To assign names to faces, it is still necessary to find personal names in the transcript. CMU again has a long history of work in NLP and is applying it to analysis of the transcripts. Some semantic problems can be quite difficult: if the announcer says, "Sinn Fein announced today that . . . " and the screen shows a picture of Gerry Adams, it is difficult to realize that Sinn Fein is not somebody's name.

The CMU project probably involves the most ambitious combination of research technologies; as mentioned, many of these have been hard problems for decades. Nevertheless, less-than-perfect performance may still be very useful in digital library work.

All of these projects, as intended by NSF, are trying to advance the technology for accessing material; merely converting material to machine-readable form is not the focus of their effort. Other projects in the United States, however, start from a more traditional goal of improving preservation or access and are more concentrated on the collection than on the technology.

11.2.7   Other U.S. Projects

The Library of Congress, for example, under James Billington, is raising $60 million to digitize 5 million items from its collections. This effort follows earlier work in their American Memory Project, in which they digitized (and have now placed on the Web) such materials as Mathew Brady's Civil War photographs, documents from the Continental Congress, sound recordings of speeches from World War I, and early motion pictures (Library of Congress 1995). LC has also led an effort in which the heads of 15 large research libraries in the United States have formed a National Digital Library Federation to pursue joint efforts in making a digital service that provides information on American heritage and history to people everywhere. For example, Yale is working on scanning some 10,000 books from microfilm in the area of diplomatic history (Project Open Book), and Cornell is converting the key publications in agricultural literature from 1850 to 1950. The project "The Making of America" combines Cornell and Michigan in efforts to digitize key works in American history. So far, journals such as *Harper's* have been scanned for a decade or so in the late 19th century.

Publishers are also running a number of projects in the United States and elsewhere. For example, the Red Sage project was a collaboration of the University of California at San Francisco, AT&T Bell Laboratories, and Springer-Verlag. It ran from 1993 to 1995 and provided about 40 Springer journals in molecular biology and radiology. The project was based on publisher scanning followed by OCR, with searching of the OCR but display of the images. AT&T used its own OCR software and was thus able to highlight matches in the images.

Similarly, the TULIP project distributed 42 Elsevier journals in materials science as scanned images to nine U.S. universities: CMU, Cornell, Georgia Tech, MIT, University of California, Michigan, Tennessee, Washington, and Virginia Tech. Usage of these materials was perhaps less than originally hoped; partly this may be the generally low usage of scientific journals in the first place, and partly the switch to the Web that was happening as the journals were put online with other interfaces.

A great many other universities in the United States have digital library projects. Virginia Tech, for example, is known for the Envision system (see Section 7.5) of Ed

Fox. Envision is a project providing access to ACM publications and includes free-text search, relevance feedback, and a Web-like display of results. The University of Virginia has an online library of works by and related to Dante Gabriel Rossetti. The University of Georgia has digitized 800 rare maps. Columbia University is trying to digitize all the works needed to get through its core curriculum for undergraduate students. Books by and about David Hume are at the University of Tennessee. In fact there are so many such projects that the best thing to know is that there are several inventories of them, including the CETH (catalog of electronic texts in the humanities) at Rutgers and Princeton, the "Digital Collections Subject Index" at Simmons, the reports of the Commission on Preservation and Access, the On-Line Books Page at CMU, and others.

11.3 *United Kingdom*

In the United Kingdom, digitization work was stimulated by the Follett report, as a result of which £20 million was set aside for new digital library projects. The resulting program (originally called FIGIT but now named E-LIB) funded 35 projects (selected from 354 applicants). There is much work on cataloging archives, providing U.K.-wide email, and providing access to Web material of all kinds (shareware, teaching materials, and current information). The projects include four document delivery systems, ten electronic journals, two digitization efforts, seven on-demand publications, four efforts in training, and five supporting studies. For example, the University of Kent is doing caching, storing local copies of information that has been asked for recently. The idea is that the second and later requests for Web pages in the United States will, if possible, be provided from the cache, avoiding the delay in fetching it again from across the Atlantic. As of early 1997, the congestion across the Atlantic on the Internet is extremely bad, and people in the United Kingdom try to do their transatlantic data communication in their morning, when most of the United States is asleep.

U.K. projects include digitizing the Burney collection of pre-1800 newspapers, with initial attention to the time of the French Revolution, and to scanning the *Batley News*. The "Treasures of St. Pancras" are being scanned via 35-mm film to PhotoCD; this will include the Lindisfarne Gospels, the Diamond Sutra, and other famous works. The Canterbury Tales project is scanning all pre-1500 manuscripts and printed editions of Chaucer's poem and adding transcriptions and scholarly commentary (Robinson 1993). Other projects are scanning the papers of Samuel Hartlib (24,000 images), the *Palestine Post* (150,000 pages), and the 4000 letters of Thomas Wentworth, first earl of Strafford (Sheffield University 1995).

Perhaps the most important model that the United Kingdom has defined is that they have persuaded publishers to treat the entire academic community of the

United Kingdom as a single site for purposes of licensing information. The United Kingdom, acting through bulk purchases, has been able to obtain unlimited use licenses for all students and faculty for a number of databases. They have effectively used the market power of academic purchasing to negotiate good terms for the use of electronic information.

A U.S./U.K. project deserving special mention is the Electronic Beowulf project of Kevin Kiernan (University of Kentucky) and Paul Szarmach (Western Michigan University), working with the British Library to scan the *Beowulf* manuscript. The *Beowulf* manuscript was damaged by a fire in the 18th century, and areas of it have become much more difficult to read. By scanning under different light conditions (including UV), it is possible to obtain scanned images that display more than an ordinary reader could see by eye. A sample image is shown in Figure 11.3 (Color Plate). Thus, in addition to providing access to a fragile and unique manuscript to scholars at a distance, it can even provide better access than the original (Kiernan 1995).

Looking at more current material, the British Library Document Supply Centre (BL-DSC) is testing the idea of scanning current journals, with publisher permission, to simplify remote delivery by fax. This project is called TEDS (Trial Electronic Delivery System). BL-DSC holds over 200,000 serial titles and supplies over 2 million copies a year, about a quarter going overseas. The British pharmaceutical company Glaxo, for example, buys about 25,000 reprints per year. The Institute for Scientific Information (ISI) is piloting a similar effort, with 1350 scientific journals to be stored online.

11.4 *France*

France centers its efforts around the new building for the national library, which is to contain 10,000 books in ASCII format and 100,000 books in image format. Originally, the plan for the building also provided for extensive automatic access to sound and video recordings, but work is still continuing on building systems to access these media. It is planned to digitize 300,000 pictures and 3000 recordings. Their digitization, however, includes 1000 extremely beautiful 14th-century manuscripts, scanned from the Bibliothèque Nationale (Renoult 1995). For example, Figure 11.4 (Color Plate) is a map of Western Europe from the *Catalan Atlas* (14th century) at the Paris collection.

About 2000 works of classic French literature were keyed by the Trésor de la Langue Française project at the University of Nancy, with the aim of creating an historical record of French. The database, known also as Frantext and (in the United States) as ARTFL, is now run by the Institut National de la Langue Française in Paris. This is one of the earliest and most systematic efforts to obtain the basic literary corpus of any language in computer-readable form.

France, along with Japan, is a leader in a Group 7 project, the Bibliotheca Universalis. This is somewhat more of a museum project: it involves digitizing key cultural resources of many nations. The intent is to preserve and make internationally available public domain works in all kinds of media. It is also planning and collecting existing work, rather than new work. A great many digitization projects are viewed as part of this (including those at the Bibliothèque Nationale de France, Library of Congress, the Royal Society, and others). Among the few cooperative projects is the CERL (Consortium of European Research Libraries) effort to create a database of books prior to 1850. A French project that provides an exhibition of Enlightenment-period painting collected from many different physical museums can be found at `http://www.culture.fr/lumiere/documents/files/imaginary_exhibition.html` on the Web.

INIST (Institut de l'Information Scientifique et Technique), a French document delivery organization, is engaged in a major digitization project. Some 2000 current serials are scanned and the images used for document provision within France. Scanning is done so that text is produced in Group IV compression (see Section 3.2), while photographs are produced in JPEG. The results are placed on CD-ROM, and CD-ROM jukeboxes are used in the running system. French copyright policy lets INIST store electronic images of articles; so far no one has sued them. They only transmit electronically when they have concluded agreements with publishers, however, and thus most of their delivery is fax or postal. INIST charges 47 Fr for postal delivery, or 212 Fr for fax, with higher charges if the article is more than 10 pages long (as of early 1997, 6 Fr = U.S. $1).

Another project of the same sort was FOUDRE (Fourniture de documents sur reseau electronique), which did on-demand scanning (Group IV) and delivery over an ISDN network. A group of 12 libraries participated. There was little reuse; only 2% of the articles requested once were ever recalled from the digital store. FOUDRE ran from 1989 to 1992 and has been followed by EDIL and then ELITE.

11.5 *Other EU Efforts*

The European Union, of course, funds a variety of international efforts in digital libraries. For example:

- De Montfort University, the Victoria and Albert Museum, IBM UK, and Tilburg University have worked together on scanned art works under the name Elise Project (not to be confused with other De Montfort efforts such as the Elinor electronic library and the Elvira digital library conference).

- Another effort combines Vasari Ltd. and the Witt Library of the Courtauld Institute in London with RKD (Rijksbureau voor Kunsthistorische Documentatie, the Netherlands Institute for Art History) and Utrecht University in The Hague and Trinity College Dublin, who are working on sharing art library information via a project called Van Eyck (Visual Arts Network for Exchange of Cultural Knowledge).

- The Gothic Cathedrals of Europe project will issue CD-ROMs with photographs of major cathedrals, combining work by the British Museum (United Kingdom), the Caisse Nationale des Monuments Historiques et des Sites (France), Cologne Cathedral (Germany), Institut de France, Kairos Vision (France), the Kunstinstitut of Munich, the Musée National des Thermes de Cluny et du Moyen-Age (France), the Museu Nacional d'Arte Catalan (Spain), and the Superindendenza di Milano (Italy).

- At the Technical University of Munich, Rudolf Bayer is building a table-of-contents cataloging system (OMNIS/Myriad) for books.

- Between 1987 and 1992, IBM scanned much of the Archives of the Indies in Seville, including 9 million pages (the full archive is 90 million pages and has 7000 maps). IBM is also helping scan about 20,000 documents from the rare manuscript collection of the Vatican Library, which has 150,000 manuscripts in total (Mintzer et al. 1995a, 1995b). Figure 11.5 (Color Plate) shows a sample image from the Vatican.

- A multimedia production of the literature, history, and culture related to Mt. Olympus is being built by the Athens Technology Centre SA, New Media Productions Ltd. (United Kingdom), and the Aristotle University of Thessaloniki (Greece).

- A multimedia dictionary of modern art is being prepared by Ediciones AKAL (Spain), Editions Fernand Hazan (France), Thames and Hudson (United Kingdom), and the Videomuseum (France), to appear on CD-ROM.

- Many other projects exist in other European countries; see the list of digital library projects maintained by Marc Fresko for the British Library (Fresko 1994) and the reports of Hans Rutimann (Rutimann 1992).

11.6 *Japan*

In Japan the digital library effort includes the preparation of a national union catalog and also a set of experiments on primary material at the National Diet Library. These experiments are testing and demonstrating digitization over a range of different kinds of library materials.

The work in Japan explores not only many different holdings but also different kinds of digitization techniques (National Diet Library 1995). Among the materials being digitized are the following:

- 7100 sheets of especially valuable rare materials, of which 1236 sheets are national treasures or important cultural properties, including woodblock prints, scrolls, and old maps. These will be digitized (via photographic film) in color, at high resolution (5000 × 4000 pixels).

- 21,000 books in the social sciences published during the Meiji (1868–1912) period. These are to be scanned in monochrome from microfilm.

- 3000 books, published during World War II on poor-quality paper, that are both deteriorating badly and present in few copies. Again, these will be scanned from microfilm.

- 20 serial titles, totalling 800,000 pages, to be scanned directly with sheet feeders.

- 260 volumes of Diet (Parliamentary) research materials, amounting to about 6000 pages, to be both scanned and processed by an OCR program that can recognize kanji.

- 7000 documents in political history related to Michitsune Mishima, comprising 340,000 frames of microfilm.

- 1,600,000 pages of material, largely Diet proceedings, to be scanned directly from paper.

The total budget for this project is about 5 billion yen ($50 million). As can be seen from the example materials, both preservation and access are important, and libraries are expected to have a key role in the distribution of electronic information.

Japan also has projects in modern document delivery, including the NACSIS (National Center for Science Information Systems) project, which is doing page images for 56 titles, and the MANDALA library in Nara, which adds OCR to journal page images.

11.7 *Australia*

Australia is also planning some important digitization efforts. The prime minister announced in December 1995 that the next budget would contain $10 million (Australian) for digitizing at national cultural institutions, such as the National Gallery of Australia and the National Library of Australia. In speeches he has called for Australia to be the "creative country" or the "clever country" (traditionally, it was the "lucky country"). Among the projects being undertaken are the digitization of important early Australian literary works, called the Ferguson 1840–1845 project after the major bibliographer of Australian publishing. This project will scan (400 dpi, 8 bits of grey level) 150,000 images representing 75 serial titles and four novels. There is also digitization of aboriginal language recordings,

Figure 11.6 Australian picture

scanning of the journals of Sir Joseph Banks, creation of a computer file of biographies of Australian scientists, and converting Australian war photographs to electronic form.

The State Library of Victoria, for example, has converted 107,000 of its 650,000 historical photographs to digital form, averaging 35 KB for the JPEG file for each picture. An item-level catalog was prepared for each picture. Figure 11.6, for example, is from the portrait file and shows four aboriginal men at Corranderrk.

11.8 *Elsewhere*

Every major country has some national digitization projects. Canada, for example, is active on many fronts. The University of Waterloo developed text search software based on the Patricia tree data structure, and a company named OpenText is selling a commercial version. The National Library of Canada is digitizing works related to the Confederation and the history of Canadian women (Turko 1996), as shown in Figure 11.7.

More interesting potentially is its effort to collect in electronic form Canadian online books and journals. Although skimpy at present, the integration of

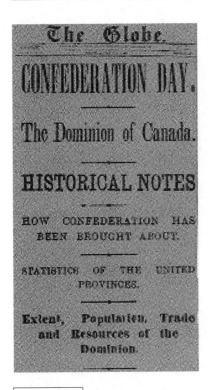

Figure 11.7 Canadian newspaper

new and old online material points the way to the unified library catalog of the future.

Singapore has announced a goal of becoming the "Intelligent Island." All libraries are to be linked with networking (in fact a high-speed network is to cover the country). The economic emphasis is explicit: "Information is becoming a critical factor of production providing many industries with the impetus to enhance their competitiveness. It is transforming the economy. For example, innovative exploitation of IT can help Singapore develop high value-added manufacturing with links to lower cost manufacturing centres in the region and markets around the world" (from the Singapore plan for the year 2000 [IT2000 1992]). So far, the libraries are emphasizing access to other information (the gateway concept).

In Korea, there is a fascinating project to digitize the wood carvings at the Haeinsa monastery, which contains 81,258 wooden printing blocks with the oldest known copy of the Buddhist canon in Chinese, the Tripitaka Koreana. The risk of mold damage to these 13th-century printing blocks (see Figure 11.8) and the desire to make them accessible to more people prompt a digitization project plus work on

(a)

(b)

Figure 11.8   *(a)* Woodblocks as stored; *(b)* block and printing

the preservation of the actual wood, although the 15th-century buildings with clay floors turn out to be excellent storehouses (Haeinsa Monks 1996).

China is developing new technology very rapidly, although much work in China's 300,000 libraries is focused on online cataloging and the development of Chinese MARC records. But the National Library of China, with 16 million books in Beijing, is planning to scan old books from the Sung and Yuan dynasties of A.D. 960–1368 (Jishi 1992), and there is research on Chinese character recognition.

CD-ROM publishing is very familiar in China, which balances the lack of good data networks. The Chinese are also considering blocking parts of the Internet for a variety of reasons, leading to a security fence described in the rest of the world as the "Great Firewall of China"; it remains to be seen if they can succeed in blocking the political content that they wish to exclude.

11.9 *International Cooperation*

There are many cooperative international projects. These include papyri, led by the University of Michigan (Bagnall 1995) and shown in Figure 11.9 (Color Plate); the Sakharov papers (Brandeis University and the Moscow Sakharov Centre, funded by the Public Commission for the Preservation of the Legacy of Academician A. D. Sakharov); the Research Library Group's (RLG) "Studies in Scarlet" (marriage and sexuality in the United States and United Kingdom, 1815–1916); CIMI (Consortium for Interchange of Museum Information), sponsored by the Getty, RLG, and Canadian Heritage; and Project Diana, an international human rights database run by the law libraries at Yale, the University of Cincinnati, and the University of Minnesota. The International Dunhuang project combines London, Berlin, Paris, and St. Petersburg institutions to scan central Asian Buddhist documents. UNESCO has a Memory of the World project, devoted to endangered material.

All the digitization activity is rapidly accumulating library-owned material on the Web, joining the publisher-owned material. For example, such newspapers as the *Times* (London), the *New York Times*, the *Telegraph*, and others are on the Web in full text (initially for free). The contrast, however, between the publisher material (generally full text, fairly complete, and often without images) and the library material (often scattered, representing exhibitions, and heavy on pictures and light on text) is dramatic.

11.10 *Summary*

Much of the library material being digitized in these projects is from special collections, preservation material, or other content that is not heavily used in traditional libraries. It is understandable that libraries are avoiding the copyright problems in choosing collections to digitize, but it does run the risk that their material will seem less important to users. It will be of the greatest value to libraries if the early digital library projects involve material that is heavily used, and patrons regularly learn that digital information is easy to use and valuable. This will help us learn how much the electronic forms of material are worth to the users and build up public support for and familiarity with digital libraries.

The international nature of the Internet revolutionizes our ability to move information around the world. U.S. undergraduates can be assigned papers with topics needing information from all over the world, and they can find this information with less effort than was traditionally required. If we can continue the library tradition of open cooperation and access, in which scholars from any country are usually welcome at any library, we should be able to increase the amount of transnational information flow and compensate for the increasing numbers of libraries that lack funds to maintain their foreign purchases of journals and books.

Internationalism interacts with the previous issues of economics and intellectual property rights. Will there be a single place where most online information is collected, or will files like books be distributed around the world? Will there be the equivalent of "flags of convenience" in shipping, as digital publishers or libraries try to locate in places whose legal system is perceived to be more generous? We are already seeing offshore gambling on the Internet. Fortunately, libraries have a history of cooperation, extending around the world for decades. As I write (early 1997) the British Library is reorganizing the reference shelves in its reading room into the Dewey classification. And the British Library's Document Supply Centre sends the United States copies of U.K. publications and doctoral theses. Libraries must continue to work together and help each other deal with the economic problems of the digital world.

12

Future: Ubiquity, Diversity, Creativity, and Public Policy

SO THE DREAM OF Vannevar Bush is about to be realized. We will have whatever we need at our fingertips. What will this mean for society? Is there something we should be changing about our law or our institutions to deal with the coming digital library?

12.1 *Dream to Be Realized*

In the future we expect that artifacts will be relatively less important. More and more, it will be the digital version that is used. Just as the reading of old newspapers moved from paper to microfilm, and music moved from performance to recordings, and the theatre from stage to cinema, we can expect a major shift toward digital reading. Just as in these other examples, the old will survive, but the new will be dominant.

Yogi Berra said it is tough to make predictions, especially about the future. Harold Stassen wrote in 1955 that nuclear energy would create a world "in which there is no disease . . . where hunger is unknown . . . where food never rots and crops never spoil" (Corn 1986). And Douglas Hartree wrote in 1951 that "we have a computer here in Cambridge; there is one in Manchester and one at the [National Physical Laboratory]. I suppose there ought to be one in Scotland, but that's about all" (Corn 1986). And, there is no fanatic like a convert. The chief engineer of the British Post Office, Sir William Preece, wrote in 1879 that "I fancy the descriptions we get of its [the telephone's] use in America are a little exaggerated, though there are conditions in America which necessitate the use of such instruments more than here. Here we have a superabundance of messengers, errand boys, and things of that kind." By 1898 he had switched sides and wrote, "If any of the planets be populated with beings like ourselves, then if they could oscillate immense stores of electrical energy to and fro in telegraphic order, it would be possible for us to hold commune by telephone with the people of Mars." Similarly, what should we make of a claim by International Data Corporation at the beginning of 1996 that within one year up to a fifth of large companies with Web sites will have closed or frozen them ("Net Outlook Gloomy" 1996)? With hindsight, we know this did not happen.

Now that you have been warned, Table 12.1 offers some predictions collected by *Wired* magazine on digital libraries ("Future of Libraries" 1995). Personally, I believe these predictions are very conservative. The Library of Congress is likely to see many acquisitions coming in electronic form; I think that long before 2040 more than half the contents of the Library of Congress will be newly purchased or deposited electronic materials. And I believe the rate of conversion of old material will accelerate and that conversion of half the existing content, shared among many libraries in the United States, is going to come in the early 21st century.

If the electronic library comes to pass, there may be, as a result, a greater distance from the real world. People will study more and do less. Simulation may replace experiment. Some of this is clearly good. Simulators can be used to teach airline pilots emergency maneuvers that would be too dangerous to try in a real airplane, for example. Simulation can let many students "visit" an ecological area

Table 12.1

	Half of the Library of Congress Is Digitized	*First Virtual Large Library*	*Free Net Access in Public Libraries*	*VR in Libraries*
Ken Dowlin	2050	2020	2005	1997
Hector Garcia-Molina	2065	unlikely	2000	2010
Clifford Lynch	2020	2005	unlikely	1997
Ellen Poisson	2050	2030	2005	2020
Robert Zich	2030	2010	2005	2000
Average	2043	2016	2003	2005

Ken Dowlin: former librarian of the city of San Francisco
Hector Garcia-Molina: Stanford professor, principal investigator on the Stanford digital library project
Clifford Lynch: director of library automation, University of California
Ellen Poisson: assistant director, New York Public Library, Science, Industry and Business Library
Robert Zich: director of electronic programs, Library of Congress

that is too sensitive to stand many users or that is too expensive for them to visit. Similarly, objects that are only in one place can be seen everywhere. Rare manuscripts, paintings, and photographs can be viewed. Material that is too bulky to be collected in many places may be available.

Yet there are also costs. Will we see buildings collapse when architects rely on simulation programs that they do not entirely understand? Will children lose even more touch with the physical world and other people, as computers add to television as an artificially created distraction? Can we tell what the consequences will be? We don't seem to know much about the effects of television on society; how will we find out about the effects of computers?

12.2 *Future Roles in Information Handling*

In this new world, if everyone can contribute information, how will we know what is good and what is bad? Our supermarkets are already full of publications claiming that Elvis is still alive or that space aliens walk among us. How will we know what is true and what is false? We have various cues today; books from university presses, or whose authors have faculty appointments, are usually more dependable than paperbacks with lurid covers. What TV network anchors say is more credible than what callers to talk radio say. In the world of the Net, many or most of these cues will be gone. What will replace them? How will we know what to believe? As mentioned previously, the replacement of a refereed letters journal by a preprint bulletin board has made it more difficult for people who are not well-known to get attention in the research physics community. This is an example of an unexpected social effect from a technological change. What other effects will we have?

One possibility is that the job of evaluating and assessing information will become more important to everyone. Perhaps, at some point, it will be more lucrative to check information than to create it. Don King (then head of King Research) suggested that engineers typically spent about one-fifth as much time finding what to read as they did reading (King 1987). Perhaps this will change, and we'll spend a higher fraction of our effort on selection. Certainly, most people I know have no more time to read additional items but could use some help picking the right thing to read.

From what source will we get information? Today we have places we go to get things that we carry away at once: bookstores, newsstands, and libraries. We get things through the mail from publishers and from bookstores. We hear information on broadcast media, television, and radio. Where does the Net fit? Information comes immediately, as from a library or bookstore, but no travel is involved. It can be generated simultaneously with our inquiry, but no broadcasting is done. Who should run such a service? It doesn't mesh with any of the existing organizations, and the field is still up for grabs.

Libraries will need to expand their cooperative activities. Today, most libraries are judged and budgeted on the basis of how many books they have. The *Chronicle of Higher Education* publishes a regular table showing the ranks of libraries, recently showing Michigan listed as sixth while Columbia is seventh, partly because Michigan has 6,584,081 books and Columbia has only 6,532,026. It cannot really matter, in evaluating a library or a university, what the third significant digit in the number of books owned might be. Access to books may, in the future, be more important than possession. And the habit of valuing libraries by the size of their collections has meant that inadequate attention is paid to the assistance provided by staff to faculty and students. The services and training given by the librarians to the university community are the aspects of the library that an outside vendor will have most difficulty providing. On many campuses the library building also doubles as a student center or a study hall, or has other functions. Libraries need to be valued for their functions beyond buying and shelving.

Similarly, we have in the past obtained information from a great variety of sources. Perhaps these will shrink. Partly this reflects the concentration in the publishing and media industries, as Viacom buys Paramount, which had previously bought Simon & Schuster, which had previously bought Prentice-Hall. Partly this reflects the low incremental cost of electronic publishing, meaning that lengthening a press run will be much easier than putting out a new book. This will be particularly true if everything has to be a "multimedia production," with art, animation, video, and sound. Any such production requires a team of specialists with expensive skills in each area.

Some years ago I was talking to an executive at Elsevier. He commented that Elsevier published a large number of elementary college physics textbooks. They were looking at producing a fancy multimedia physics textbook, but given the costs involved he feared they might only be able to finance one such CD-ROM. Now it may not matter if everyone in the United States learns first-year college physics from the same book. But would we like a world in which everyone learned history or philosophy from the same book? Are there advantages to a local textbook that is tailored to the particular environment?

The danger to all of us is that much lightly used research material may be bypassed in a rush to provide the heavily used and commercially lucrative current textbooks and important reference material online, and that the broader mission of keeping our entire cultural heritage will be overlooked. Digitization should be a way of increasing memory and diversity, not a way of standardizing everything and abolishing university institutions.

And how individual can a CD-ROM created by a committee really be? Would we expect the same level of individuality, even in physics, from a committee-produced CD-ROM that we find in, say, Richard Feynman's textbook? Secondary-school texts are already committee productions, and few feel they demonstrate eloquence, creativity, or an individual spirit. Will we lose something if all texts, and even all publications, move toward committee work?

12.3   *Effect of Digital Technology on Universities*

If using a library merely means connecting to its computer from a dorm room, it doesn't matter where the library is. Earlier this was discussed as an advantage, letting libraries avoid the need for expensive central-campus buildings. But, like the Force, it also has a dark side. When someday Berkeley has digitized all or most of its library, and students everywhere can access it, why does a small college need a library? What will it have that is not easily accessible from a larger library? If the students in a university library cannot tell whether the books they are reading come from the local network or from a remote library, does it matter whether the university library actually owns any of its own books? Soon larger universities may approach smaller colleges and offer to provide library services for them at a lower cost than the small college could do for itself. And in the current university financial world, the small-college president may jump at the chance.

But then, what about teaching? Stanford already sells all of its computer science courses on videotape. If the Berkeley library were online, why would a small college need a library? If the Stanford courses were online, perhaps some college would question its need for a faculty. "Distance learning" is all the rage, and universities propose that they will create campuses with no resident faculty, merely places where students can access remote information. If libraries can be merely nodes on the Net, what about universities? Again, how long can it be before a large university offers to take over the teaching of a small college, pointing out their wider array of courses, more famous faculty, and economies of scale. Does the variety and individuality of different colleges and universities have value? Is the ability of the students to ask questions, and the ability of the professor to adjust the lecture to the student reaction, worth something? Or would we rather have each student given a selected and preserved lecture by the best professor, even if that professor is on video or on the Web? What if the best professor has even been dead for years? Will students watching on the Web know or care?

12.4   *Society and Creativity*

Perhaps it does not matter if universities are decimated. Once upon a time there was a vaudeville theatre in most American towns. The radio and the movies did them in, and lots of vaudeville comedians lost their jobs. A few were able to go into politics, but most had to find other employment. So what? I once heard the argument that after all, Jack Benny was funnier than all these individual comedians, so when he went on the radio and the individual theatres closed, the total amount of laughter in the United States increased. Perhaps; perhaps not. Perhaps the ability of the individual comics to make jokes about that particular town let them do better than Jack Benny, whose jokes had to cover the entire nation.

Is there value to the wide variety of universities, of books, of sources of information? Each year the United States publishes 50,000 books and produces 500 movies. There are 2000 legitimate stage productions, and there are about 85 network prime-time show slots each week. Will there be an enormous variety of Web pages, as we now see? Or will a few massive information providers send us everything?

Some of the answers to these questions depend on what we ask for. If we demand that each Web page we look at has to have animation, cartoons, music, and sound effects, then producing a Web page is going to take substantial capital resources, and there may not be many. Each would be made by committee and intended for a wide audience and probably therefore fairly bland. If, in contrast, people are satisfied with a Web page that just contains somebody's poetry, we can have many more, and they can be much more specialized. Would Rembrandt have succeeded as a painter if he had to sing and dance as well? Just as a theatrical audience accepts that the car chases that characterize action films can't really be done on the stage, if we want variety in our information sources, we can't expect them all to be multimedia extravaganzas.

12.5 *Public Policy Questions*

As the Web merges with paper libraries, public policy questions related to the role and organization of libraries are raised. Do we want single large libraries, or library cooperatives, or many small ones? Small libraries might well go the way of the corner hardware store as technology lets large libraries deliver services to homes. Should libraries be linked to educational institutions, or businesses, or what? Traditionally our libraries for books are public, but our video stores are private. Will the "cyber cafe" turn into a viable commercial business, or should libraries provide public access, or both? Librarians are in an unenviable position: they must cope simultaneously with budget difficulties, threats of commercial competition for some of their most valuable uses, and the need to educate an entire population of users.

Broader questions also arise. How do we ensure universal access to the Web so that we do not have a country in which the amount of information available to the rich and the poor is even more distorted than it is today? How do we ensure access for writing as well as reading? Some of the technological proposals (e.g., systems based on video-on-demand as the business driver) provide only one-way communications. It is a truism that freedom of the press helps most if you can afford to buy a newspaper; how do we keep Web publishing open to all?

There are many controversial questions about control of the Internet, arising from desires for censorship, or fears that the Internet will be used by terrorists or drug dealers, or concerns for privacy of individual citizens (would you like it, for example, if your electronic mail provider read your mail to decide which advertising to send you?). Even on a more mundane level, who should decide the format of works presented on your screen? Is this something publishers need to control, or will users wind up arranging books to suit their individual tastes, just as they once had custom binding of printed books?

International public policy issues will also rise in importance. Today the Web largely originates in the United States. Most of the new technological developments are also coming from the United States, but the Internet is international, and just as new companies often lead new industries, new countries could lead the Web business. Unlike manufacturing, there is little fixed capital investment that would stop people from suddenly accessing only pages in some new country. The Internet might, of course, reverse some current business imports. U.S. libraries and scholars buy many books and journals from foreign-based publishers that contain mostly papers written by American faculty. If the current scholarly publishing system is largely overthrown, this might decrease that particular item in the balance of payments. But whether we should simply hope for it, or try to do something about it, has attracted no real political interest. Does it even matter where intellectual property leadership is found? Perhaps not, if we judge by the attention given to it in recent elections.

It is not just economics and technology that decide how many information creators we will have or where they will be. Engineers tend to believe in technological determinism: if it can be built, it will be built. Bigger guns, bigger buildings, and bigger disk drives are all foreordained and unstoppable. But this is not true. Public concerns, law, or society can, in fact, stop a technology. Centuries ago, Japan, having seen early European guns, decided they did not want them and resumed using swords instead of muskets and artillery (Perrin 1980). More recently, we have seen public concerns and liability lawsuits end such technologies as nuclear power or new research on birth control methods. Childhood vaccines are a particularly frightening example. Only one manufacturer of whooping cough vaccine survives in the United States, for fear of liability lawsuits. Whooping cough (pertussis) vaccine may carry a risk of encephalitis, which, if real, affects about 1 in 100,000 children who get the vaccine. Of course, before 1930 about 1 child in 80 *died* of whooping cough. Nevertheless, we can barely keep the vaccine on the market. Liability lawsuits have also meant that streptomycin, once a wonder drug for which Selman Waksman got the Nobel Prize, is no longer available in the United States. It is possible for technology to be brought to a halt, and we have to think whether we want digital libraries and in what form.

The greatest benefit and the greatest risk of digital libraries are the same: we can foresee a world in which everyone can get any source of information, at their fingertips. We have to remember that many earlier technologies had great promise for teaching; both the phonograph and television were first thought of as educational tools. Both turned almost entirely into entertainment. Perhaps that is acceptable as one use of these technologies. But with the capacity available in digital networks, and the wide variety of sources of information that might be available, it would be a shame if the only future pages on the Web were those for pop music videos and special-effects movies. Let's design our networks to support open access for everyone, our copyright laws to provide access for the small as well as the large, and our educational system to encourage diversity and local option.

In his August 1996 acceptance speech to the Democratic National Convention, President Clinton called for a school system that has "every single library and classroom in America connected to the Information Superhighway" and for a country in which "every 12-year-old will be able to log in on the Internet" and "all Americans will have the knowledge they need to cross that bridge to the 21st century." But if we want true diversity, we need not just for everyone to have access to read but also the ability to create and distribute information.

12.6 *Projections*

Vannevar Bush's dream is going to be achieved, and in one lifetime. Seventy years from 1945, when he wrote his paper, it will be 2015, and it is clear that before then we will have the equivalent of a major research library on each desk. And it will have searching capabilities beyond those Bush imagined. We can capture newly written documents, we can convert old documents, and we are rapidly figuring out how to provide access to pictures, sound recordings, and videos.

We still lack a clear picture of how we're going to pay for all of this, but the explosion of the Web cannot be turned back. Whatever combination of greed and fear winds up supporting millions of Web sites, we will find some solution. Most likely, someday each scholar will have subscriptions to a variety of online services just as they own a computer and word processor today. Remember that the PC industry is selling over 50 million machines a year at $2000 each; its revenues are over $100 billion, larger than the entire publishing industry. So there is enough money to pay for a switch from paper information to electronic information; we only lack the procedures and organization.

And what will become of librarians? Bush described a profession of "trailblazer" to describe people who found and organized information. Perhaps the Web page evaluators of Yahoo and Magellan are the next step toward this profession. As information becomes easier to use, we can expect those who help others to find it to become more important, just as accountants changed from people who were good at arithmetic to those who run corporations. Similarly, in the sea of information of the future, librarians will not be those who provide the water but those who navigate the ship.

Shakespeare, in *As You Like It*, described seven ages of man. His ages correspond roughly to the development of this field. First there was the infant, the time until perhaps 1955 when only a few even thought about electronic information. Then the schoolboy, the period of initial experiments and research in the 1960s. Then the lover, the first flush of excitement about computers and word processors and our ability to put information online. The soldier followed on, working through the 1980s producing the technological development to make this all possible. The justice, probably about our state today, has to decide how the new technology will be used. And we look forward to the elderly character who can simply use it, and finally, we hope, not senility but perhaps the movement of advanced research to new areas. The story will play out in one lifetime, and we will move from a world of paper information, decaying and hard to find, to a world of screens, with fast access to almost everything. Those born in 1945 will see the entire play, from the days when computers were strange new machines in science fiction stories to the days when computers are our normal source of information.

References

Ackerman, M. 1994. "Augmenting the Organizational Memory: A Field Study of Answer Garden." *Proc. ACM Conf. on Computer Supported Cooperative Work (CSCW)*, pp. 243–252.

Ackerman, M., and T. Malone. 1990. "Answer Garden: A Tool for Growing Organizational Memory." *Proc. ACM Conf. on Office Information Systems*, pp. 31–39.

Aho, A., R. Sethi, and J. Ullman. 1986. *Compilers, Principles, Techniques and Tools*. Reading, MA: Addison-Wesley.

"Alexandria Digital Library." 1996 (date accessed). http://alexandria.sdc.ucsb.edu/.

Alston, R. C. 1986. *The Arrangement of Books in the British Museum Library*. London: British Library Humanities & Social Sciences.

Amsler, R., and D. Walker. 1985. "The Use of Machine-Readable Dictionaries in Sublanguage Analysis," in *Sublanguage: Description and Processing*, R. Grishman and R. Kittredge, eds., Hillsdale, NJ: Lawrence Erlbaum.

ANSI. 1992. *ANSI/NISO Z39.50-1992 (version 2) Information Retrieval Service and Protocol*. New York: American National Standards Institute.

Bagnall, R. S. 1995. *Digital Imaging of Papyri*. Washington, DC: Commission on Preservation and Access. September.

Baird, H. S. 1987. "The Skew Angle of Printed Documents." *Proceedings SPSE 40th Conf. on Hybrid Imaging Systems*, Rochester, NY, May, pp. 21–24.

Berghel, H., and L. O'Gorman. 1996. "Protecting Ownership Rights through Digital Watermarking." *IEEE Computer* 29(7):101–103.

Berners-Lee, T., R. Caillau, J. Groff, and B. Pollerman. 1992. "World-Wide Web: The Information Universe." *Electronic Networking: Research, Applications, Policy* 1(2):52–58.

Bielawski, M. 1996. Personal communication.

Birmingham, W. 1995 (date accessed). "University of Michigan Digital Library Project." http://http2.sils.umich.edu/UMDL/HomePage.html.

Blyskal, J. 1983. "Technology for Technology's Sake? (Database Publishing)." *Forbes* 131(May 9):196.

Borgman, C. 1986. "Why Are Online Catalogs Hard to Use? Lessons Learned from Information Retrieval Studies." *J. Amer. Soc. for Information Science* 37:387–400.

Borgman, C. 1996. "Why Are Online Catalogs Still Hard to Use?" *J. Amer. Soc. for Inf. Sci.* 47(7):493–503.

Born, G. 1995. *The File Formats Handbook.* New York: Van Nostrand Reinhold.

Boursin, F. 1995. "Stemming the Flood of Paper." *Chemistry and Industry* 23:992.

Bowen, W. G. 1995. *JSTOR and the Economics of Scholarly Communication.* Washington, DC: Council on Library Resources. Sept. 18. http://www-clr.stanford.edu/clr/econ/jstor.html.

Brassil, J. T., S. Low, N. Maxemchuk, and L. O'Gorman. 1994. "Marking of Document Images with Codewords to Deter Illicit Dissemination." *Proc. INFOCOM 94 Conference on Computer Communications*, pp. 1278–1287.

Broxis, P. F. 1976. "Syntactic and Semantic Relationships—or, a Review of 'PRECIS: A Manual of Concept Analysis and Subject Indexing, by D. Austin.'" *Indexer* 10(2):54–59.

Brynjolfsson, E., and L. Hitt. 1996. "Paradox Lost? Evidence on the Returns to Information Systems Spending." *Management Science* 42(4):541–558.

Burrell, Q. 1985. "A Note on Ageing in a Library Circulation Model." *J. Doc.* 41(2):100–115.

Bush, V. 1945. "As We May Think." *Atlantic Monthly* 176(1):101–108.

Canfora, L. 1990. *The Vanished Library: A Wonder of the Ancient World*, translated by Martin Ryle. Berkeley, CA: University of California Press.

Chang, S.-F., and J. R. Smith. 1995. "Extracting Multi-Dimensional Signal Features for Content-Based Visual Query." *SPIE Symposium on Visual Communications and Signal Processing* 2501(2):995–1006.

Chankhunthod, A., P. Danzig, C. Neerdaels, M. Schwartz, and K. Worell. 1996. "A Hierarchical Internet Object Cache." *Proceedings 1996 USENIX Conference.*

Charles, D. 1994. "A Look at the Clothing Industry of Today." *Morning Edition*. National Public Radio (Dec. 19).

Christel, M., T. Kanade, M. Mauldin, R. Reddy, M. Sirbu, S. Stevens, and H. Wactlar. 1995. "Informedia Digital Video Library." *Communications of the ACM* 38(4):57–58.

Church, K. 1988. "A Stochastic Parts Program and Noun Phrase Parser for Unrestricted Text." *Second Conference on Applied Natural Language Processing, ACL*, Austin, TX, pp. 136–143.

Church, K., and L. Rau. 1995. "Commercial Applications of Natural Language Processing." *Comm. ACM* (Nov.):71–79.

Cleverdon, C. W., J. Mills, and E. M. Keen. 1966. *Factors Determining the Performance of Indexing Systems.* Aslib Cranfield Research Project.

Cooper, M. D. 1989. "Cost Comparison of Alternative Book Storage Strategies." *Library Quarterly* 59(3):239–260.

Cormack, G. V., R. N. Horspool, and M. Kaiserswerth. 1985. "Practical Perfect Hashing." *Computer Journal* 28(1):54–58.

Corn, J. 1986. *Imagining Tomorrow: History, Technology, and the American Future.* Cambridge, MA: MIT Press.

Croft, W. B., S. M. Harding, K. Taghva, and J. Borsack. 1994. "An Evaluation of Information Retrieval Accuracy with Simulated OCR Output." *Symposium on Document Analysis and Information Retrieval*, Las Vegas, NV.

Cummings, A. M., M. L. Witte, W. G. Bowen, L. O. Lazarus, and R. H. Ekman. 1992. *University Libraries and Scholarly Communication: A Study Prepared for the Andrew W. Mellon Foundation.* Washington, DC: Association of Research Libraries. November.

Deerwester, S., S. Dumais, G. Furnas, T. Landauer, and R. Harshman. 1990. "Indexing by Latent Semantic Analysis." *J. American Society for Information Science* 41(6):391–407.

de la Solla Price, D. 1986. *Little Science, Big Science—and Beyond.* New York: Columbia University Press.

Drucker, P. F. 1970. *Technology, Management & Society; Essays.* New York: Harper & Row.

Egan, D. E., M. E. Lesk, R. D. Ketchum, C. C. Lochbaum, J. R. Remde, M. Littman, and T. K. Landauer. 1991. "Hypertext for the Electronic Library? CORE Sample Results." *Proc. Hypertext '91*, San Antonio, TX, Dec. 15–18, pp. 299–312.

Egan, D. E., J. R. Remde, T. K. Landauer, C. C. Lochbaum, and L. M. Gomez. 1989. "Behavioral Evaluation and Analysis of a Hypertext Browser." *Proc. CHI '89, Human Factors in Computing Systems*, pp. 205–210.

Eliot, C. W. 1978. "The Division of a Library into Books in Use, and Books Not in Use, with Different Storage Methods for the Two Classes of Books." *Collection Management* 2(1):73–82. Reprint of original 1902 essay.

Ester, M. 1990. "Image Quality and Viewer Perception." *Leonardo*, SIGGRAPH 1990 special issue, pp. 51–63.

Finlay, M. 1993. *The CD-ROM Directory 1994.* London: TFPL Publishing.

Fletcher, L. A., and R. Kasturi. 1987. "Segmentation of Binary Images into Text Strings and Graphics." *Proc. SPIE Conf. on Applications of Artificial Intelligence V* 786:533–540.

Flickner, M., H. Sawhney, W. Niblack, J. Ashley, Q. Huang, B. Dom, M. Gorkani, J. Hafner, D. Lee, D. Petkovic, D. Steele, and P. Yanker. 1995. "Query by Image and Video Content: The QBIC System." *Computer* 28(9):23–32.

Fresko, M. 1994. "Sources of Digital Information." Report 6102, British Library R&D Department.

Furnas, G. W., T. K. Landauer, L. M. Gomez, and S. T. Dumais. 1983. "Statistical Semantics: Analysis of the Potential Performance of Keyword Information Systems." *Bell Sys. Tech. Jour.* 62(6):1753–1806.

"The Future of Libraries." 1995. *Wired* (Dec.):68.

Garrett, J., and D. Waters. 1996. *Preserving Digital Information*. Washington, DC: Commission on Preservation and Access and Research Libraries Group.

Garside, R., G. Leech, and G. Sampson. 1987. *The Computational Analysis of English: A Corpus-Based Approach*. White Plains, NY: Longman's Publishing.

Geller, V. J., and M. Lesk. 1983. "User Interfaces to Information Systems: Choices vs. Commands." *Proc. 6th Int. ACM SIGIR Conference*, Bethesda, MD, June, pp. 130–135.

Gordon, S., J. Gustavel, J. Moore, and J. Hankey. 1988. "The Effects of Hypertext on Reader Knowledge Representation." *Proceedings of the Human Factors Society—32nd Annual Meeting*, Santa Monica, CA, pp. 296–300.

Gould, J. D., L. Alfaro, R. Fonn, R. Haupt, A. Minuto, and J. Salaun. 1987. "Why Reading Was Slower from CRT Displays than from Paper." *Proc. ACM CHI+GI 87*, Toronto, April, pp. 7–11.

Gould, J. D., and N. Grischokowsky. 1984. "Doing the Same Work with Hard Copy and with Cathode-Ray Tube (CRT) Computer Terminals." *Human Factors* 26(3):323–337.

Griffiths, J.-M., and D. W. King. 1993. *Special Libraries: Increasing the Information Edge*. Washington, DC: Special Libraries Association.

Guiliano, V. E., and P. Jones. 1963. "Linear Associative Information Retrieval." In P. Howerton, ed. *Vista in Information Handling*. Washington, DC: Spartan Books.

Haber, S., and W. S. Stornetta. 1991. "How to Time-Stamp a Digital Document." *Journal of Cryptology* 3:99–111.

"Haeinsa Monks Computerize the Tripitaka Koreana." 1996 (date accessed). `http://www.nuri.net/~hederein/intro/korecult.htm`.

Haigh, R., G. Sampson, and E. Atwell. 1988. "Project APRIL—A Progress Report." *Proc. 26th Annual Meeting of the Association for Computational Linguistics*, Buffalo, NY, June, pp. 104–112.

Hammann, D. 1983. "Computers in Physics: An Overview." *Physics Today* 36(5):25–33.

Hamming, R. W. 1969. "One Man's View of Computer Science." (Turing Award Lecture) *J. Assoc. Comp. Mach.* 16(1):3–12.

Harman, D. 1995. *Overview of the Third Text Retrieval Conference (TREC-3)*. NIST Publication 500-225. Gaithersburg, MD: NIST.

Hawkins, B. L. 1994. "Planning for the National Electronic Library." *EDUCOM Review* 29(3):19–29.

Hawkins, D. 1989. "In Search of Ideal Information Pricing." *Online*. 13:15–30.

Hawley, M. 1993. "Structure out of Sound." PhD thesis, MIT.

Hearst, M. A. 1995. "TileBars: Visualization of Term Distribution Information in Full Text Information Access." *Proceedings of the ACM SIGCHI Conference on Human Factors in Computing Systems*, Denver, CO, pp. 59–66.

Heath, L., D. Hix, L. Nowell, W. Wake, G. Averboch, and E. Fox. 1995. "Envision: A User-Centered Database from the Computer Science Literature." *Commun. of the ACM* 38(4) (Apr. 1995):52–53.

Hill, G. C., and M. Baker. 1996. "Companies Remain in the Dark about Size of On-line Markets." *Wall Street Journal–Interactive Edition*, June 17.

Hill, W., L. Stead, M. Rosenstein, and G. Furnas. 1995. "Recommending and Evaluating Choices in a Virtual Community of Use." *Proc. CHI Conference on Human Factors in Computing Systems*, Denver, CO, pp. 194–201.

Hillstrom, K., ed. 1994. *Encyclopedia of American Industries, Volume Two: Service and Non-Manufacturing*. Detroit: Gale Research.

Hough, R. 1970. "Future Data Traffic Volume." *IEEE Computer* 3(5):6.

Huang, X., F. Alleva, H.-W. Hon, M.-Y. Hwang, and R. Rosenfeld. 1992. "The SPHINX-II Speech Recognition System: An Overview." Report CMU-CS-92-112. See also http://www.informedia.cs.cmu.edu/report/results.html.

Humphrey, S. 1989. "A Knowledge-Based Expert System for Computer-Assisted Indexing." *IEEE Expert* 4(3):25–38.

Humphrey, S. 1992. "Indexing Biomedical Documents: From Thesaural to Knowledge-Based Retrieval Systems." *Artificial Intelligence in Medicine* 4:343–371.

IT2000. 1992. *A Vision of an Intelligent Island: IT2000.* Singapore: National Computer Board.

Jishi, B. 1992. "Optical Disk Document Storage and Retrieval System of the National Library of China." *Library in the 90's: Int'l Symposium on the Latest Developments in Technologies of Library Service*, National Library of China, Beijing, Sept. 7–11, pp. F6-1 to F6-8.

Johnson, B., and B. Shneiderman. 1991. "Treemaps: A Space-Filling Approach to the Visualization of Hierarchical Information Structures." *Proc. 2nd Int'l. IEEE Visualization Conference*, San Diego, Oct., pp. 284–291.

Jones, W., and S. Dumais. 1986. "The Spatial Metaphor for User Interfaces: Experimental Tests of Reference by Location Versus Name." *ACM Trans. Office Information Systems* 4(1):42–63.

Kenney, A., and L. Personius. 1992. *Joint Study in Digital Preservation*. Washington, DC: Commission on Preservation and Access.

Kiernan, K. 1995. "The Electronic Beowulf." *Computers in Libraries* (Feb.):14–15. http://www.uky.edu/~kiernan.

King, D. 1987. Lecture. British Library (April).

King, D. W., J. Castro, and H. Jones. 1994. *Communication by Engineers: A Literature Review of Engineers' Information Needs, Seeking Processes and Use*. Washington, DC: Council on Library Resources.

Knecht, G. Bruce. 1996. "How Wall Street Whiz Found a Niche Selling Books on the Internet." *Wall Street Journal*, May 16, p. 1.

Komatsu, N., and H. Tominaga. 1990. "A Proposal on Digital Watermark in Document Image Communication and Its Application to Realizing a Signature." *Electronics and Communications in Japan, Part 1 (Communications)* 73(5):22–23.

Krasilovsky, P. 1995. "Into the Black." *American Demographics: Marketing Tools Supplement* (July/Aug.):22–25. http://www.marketingtools.com/mt_current/MT285.html.

Krentz, D. M. 1978. "On-line Searching: Specialist Required." *J. Chem. Inf. Comp. Sci.* 18(1):4–9.

Landauer, T. 1995a. Unpublished work on closed captioning.

Landauer, T. 1995b. *The Trouble with Computers.* Cambridge, MA: MIT Press.

Landauer, T. K., and M. L. Littman. 1990. "Fully Automatic Cross-Language Document Retrieval Using Latent Semantic Indexing." *Proceedings of the Sixth Annual Conference of the UW Centre for the New Oxford English Dictionary and Text Research.* UW Centre for the New OED and Text Research, Waterloo, Ontario, pp. 31–38.

Leach, S. 1976. "The Growth Rate of Major Academic Libraries: Rider and Purdue Reviewed." *College and Research Libraries* 37(Nov.):531–542.

Lemberg, W. 1995. "A Life-Cycle Cost Analysis for the Creation, Storage and Dissemination of a Digitized Document Collection." PhD dissertation, University of California, Berkeley.

Lenat, D., and R. V. Guha. 1990. *Building Large Knowledge-Based Systems: Representation and Inference in the CYC Project.* Reading, MA: Addison-Wesley.

Lesk, M. E. 1986. "Automatic Sense Disambiguation Using Machine Readable Dictionaries: How to Tell a Pine Cone from an Ice Cream Cone." *Proc. SIGDOC Conference,* Toronto, June, pp. 24–26.

Lesk, M. E. 1991. "Television Libraries for Workstations: An All-Digital Storage, Transmission and Display System for Low-Rate Video," in M. Feeney and S. Day, eds., *Multimedia Information. Proceedings of the Second International Information Research Conference Held at Churchill College,* Cambridge, UK, July 15–18, pp. 187–194.

Library of Congress. 1995. *The National Digital Library Program—A Library for All Americans.* February. See also the American Memory Project: `http://lcweb2.loc.gov/amhome.html`.

Lin, X., and D. Soergel. 1991. "A Self-Organizing Semantic Map for Information Retrieval." *Proc. 14th Int'l SIGIR Conference,* Chicago, IL, October, pp. 262–269.

Lovins, J. B. 1968. "Development of a Stemming Algorithm." *Mechanical Translation and Computational Linguistics* 11(2):22–31.

Machlup, F. 1962. *The Production and Distribution of Knowledge in the United States.* Princeton, NJ: Princeton University Press.

Marks, K. E., S. P. Nielsen, H. Craig Petersen, and P. E. Wagner. 1991. "Longitudinal Study of Scientific Journal Prices in a Research Library." *College and Research Libraries* 52(2):125–138.

Matsui, K., and K. Tanaka. 1994. "Video-Steganography: How to Secretly Embed a Signature in a Picture." *Technological Strategies for Protecting Intellectual Property in the Networked Multimedia Environment* 1(1):187–206.

Mauldin, M. 1996 (date accessed). "Informedia Digital Video Library." `http://fuzine.mt.cs.cmu.edu/im/index.html`.

McKnight, L., A. Dillon, and J. Richardson. 1991. "A Comparison of Linear and Hypertext Formats in Information Retrieval," in R. Macaleese and C. Green, eds., *HYPERTEXT: State of the Art,* Oxford: Intellect.

Meadows, J. 1993. "Too Much of a Good Thing?" in H. Woodward and S. Pilling, eds., *The International Serials Industry*, Aldershot, Hampshire: Gower Publishing, pp. 23–43.

Meyer, S., and L. Phillabaum. 1996 (date accessed). "What Is a University Press?" `http://aaup.princeton.edu/central/press.html`.

Milliot, J. 1996. "Publishers Still Searching for Profits in New Media." *Publishers Weekly* 243(1):22.

Minsky, M. 1975. "A Framework for Representing Knowledge," in P. H. Winston, ed., *The Psychology of Computer Vision*, New York: McGraw-Hill.

Mintzer, F. C., L. E. Boyle, A. N. Cazes, B. S. Christian, S. C. Cox, F. P. Giordano, H. M. Gladney, J. C. Lee, M. L. Kelmanson, A. C. Lirani, K. A. Magerlein, A. M. B. Pavini, and F. Schiattarella. 1995a. "Toward On-line, Worldwide Access to Vatican Library Materials." *IBM J. of Research and Development* 40(2):139–162.

Mintzer, F., A. Cazes, F. Giordano, J. Lee, K. Magerlein, and F. Schiattarella. 1995b. "Capturing and Preparing Images of Vatican Library Manuscripts for Access via Internet." *Proc. 48th Annual Conf. Society for Imaging Science and Technology: Imaging on the Information Superhighway*, Washington, DC, May, pp. 74–77.

Morris, R. 1968. "Scatter Storage Techniques." *Comm. of the ACM* 11:38–43.

Mosteller, F., and D. Wallace. 1984. *Applied Bayesian and Classical Inference: The Case of the Federalist Papers, 2d ed.* New York: Springer-Verlag.

National Diet Library. 1995. *NDL Newsletter*, Tokyo, pp. 2–5.

Negroponte, N. 1996. "Caught Browsing Again." *Wired* 4.05 (May 1996).

Nelson, T. 1996. "Rants and Raves (letters column)." *Wired* 3.06.

"Net Outlook Gloomy in 96." 1996. *Times* (London) (Jan. 24).

Nielsen, J. 1990. "Evaluating Hypertext Usability," in D. H. Jonassen and H. Mandl, eds., *Designing Hypermedia for Learning. Proceedings of the NATO Advanced Research Workshop*, Berlin: Springer, pp. 147–168.

Noll, A. M. 1991. "Voice vs. Data: An Estimate of Broadband Traffic." *IEEE Communications* 29(6):22, 24, 29, 78.

Odlyzko, A. 1995. "Tragic Loss or Good Riddance: The Impending Demise of Traditional Scholarly Journals." *International Journal of Human-Computer Studies* 42(1):71–122.

Ogle, V. E., and M. Stonebraker. 1995. "Chabot: Retrieval from a Relational Database of Images." *Computer* 28(9):40–48.

Okerson, A., and J. O'Donnell. 1994. *Scholarly Journals at the Crossroads: A Subversive Proposal for Electronic Publishing*. Washington, DC: Association of Research Libraries.

Okerson, A., and K. Stubbs. 1992. "ARL Annual Statistics 1990–91: Remembrance of Things Past, Present . . . and Future?" *Publishers Weekly* 239(34):22.

Ousterhout, J. 1994. *Tcl and the Tk Toolkit*. Reading, MA: Addison-Wesley.

Paice, C. D. 1990. "Another Stemmer." *ACM SIGIR Forum* 24:56–61.

Peacocke, R. D., and D. H. Graf. 1990. "Introduction to Speech and Speaker Recognition." *IEEE Computer* 23(8):26–33.

Pearce, C., and C. Nicholas. 1996. "TELLTALE: Experiments in a Dynamic Hypertext Environment for Degraded and Multilingual Data." *J. Amer. Soc. for Inf. Sci.* 47(4): 263–275.

Pentland, A. 1996. "Smart Rooms." *Scientific American (international edition)* 274(4): 54–62.

Perrin, N. 1980. *Giving Up the Gun.* New York: Random House.

Renoult, D. 1995. "The Digitizing Program of the French National Library." *International Symposium on Digital Libraries 1995*, University of Library and Information Science, Tsukuba, Ibaraki, Japan, August 22–25, pp. 87–90. Also: http://www.bnf.fr/enluminures/aaccueil.shtm.

Rice, S., F. Jenkins, and T. Nartker. 1996. "Fifth Annual Test of OCR Accuracy." TR-96-01, Information Science Research Institute, University of Nevada, LV, April.

Rider, F. 1944. *The Scholar and the Future of the Research Library.* New York: Hadham Press.

Roach, S. S. 1996. "The Hollow Ring of the Productivity Revival." *Harvard Business Review* 74(6):81–89.

Robinson, P. 1993. *The Digitization of Primary Text Sources.* Oxford: Office for Humanities Communication, Oxford University Computing Services.

Ross, P., and N. Hutheesing. 1995. "Along Came the Spiders." *Forbes* 156(10):210–217.

Rothman, T. 1992. "Reader Ripoff: Why Are Books So Expensive?" *New Republic* 206(Feb. 3):14.

Rudnicky, A., A. Hauptmann, and K.-F. Lee. 1994. "Survey of Current Speech Technology." *Comm. ACM* 37(3):52–57.

Rutimann, H. 1992. *The International Project 1992 Update.* Washington, DC: Commission on Preservation and Access. http://palimpsest.stanford.edu/cpa/reports/intern92.html.

Salton, G. 1968. *Automatic Information Organization and Retrieval.* New York: McGraw-Hill.

Salton, G. 1970. "Automatic Processing of Foreign Language Documents." *J. Amer. Soc. for Inf. Sci.* 21(3):187–194.

Salton, G. A., and C. Buckley. 1991. "Automatic Text Structuring and Retrieval: Experiments in Automatic Encyclopedia Searching." *Proc. 14th SIGIR Conference*, Chicago, October, pp. 21–30.

Salton, G. A., and E. Voorhees. 1985. "Automatic Assignment of Soft Boolean Operators." *Proc. 8th Annual SIGIR Conference on Research and Development*, Montreal, pp. 54–69.

Sampson, G., R. Haigh, and E. Atwell. 1989. "Natural Language Analysis by Stochastic Optimization: A Progress Report on Project APRIL." *Journal of Experimental and Theoretical Artificial Intelligence* 1(4):271–287.

Samuel, A. L. 1964. "The Banishment of Paperwork." *New Scientist* 21(380):529–530.

Samuelson, P. 1993. "Legally Speaking: Liability for Defective Electronic Information." *Communications of the ACM* 36:21.

Samuelson, P. 1995. "Copyright's Fair Use Doctrine and Digital Data." *Publishing Research Quarterly* 11(1):27–39.

Sapir, E. 1949. *Language: An Introduction to the Study of Speech*. New York: Harcourt.

Savoy, J. 1990. "Statistical Behavior of Fast Hashing of Variable-Length Text Strings." *ACM SIGIR Forum* 24(3):62–71.

Sayood, K. 1996. *Introduction to Data Compression*. San Francisco: Morgan Kaufmann.

Schank, R. C., and K. Colby. 1973. *Computer Models of Thought and Language*. San Francisco: W. H. Freeman.

Schatz, B. R. 1996 (date accessed). "Building the Interspace: Digital Library Infrastructure for a University Engineering Community." http://surya.grainger.uiuc.edu/dli/.

Schatz, B. R. 1997. "Information Retrieval in Digital Libraries: Bringing Search to the Net." *Science* 275(5298) (Jan 17, 1997):327–334.

Seybold. 1996. "Kodak Enhances Photo CD." *Seybold Report on Desktop Publishing* 10(10):25.

Shannon, C. E. 1951. "Prediction and Entropy of Printed English." *Bell Sys. Tech. Jour.* 30:51–64.

Shardanand, U., and Pattie Maes. 1995. "Social Information Filtering: Algorithms for Automating 'Word of Mouth.'" *Proc. CHI Conference on Human Factors in Computing Systems*, Denver, CO, pp. 210–217.

Sheffield University. 1995. *Generating Electronic Text in the Humanities*. University of Sheffield Workshop. June.

Shneiderman, B. 1978. "Improving the Human Factors Aspect of Database Interactions." *ACM Trans. on Database Systems* 3(4):417–439.

Shneiderman, B. 1987. "User Interface Design and Evaluation for an Electronic Encyclopedia," in G. Salvendy, ed., *Cognitive Engineering in the Design of Human-Computer Interaction and Expert Systems*, Amsterdam: Elsevier Science Publishers, pp. 207–223.

Shneiderman, B. 1992. "Tree Visualization with Tree-maps: A 2-d Space-Filling Approach." *ACM Transactions on Graphics* 11(1):92–99.

Sincoskie, W. D. 1996. Personal communication.

Sirbu, M., and J. D. Tygar. 1995. "NetBill: An Internet Commerce System Optimized for Network Delivered Services." *Proc. IEEE COMPCON '95*, pp. 20–25.

Sparck-Jones, K., and M. Kay. 1973. *Linguistics and Information Science*. New York: Academic Press.

Srihari, S. N., S. W. Lam, J. J. Hull, R. K. Srihari, and V. Govindaraju. 1994. "Intelligent Data Retrieval from Raster Images of Documents." *Digital Libraries '94 Proceedings*, San Antonio, TX, June 19–21, pp. 34–40.

Stanfill, C., and B. Kahle. 1986. "Parallel Free-Text Search on the Connection Machine System." *Commun. ACM* 29(12):1229–1239.

Stanfill, C., and R. Thau. 1991. "Information Retrieval on the Connection Machine: 1 to 8192 Gigabytes." *Information Processing and Management* 27(4):285–310.

Stanfill, C., R. Thau, and D. Waltz. 1989. "A Parallel Indexed Algorithm for Information Retrieval." *Proc. 12th ACM SIGIR Conference*, Cambridge, MA: pp. 88–97.

Stanford University. 1996 (date accessed). "The Stanford University Digital Libraries Project." `http://www.diglib.stanford.edu/diglib/pub/`.

Stein, R. M. 1991. "Browsing through Terabytes." *BYTE* 16(5):157–164.

Stevens, S., M. Christel, and H. Wactlar. 1994. "Informedia: Improving Access to Digital Video." *Interactions* 1(4):67–71.

Stinson, D. R. 1995. *Cryptography: Theory and Practice*. Boca Raton, FL: CRC Press.

Stipp, D. 1995. "2001 Is Just Around the Corner, Where's HAL?" *Fortune* (Nov. 13).

Stowe, D. W. 1995. "Just Do It." *Lingua Franca* (Nov./Dec.):32–42.

Swanson, D. R. 1987. "Two Medical Literatures That Are Logically But Not Bibliographically Connected." *J. Amer. Soc. Inf. Sci.* 38(4):228–233.

Swanson, D. R. 1991. "Analysis of Unintended Connections between Disjoint Science Literatures." *Proc. 14th ACM SIGIR Conference*, Chicago, Oct., pp. 280–289.

Taubes, G. 1993. "E-mail Withdrawal Prompts Spasm." *Science* 262(5131):173–174.

"Taxed in Cyberspace." 1996. *Economist* 340(7974):67.

Tenenbaum, J. M., C. Medich, A. M. Schiffman, and W. T. Wong. 1995. "CommerceNet: Spontaneous Electronic Commerce on the Internet." *Proc. IEEE COMPCON '95*, San Francisco, pp. 38–43.

"Text Retrieval: The Next Steps." 1996. *Online & CD-ROM Review* 20(3):150–152.

Tou, F. N., M. D. Williams, R. Fikes, A. Henderston, and T. Malone. 1982. "Rabbit: An Intelligent Database Assistant." *Proc. AAAI Conference*, Pittsburgh, PA, August, pp. 314–318.

Turing, A. 1950. "Computing Machinery and Intelligence." *Mind* 54 (Oct.):433–460.

Turko, K. 1996. *Preservation Activities in Canada*. Washington, DC: Commission on Preservation and Access. February.

University of California at Berkeley. 1995 (date accessed). "UC Berkeley Digital Library Project." `http://elib.cs.berkeley.edu`.

Van Bogart, J. 1995. *Magnetic Tape Storage and Handling: A Guide for Libraries and Archives*. Washington, DC: Commission on Preservation and Access. June.

Varian, H. R., and R. Roehl. 1997 (date accessed). "Circulating Libraries and Video Rental Stores." `http://www.sims.berkeley.edu/~hal/Papers/history.html`.

Wactlar, H. D., T. Kanade, M. A. Smith, and S. M. Stevens. 1996. "Intelligent Access to Digital Video: Informedia Project." *IEEE Computer* 29(5):46–52.

Waibel, A. 1996. "Interactive Translation of Conversational Speech." *IEEE Computer* 29(7):41–48.

Wang, D., and S. N. Srihari. 1989. "Classification of Newspaper Image Blocks Using Texture Analysis." *Computer Vision, Graphics, and Image Processing* 47:327–352.

Weaver, W. 1955. "Translation." (Reprint of 1949 memo.) In W. N. Locke and A. D. Booth, eds. *Machine Translation of Languages*. New York: John Wiley, pp. 15–27.

Wilcox, L., D. Kimber, and F. Chen. 1994. "Audio Indexing Using Speaker Identification." Information Science and Technologies Laboratory report ISTL-QCA-1994-05-04, Xerox Palo Alto Research Center, Palo Alto, CA.

Wilhoit, K. 1994. "Outsourcing Cataloging at Wright State University." *Serials Review* 20(3):70–73.

Wilkins, J. 1668. *An Essay Towards a Real Character and a Philosophical Language*. Printed for S. Gellibrand, London. Reprinted by Scolar Press, 1968.

Williams, M. 1995. "Database Publishing Statistics." *Publishing Research Quarterly* 11(3): 3–9.

Williams, M. ed. 1996. "State of Databases Today: 1996." *Gale Directory of Databases*. Detroit: Gale Research.

Witten, I., A. Moffat, and T. Bell. 1994. *Managing Gigabytes: Compressing and Indexing Documents and Images*. New York: Van Nostrand Reinhold.

Zhang, H.-J., A. Kankanhalli, and S. Smoliar. "Automatic Partitioning of Full-Motion Video." *Multimedia Systems* 1:10–28.

Index